9   Nations and Empires

1854   1855   1857

The Reader's Digest Association Limited
London New York Montreal Sydney Cape Town
in association with
Newsweek Books New York

Editor Alan Palmer

1859 1860 1863 1870

Milestones
of History

9

Nations and Empires

1871   1876   1879

© George Weidenfeld and Nicolson Ltd, 1970 and 1974
First published 1970. Revised and expanded edition 1974

Printed and bound in Italy
by Arnoldo Mondadori Editore—Verona

1881   1886   1886

1897   1898   1900

Contents

Introduction

The ideals and aspirations of the second half of the nineteenth century differed astonishingly from those that had inspired the Age of Optimism. The year 1850, in which Wordsworth died and Tennyson's *In Memoriam* anticipated the imagery of evolution, marked the end of an era. During the four decades following Napoleon I's coronation, thought and action throughout the European world had been dominated by the Romantic imagination, the natural supremacy of feeling over reason. But the events of 1848-49, when the barricades had gone up in so many cities, shattered the assumptions of both the young and the politically mature. No one doubted the essential rightness of national sentiment and most people remained certain that "progress" would bring material prosperity; but there was a new conviction that political and social objectives could be attained only through a realistic assessment of what was practicable. A sense of scientific discipline began to permeate the beliefs of the age, reaching its climax in the 1870s with the conception of international relations as a perpetual struggle for existence between weak and strong species of social organism. It was all too easy to transform the pride that people felt in identifying themselves with a nation into an assumption that imperial power was an end in itself. "O Evolution, what crimes are committed in Thy name!" wrote a contributor to the *Westminster Review* in the closing months of the century. In two generations the European peoples on both sides of the Atlantic became so convinced of their physical and mental fitness to dominate the world that they molded all society in their Westernized image—barely noticing, in their aggressive ebullience, that they were selling their souls to industry and materialism.

The contrast between the Romanticism of the earlier age and the Realism that succeeded it was clearly shown in the creation of an Italian state during the years 1859 and 1860. The attempts of Garibaldi and Mazzini to establish a national and democratic republic had come to nothing in 1848-49 because of the inability of the Italian patriots to defy successfully the collective will of Catholic Europe. It was left to Count Camillo Cavour, the austerely un-Romantic Prime Minister of Sardinia-Piedmont, to secure the unification of Italy by playing off rival great powers against each other and by harnessing Garibaldian enthusiasm to practicable politics—"A sense of what is possible," to use Cavour's own phrase. Cavour, who had observed the upheavals of 1848 from a newspaper editor's desk in Turin, had few illusions about his methods. "Were we to do for ourselves what we are doing for Italy, we should be very great rogues indeed," he remarked to his successor toward the end of his life. But Cavour knew the only effective means to maintain an Italian state was by using the armed strength and diplomatic machinery of one of the existing kingdoms to absorb the peninsula. Basically Cavour's united Italy was a greater Piedmont, even though the capital was moved from Turin first to Florence and, after Cavour's death, to Rome. But, though Cavour's achievement fell short of the full ideals of 1848-49 and though his policy seemed to owe more to Machiavelli than to the nobler prophets of Italian unity, most of those who had sought to build an Italian nation state recognized him as the master architect of their work. Liberal sentiment, inside and outside the peninsula, paid tribute to Garibaldi and his thousand followers; detached observers acknowledged that their hot-headed patriotism would have been disastrous without Cavour's diplomatic virtuosity.

Cavour's technique seemed ruthlessly realistic in the late 1850s, but it was surpassed in the next decade by the power politics of Otto von Bismarck. Throughout his life Bismarck remained unsympathetic toward the liberal and nationalistic sentiments of the German bourgeoisie. In 1848 he had opposed the revolutionary movement both in his Prussian homeland and in Germany as a whole, and he continued to dislike all forms of political dogmatism. Yet Bismarck possessed a shrewd awareness of historical perspective. By 1850 he had convinced himself that the Prussian kingdom would need to expand into a German state, though one which was less extensive territorially than the greater Germany of liberal ambition. He believed Prussia needed a wider field of action for her growing economic power and he feared that, unless it were possible to control Pan-German feeling throughout the Confederation, the champions of a unified Germany would destroy the existing social order and challenge the primacy of the landowning class in Prussia and her dependencies. If necessary, he was willing to give battle to all the other German states in order to create a national Germany acceptable alike to liberal academics and Prussian conservatives. In old age Bismarck claimed to have unified Germany: in reality he had brought into being a greater Prussia, though he had made it the strongest power on the Continent. Fundamentally Bismarck's achievement was similar to Cavour's except for its greater scope and efficiency.

Both Cavour and Bismarck reflected the hard and unsentimental attitude to power politics that predominated in the middle of the century. Neither statesman welcomed war nor believed in brute force as the sole arbiter of political disputes. "Woe to the national leader who goes to war for a cause which will not stand up to examination when the battles are over," Bismarck once declared. There is, however, little doubt that military conflict was regarded with far less revulsion in the third quarter of the nineteenth century than in the Age of Metternich and Alexander I. The decade of the 1860s, in particular, saw almost constant war—in Italy, Germany and South America, between the states of the American Union, between an Anglo-French expeditionary force and the Chinese, and in other regions where colonial expansion aroused native resistance. Finally in 1870 the Second Empire of Napoleon III fell to the armed might of Bismarck's Prussia and, within a few months, a conquering army entered Paris for the third time in sixty years. Advances in technological science, and in the system of commanding large armies in the field, made these wars increasingly terrible. After 1870 the introduction of small-bore breech-loading repeating rifles, the development of a single-barrel machine gun firing more than 600 rounds a minute and (in the early 1890s) of the artillery, all made the prospect of future wars even more hideous. There was a reaction, especially in Europe, which favored the acceptance of peaceful arbitration for international disputes, and a strong peace movement developed seeking, in the first instance, to limit the armaments race of the great powers. The growth of steamships and transcontinental railways was helping to contract world society, drawing peoples into greater dependence upon one another but also making it harder to confine future conflicts between the great powers to any one particular region. All European wars between 1814 and 1914 were limited in area and duration, but the experience of the American Civil War and of the Paraguayan War of 1865–70 held a frightening warning.

It is nevertheless strange that during the last thirty years of the century there were distinguished writers and thinkers who were prepared to accept military conflict as a natural condition of human progress. Herbert Spencer, who in founding evolutionary philosophy pioneered the study of sociology, argued that without mankind's instinct to fight "the world would still have been inhabited by men of feeble types sheltering in caves and living on wild food." Charles Darwin's *The Origin of Species* (1859) and *The Descent of Man* (1871) did far more than stimulate biological and anthropological science. They provided the intelligentsia of Europe and America with a ready-made deterministic doctrine of natural history with which to oppose the Romanticist concept of the individual man as good and sacred in himself as well as the conventional certitudes of religious dogma. The predominant thought of the later nineteenth century emphasized the order and continuity of natural selection at the expense of other standards by which to assess the magnitude of man's achievements and his potentiality for good or evil.

Inevitably, by the closing years of the century, these narrowly materialistic explanations were beginning to be called into question. Could the processes of the mind itself be understood in purely physical terms? Did a blind faith in the laws of scientific progress lessen man's dignity by denying him responsibility, imposing a framework as narrowly constraining as the Calvinist doctrines of the sixteenth century? By 1900, the year in which Freud published his *The Interpretation of Dreams*, doubts were growing as readily as they had among the Christian waverers who welcomed Darwinism in the previous generation. The new psychoanalysis provided an interpretation of the mind but it did not claim the finality of proof with which the Darwinians had sought to dispose of man's sense of purpose. Yet Freud's theories were welcomed by painters, novelists and dramatists who were tending to turn more and more toward their own inner thoughts and sensations for inspiration. Half a century previously the French artist Gustave Courbet believed he had found freedom of expression in the purity of Realism. Long before 1900 the great artists of Paris had found that Realism, too, had its limitations, that it was necessary to perceive more than touches the eyes. As the shadows of the twentieth century became clearly defined, what mattered was the individual artist and writer's attempts to recreate nature himself rather than accept established traditions.

Popular culture, of course, virtually ignored fashionable changes in artistic expression. It barely reflected the Darwinian dethronement of accepted beliefs. The most widespread sentiment during the closing decades of the century was a consciousness of national pride. In Britain it manifested itself in the jingoism of the music halls during the Eastern Crisis of 1877-78. French patriotism, gravely wounded by the war of 1870 and the Paris Commune, recovered sufficiently in the 1880s to find in General Boulanger a hero fit for the Republic to laud. Germany, an empire in name only since 1871, delighted in the empty pageantry of military reviews so as to assert a national unity easy to forget in a continent at peace. Yet the greatest source of patriotic self-congratulation was the scramble for colonies that reached a climax in the last two decades of the century. Of the great powers, only Austria-Hungary denied herself colonial possessions, the monarchy being content to exploit the protectorate over Bosnia-Herzegovina accorded by the Treaty of Berlin in 1878. But in Britain, France, Italy, Germany and Belgium all classes were united in welcoming imperial expansion, sometimes for economic motives but often from collective pride. In Russia, where the eastern railways penetrated new lands of Asia, and in the United States, looking out across the Pacific and southward to the Caribbean, the sentiment of imperialism was also present, though in a different form. To the mass of people it made little difference if Empire grew from the enterprise of explorers or the zeal of idealists stamping out a system they considered evil. The bronzed heroes who planted the tricolor flag of France on the banks of the White Nile or who hoisted the Stars and Stripes over the Cuban Sierra were honored in the press of their homelands and feted on their return. Only a few radical critics, conscious of growing social pressures at home, questioned the justice of imperial expansion. Already some writers were arguing that imperialism was the final manifestation of capitalism and that the socialist revolution predicted by Marx and Engels more than half a century previously was at hand. But in 1900 the sun of Empire still seemed to be shining brightly; only Ethiopia on the African continent and Tibet and Afghanistan in Asia remained virtually free from European influence.

ALAN PALMER

The Unnecessary War 1854

*Expansionist, imperial Russia, eyeing the tottering Ottoman Empire on its southern border, used a
pretext to move into Turkish-held land. This alarmed the British and French, who feared that the
balance of power in Europe might tilt toward Russia. They invaded Russia's Crimean Peninsula in a
contest distinguished on both sides by unbelievable incompetence. The Crimean War slaughtered
troops in the thousands on both sides and settled nothing. Its only lasting effects were the setting up of
Rumania as a sovereign state and shocking the British into long-overdue military reforms.*

The Crimean War has been called "the unnecessary war." Most conflicts have been given that name by someone, but the Crimea leads them all in futility and beastliness. Fifty thousand French and British soldiers, and countless thousands of Russians, died in the mud around Sevastopol because the Western powers were unable to head off Russian ambitions by diplomatic means. Resorting to war, they found themselves committed to a distant campaign that they could neither direct nor supply effectively. The war came about because of the threat of Russian expansion southward into Eastern Europe at the expense of the Turkish Empire. Britain feared the consequences of Russian supremacy in the eastern Mediterranean, and the newly created French Emperor Napoleon III was equally anxious to divert Russian ambitions away from Europe. He also wished to pose as the champion of Roman Catholicism before Russian Orthodoxy. Both Britain and France also wanted to preserve the Turkish Empire; an inefficient, listless Turkey was no military threat and, as the French had demonstrated in North Africa, there were rich spoils to be had as successive limbs of the once-mighty Ottoman Empire broke off at the touch of the interfering Western powers.

The events that led to the outbreak of hostilities took place in Palestine. There, a conflict between Roman Catholic and Greek Orthodox monks at the Holy Places had been settled by the Sultan in 1852 in favor of the Latins, much to the chagrin of Tsar Nicholas I. After inconclusive talks with the British about dismembering the Ottoman Empire, the Russians invaded Turkey's Danubian principalities (later to become Rumania) in order to pressure the Sultan on their claims to a protectorate over the Holy Places and over Turkish Christian subjects.

Actual hostilities, however, were started by the Turks in October, 1853, in the wake of the Russian rejection of their amendments to the Vienna Note (a Franco-Austrian formula aimed at satisfying Russian claims in principle without offending the Turks). Britain and France became concerned when the destruction of the Turkish fleet off Sinope in northern Anatolia left a power gap, which they feared would enable the Russian Black Sea fleet to dominate the eastern Mediterranean.

At Napoleon's suggestion, the British and French sent their fleets into the Black Sea, and in February, 1854, presented Russia with an ultimatum demanding evacuation of the Danubian principalities. When this was not met, they declared war in March. Austria then made a treaty with Turkey by which she would occupy the principalities until the end of the war and intervene in the western Balkans if disturbances broke out there. The Russians responded to Austria's ultimatum, however, and evacuated the principalities, which the Austrians promptly occupied. This neutralization of the Balkan and Danubian territories left the Crimea as the only possible theater of operations in southeastern Europe.

The allies now planned to invest and capture the naval base of Sevastopol, on the southern shore of the Crimea; such a move would ruin Russian naval strength in the Black Sea, and greatly reduce her means of threatening the Turkish capital of Constantinople. It was accordingly decided to send thirty thousand British and an equal number of French troops to the Black Sea to set about the virtually impossible task of defeating Holy Russia.

The army's first base was at Varna, in Bulgaria. In the three months spent there, typhus and cholera soon transformed the promenade atmosphere in which the campaign had begun. It became clear that no one had foreseen the transport and supply problems involved in this campaign, and that the medical authorities had no idea of how to deal with mass infection and disease. By the time the allies landed in the Crimean Peninsula on September 14, 1854, the fighting efficiency of both contingents was severely reduced. The Russians did nothing to

General Canrobert, commander of the French army in the Crimea. His efficiency did much to rectify the errors of the British command.

Opposite British troops storming the Heights of Alma. Discipline and valor were not enough on their own to make up for the deficiencies in British military planning.

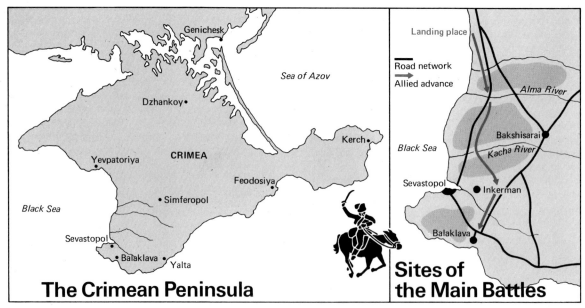

The Crimean Peninsula

Sites of the Main Battles

oppose the landing; their commander, Prince Menshikov, was arrogantly certain of his ability to destroy the invaders once they were ashore, and was content to observe them as they toiled in the muddle of disembarkation. The French were much quicker and more efficient, and British slowness and amateurishness became a bone of contention that continued throughout the war. It took two days to reorganize the army and begin the march inland through a pretty, sun-drenched landscape dotted with whitewashed farmhouses and banks of wild flowers. Menshikov allowed the allies to advance far enough for the heat and poor condition of the troops to tell on them, and then occupied a strong defensive position across the Alma River, blocking the way to Sevastopol.

The ensuing Battle of the Alma River set the tone for the entire war. The French proved unstable and occasionally frighteningly inept at the business of fighting battles, while the discipline and courage of the British infantry ensured an allied victory at a cost that dismayed the commanding generals and the government that had sent them there. The Russians themselves fought stubbornly and well, but their huge, dense formations did not allow them any scope for tactical surprises, even if their commanders had been able to think of any. Menshikov had been castrated by a Turkish bullet in his last campaign, and personal hatred combined with aristocratic hauteur to make him one of the least loved and least competent generals of the nineteenth century. Lord Raglan, the British commander, was, at seventy-three, the youngest of Britain's senior generals. He had lost an arm at Waterloo, and his kindness, gentleness and popularity with the troops ensured that his acceptability as a commander-in-chief would long outlast his usefulness. The French commander, Marshal Saint-Arnaud, was a political appointee, and a general of untried ability. In fact, he turned out to be a successful and active commander, but he succumbed to cholera shortly after the battle at the Alma River and his successor, Canrobert, was indecisive and nervous. The open-

ing of the Crimean campaign was hardly auspicious.

The Battle of Balaklava which followed is generally thought of as a British victory, if only because of the astonishing courage of the two cavalry brigades and the "thin red line" of Highlanders led by Sir Colin Campbell. In fact, the Russians gained control of the only usable road connecting the Western allied army with its base, wrecked their cavalry for the duration of the war and so exposed their military incapacity that confidence in the army, and especially its leaders, was seriously impaired. The British owed the safety of the survivors of the Light Brigade's suicidal charge to the French Chasseurs d'Afrique, and the tenuous preservation of their communications to the timidity and blundering of Prince Menshikov.

The battle was fought because the British lines of communication were long, poorly defended and near enough to the Russian positions to offer a temptation which even a commander as mediocre as Menshikov could not ignore. Balaklava, five miles to the rear of the army, was chosen as the main British base on the advice of the naval chiefs; the French, with their convenient base at Kamiesch, faced none of the problems that this decision posed for Lord Raglan. The Russians perceived that if they could rupture and hold onto the lines of communication with Balaklava the weakly protected British positions would have either to surrender or to improvise a hasty Dunkirk-like evacuation.

The Russian attack, on October 25, caught the allies entirely by surprise, despite warnings received from Russian deserters (mostly Poles). Facing the enemy advance were the 93rd Highlanders and the two cavalry brigades. The Highlanders, superbly disciplined and brilliantly commanded, faced about again and again to baffle the clumsy and tentative advance of the Russian cavalry, while the Turks, after a stout resistance, broke and fled when it became clear that no support could reach them. At this, the Russians swarmed across the Causeway Heights, beyond which lay the Balaklava road, and advanced down the valley toward the main British camp. In so doing, they ran straight into the Heavy Brigade; Sir James Scarlett, the brigade commander, was dressing his lines in preparation for an advance of his own, and had no idea that the Russian advance had reached him until line after line of their uhlans and hussars breasted the Causeway Heights and came trotting down toward him. Scarlett was quite undismayed. He finished his alignment, let out a valedictory "Damn" and ordered his trumpeter to sound the charge. The Russians halted in astonishment, and so received the full impact of the charge right in the stomach; the five hundred British cavalrymen hacked and cursed their way through nearly four thousand Russians "like butchers." The Russians, taken completely off guard by the fury of the attack and convinced that the whole allied army must be at hand, began to withdraw in disorder, their ranks awry and both men and horses scared and bewildered. Now was the time to press home the advantage so unexpectedly gained. But the Light Brigade, only five hundred yards away, merely sat on their horses and looked on. The commander, Lord Cardigan, flatly refused to budge, thinking that strict adherence to orders was more important than following up a retreating and demoralized enemy. From the distant heights behind the battlefield, the French generals watched the British with a mixture of admiration and perplexity, while Lord Raglan watched the cavalry with "dismay and anguish."

Confusion was to be worse confounded; Raglan, from his vantage point, had seen the Russians preparing to carry off the field guns overrun in their first attack, and he accordingly sent the order to Lord Lucan "to advance rapidly to the front, follow the enemy and try to prevent the enemy from carrying away the guns." Unfortunately Lucan could not see the guns to which Raglan referred. He asked the aide-de-camp who carried the order, Captain Nolan, to explain the order. Nolan detested Lucan and, infuriated by what he thought to be further evidence of Lucan's stupidity, he flung his arm out behind him shouting, "There my Lord! There is your enemy and there are your guns!" The only guns Lucan could see were in position at the end of a long, shallow valley which led right to the heart of the Russian army. Deliberately, with cold politeness, he ordered the Light Brigade to advance and take the guns.

Lord Cardigan, immaculate in cherry-colored overalls and fur-trimmed cloak, led his force toward the Russians at a steady trot; he had with him six hundred and seventy-three of "the finest cavalry in the world" as he proudly claimed. At first, nobody spotted the disastrous error that had been made; then Nolan, realizing what was about to happen, galloped furiously across the front of the advancing brigade, shouting and waving his arm in an effort to head off the charge. Cardigan was furious, thinking that Nolan was trying to force the pace and get ahead of his commanding officer. Before Nolan could clear up this fresh misunderstanding, a Russian shell blew a hole in his chest and, still screaming his incomprehensible warning, his rigid body was carried back through the disciplined lines of the advancing cavalry. Raglan could do nothing; his French allies could do little but watch with him, "with a thrilling anxiety and a sentiment scarce short of horror." The French General Bosquet immortalized what he saw in the phrase "*c'est magnifique, mais ce n'est pas la guerre*" (it's magnificent, but it's not war).

In purely physical terms, the Russians suffered little from the charge, but their morale suffered badly. When the Light Brigade drew off, after losing three hundred men and five hundred horses, and made its painful way back down the valley, the Russians began a sullen retreat. Their attempt to cut

The Battle of Balaklava. Hopes of decisive victory were lost as a result of the futile Charge of the Light Brigade.

British and French troops enjoying a lull in the campaign during 1855.

Far right The debris of war: the interior of the Redan, 1855.

Far right below An allied council of war, with Lord Raglan (left), Pacha (center) and General Pélissier (right), photographed by Roger Fenton.

Below The attack on the Malakhov, 1855, with General MacMahon planting the tricolor. The capture of the Malakhov laid Sevastopol open to allied attack.

the British lines of communication with Balaklava had failed. The Light Brigade, despite the folly of its action, helped to blunt the Russian advance, "charging an army while all the world wondered."

Balaklava was not an unqualified success for the British. The army's self-confidence was badly shaken, and the imminence of winter made the prospect of life in the trenches bleak. It was clear that the army was not equipped to face up to the rigors of a Russian winter, least of all when combined with the wearisome duties of a siege. The novelist G. A. Henty, who was Special Correspondent of the London *Morning Advertiser*, wrote that:

The British force has suffered severely, not so much from the ravages of unavoidable disease as from the pressures of fatigue and long exposure. The difference between the appearance of the French troops and our own is surprising: the French are so clean, appear well fed and their elastic step and high spirits show how little they are affected by the hardships of the campaign: our men, on the contrary, look worn and ill and are unable to keep themselves smart and soldier-like.

Lord Raglan was well aware of the lack of proper equipment and the need for reinforcements; but his sense of tact stopped him from presenting an adequate picture of his army's difficulties to those who might have been able to do something about them. At the same time he was too aloof to bring himself to utter those words of praise or encourage-ment that were the stock in trade of many less distinguished commanders, and as the situation worsened the confidence and affection with which Raglan was regarded by the army turned to dis-appointment, anger and revulsion.

The Russians did not give the allies much of a rest after their failure at Balaklava. There were incessant raids on the French and British positions, and scarcely a night passed without some disturbance, and the accompanying fear of renewed attack. At dawn on November 5, less than a fortnight after Balaklava, the Russians struck again, pouring men out of Sevastopol in an attempt to smash through the allied line by brute force. They very nearly succeeded, and that they again failed was due to the incredible courage of the British infantry who held the Inker-man Heights. As it was, the Battle of Inkerman was once again a strategic defeat for the allies, guarantee-ing Sevastopol a winter of survival.

In January, 1855, the British Prime Minister, Lord Aberdeen, at last fell from power, and Viscount Palmerston became Prime Minister. "Lord Pummice-stone," as he was sometimes called, seemed to combine the pugnacity and joviality expected of a war leader with that sublime indif-ference to the claims or status of other nations that the crowd believed to be statesmanship. He was, at seventy, a shrewd politician, endowed with the necessary energy and will power to see the war through to a successful conclusion. Several other factors combined to give a rosier appearance to the war before the end of the winter. Florence Nightin-gale arrived in the Crimea with her enthusiastic helpers from the main hospital at Scutari, on the

Asian shore of the Bosphorus opposite Constantinople. Throughout the war she was at loggerheads with the medical authorities and their handful of nurses. Nonetheless the death rate in the hospitals, at forty-two percent in February, 1855, fell to two percent by June of that year. Vast quantities of war material and comforts for the army were sent out as a result of private initiative as well as government action. The entry of Austria and Sardinia (Piedmont) into the war further aided the allies. Then in March, 1855, Tsar Nicholas I died, leaving as his successor the more liberal Alexander II, who would eventually be persuaded to end the war. But most significantly, in May, General Canrobert resigned his command, and into the center of the stage stepped the dirty, churlish figure of General Aimable Pélissier. Pélissier was one of the ablest French generals, who had been kept in relative obscurity by Napoleon III because of his doubtful political reliability. Now the urgent need to capture Sevastopol induced the Emperor to appoint him to the chief command.

The weary months of siege had not brought the allies any nearer to their goal; Pélissier assumed command of the French forces on May 19, and at once declared his intention of pressing ahead with the plan for an assault on Sevastopol first mooted eight months before. The British leaders were left in no doubt as to the vigor of the new commander; one staff officer wrote that "Pélissier is so fat and has so short a neck that he will go off like a ginger-beer bottle."

The top flew off the bottle on June 6. The French troops stormed the heavily guarded outworks to the

Satire on the British mis-
management of the Crimean
War. Inefficient supply was a
major cause of the difficulties
of the British army.

The charge of Scarlett's 300
men at Balaklava. The Heavy
Brigade under Scarlett threw
the Russians into disorder.

intended, and met the oncoming waves of infantry with a fire so concentrated and devastating that whole companies were blown aside like chaff as they moved forward to the attack. As dawn broke, it became clear that the French had suffered a terrible rebuff, and Raglan thereupon turned error into tragedy by insisting that the British should do their bit despite the obvious failure of the operation.

The British had to advance across a quarter of a mile of open ground, in clear light, to confront a victorious and well-entrenched enemy armed with more than four hundred cannon. The British soldiers were shot down in hundreds; no unit could keep formation in face of the fire that greeted them, and the assault troops dissolved into a bloody shambles after barely ten minutes in the open. The whole engagement lasted less than half an hour, and the scale of the losses combined with the congestion on the narrow battlefield to "give an adequate impression of Hell on a busy night." The morale of the army was shaken, and Lord Raglan himself returned to his headquarters a dying man.

Lord Raglan died in June, 1855. Those closest to him believed that disappointment with the army's situation and too great a sensitivity to the problems of the alliance were the true cause of death; in fact, cholera and general ill health sufficed. His successor had been in the Crimea for only a few weeks and had already given ample proof of his caution and mediocrity as chief of staff to the army, and Pélissier was soon recognized as the allied leader. Believing that a determined attack on the allied flank might induce them to give up what the Russians persisted in believing was a hopeless siege, the Russians attempted to relieve Sevastopol. They attacked on August 8, advancing down the Tchernaya Valley in great

Malakhov defenses with great bravery, despite the loss of nearly five thousand men. The British, too, invigorated by the warm weather and inspired perhaps by the French example, took the outworks in front of the Redan after a bitter struggle. It looked as though the army was poised for the final capture of the Russian fortress. Unfortunately Pélissier misjudged the Russian power of resistance, and failed altogether to coordinate his plans effectively with Lord Raglan. The French attacked without a preliminary bombardment at 3 A.M. on June 18. The Russians could see exactly what was

strength, a move that successive French commanders had anticipated since the very beginning of the siege. Pélissier, sensing his opportunity, took personal command of the French and Sardinian forces that opposed the Russian advance. The flexible and speedy French first baited the lumbering Russians, then went at them full force. The tattered and bleeding survivors turned northward toward Mother Russia, and Sevastopol was left unprotected, its supply lines cut and its fate sealed.

The final allied assault on Sevastopol was timed for September 8. The planning and preparation of this coup de grace were entirely the work of Pélissier; British views were not considered, and only two thousand British troops were detailed for the initial attack. These troops were hardly confident that the new attempt would succeed. Unnerved by the terrible losses on June 18, and utterly mistrustful of their senior commanders, the British army was in no condition to repeat the heroism and disciplined fury of earlier battles. Consequently the British assault on the Redan was "a shameful and disastrous failure."

The French, by contrast, captured the Malakhov in half an hour, storming forward and overrunning the Russian defenses. The British officers were dismayed by their own failure, and inclined to be resentful of the French success. The spectacle of British troops shouting obscene abuse at their officers contrasted unhappily with the brave figure of General MacMahon planting his tricolor flag on the Malakhov with the words "*J'y suis et j'y reste*" (I'm here and I'm staying here). Recrimination between the armies was short lived; the Malakhov was, as Pélissier had always maintained, the key to Sevastopol, and the Russians at once began to withdraw from the city, blowing up their arsenals and wrecking those defenses that still remained intact.

The taking of Sevastopol was swiftly consolidated in the international arena. In November, Sweden concluded a treaty with the allies, and in December Austria threatened intervention. The allied armies stayed in the Crimea until the following spring. This time the British were properly equipped and it was the French who had to endure hardship and disease. Their army was largely ignored once the war appeared to be won, and Pélissier, despite his recent laurels, complained with some justice that the Emperor was ungrateful and unjust.

Napoleon III, in fact, was in the process of carrying out one of those daring diplomatic somersaults of which he was so fond; he was already preparing the way for his anti-Austrian policy, determined to patch up a new friendship with his late enemy, Russia, before sending his victorious army to liberate Italy from Austrian domination. As a result, the 1856 Treaty of Paris that marked the official end of the Crimean War was strangely inconclusive: Russia agreed to demilitarize the Black Sea, and accepted that the Danube should be an international waterway; the Turkish Empire was given another lease on life, and Russia turned aside from her European policies in favor of armed expansion into Asia.

The Crimean War set several important precedents. The campaign saw the first use of explosive shells as opposed to cannon balls, the use of warships with auxiliary engines and of steam tugs, and the use of traction engines for hauling supplies over country unfit for horse. Nursing services improved on both sides—Grand Duchess Elena Pavlovna doing for the Russians what Florence Nightingale did for the British. More importantly, this was the only all-out war fought between Britain and Russia despite their long global rivalry. It showed the difficulty of the two countries actually coming to blows, because of the lack of a theater of operations. The British, not fully realizing the inaccessibility of Russia, had thought the problem of supply would be merely an extension of Wellington's supply problems in the Peninsular Campaign. Nonetheless, this war was a remarkable attempt to settle an essentially naval problem of strategic power by using armies in an attempt to destroy the rival state's base of operations.

The treaty itself solved nothing; all it did was confirm the political and military preeminence of France, and briefly postpone the confrontation between a modern Russia, conscious of its growing strength, and an antiquated and badly governed Turkish Empire, all too aware of its impoverished status and political decline. The one concrete act of the treaty, the establishment of Rumania, provided, as Palmerston feared it would, an excellent base for Russia's aggressive policy in the future. Twenty thousand British soldiers had died in the course of the war, and it might be said that the only lasting effect of the war was the reform and modernization of the British army in the wake of that unnecessary slaughter.   WILLIAM ALLAN

The British colors advancing at the Alma.

The Treaty of Paris

The Treaty of Paris, though it officially ended the Crimean War, was not a good settlement, for it merely postponed Russia's southward advance. The neutralization of the Black Sea remained valid only so long as the attention of Europe was not distracted elsewhere, and when in 1870 the Russians announced that they no longer felt themselves bound by the demilitarization clauses, the European powers were too preoccupied by the struggle between France and Prussia to take any action stronger than the delivery of written protests. So long as the Turkish government remained unreformed and unrepentant, the capricious cruelty of its officials in the Balkan lands kept the Eastern Question alive. Within twenty years of the signature of the Treaty of Paris it became clear that the Crimean War had solved nothing. The extent of Russia's imperial ambitions became more and more obvious as the nineteenth century progressed. China, Japan and Korea all found themselves threatened by Russia. The Ottoman Empire, growing steadily weaker as it was, was unable to offer any effective opposition to Russia's imperial designs. In Central Asia, Russian influence and power grew steadily, and a Russian threat to Afghanistan was soon apparent. Even the United States and Canada felt the effect of Russia's power because of its North American colony in Alaska, which was eventually purchased by the United States in 1867.

Antipodean gold

America's interest in its west coast had blossomed suddenly, largely as a result of the discovery of gold in California. Many aspects of the American experience were repeated in Australia in August, 1851, when gold was discovered in a colony that had been officially created a mere six weeks before (and named after Queen Victoria). Men rushed out from Melbourne so precipitately that the newly designated capital was left with only a handful of officials and two policemen to control the hordes of fortune hunters who were flocking ashore from ships in Port Phillip Bay.

Seven times as many immigrants arrived in Victoria in 1852 as in 1850. The population rose rapidly; from 77,000 in 1850 to 540,000 eleven years later, and the total population of Australia trebled during the same period. An average of three ships a day sailed up the Yarra River to Melbourne

in 1853, and for a few months real estate in the city was five times as expensive as in London. At Ballarat, Bendigo, Eaglehawk and Castlemaine, prospectors found nuggets of gold only a few inches below the surface of the sandy soil. Drunkenness, gambling, threats and murder became common in the mining camps and even in the streets of Melbourne itself. But—as in California—the boom years lasted only as long as did the alluvial deposits. Mining companies that sank deep shafts and employed laborers at a fixed wage replaced the pick-and-shovel prospectors, and rough discipline eventually tamed the threat of social anarchy (although not in time to prevent a rebellion by Irish and German immigrants in the gold fields in 1853). Many of the later settlers went not to the "diggings" that had lured them across the globe, but to farms where wool and wheat assured a less capricious income.

Australia transformed

The Victoria gold rush completed the transformation of the Australian scene that had begun in New South Wales in 1819 with the foundation of Bathurst, the first town in the interior. The fact that New South Wales had been established as a penal settlement gave the Australian colonies a bad name for years. Convicts were transported to New South Wales from 1788 to November, 1840 (and on a more liberal basis from 1848 to 1851). They were also settled in Tasmania from 1803 to 1853. Although the free population outnumbered the convicts or "emancipists" (ex-convicts) as early as 1834, the existence of a large number of prisoners and former prisoners in the population

delayed its political development.

Nor was the early political development of Australia one to inspire confidence. The 1830s had been a period of uncontrolled financial speculation, which had only ended in 1843 with a serious drought, a collapse in the wool sales on which the Australian colony depended and a run of bank failures.

The administrative authorities' distrust of their constituents was well illustrated by the fate of the original discoverer of gold at Ballarat. Because he had a criminal record, it was assumed that he had stolen the metal, melted it down and put forward his claim in order to speculate on land values. He was duly whipped for having made known his discovery, and it was

A view of Sydney harbor in 1860. Australia rapidly developed from a penal colony into a great nation.

only when a clergyman arrived back at Melbourne with a nugget that the authorities acknowledged that there really was gold along the inland rivers. And even then the governor of the colony tried to keep the news secret for fear of its effect on Australia's criminal element.

The governor's attitude was not shared by the members of the National Colonization Society in London. Edward Gibbon Wakefield, by far the most persuasive propagandist of Australasian immigration in Britain, declared that with the increase of settlers after the gold rush, "a colony was precipitated into a nation."

Wakefield was right. The Australian Colonies Government Act, which permitted the colonies to draft constitutions and form legislatures on whatever franchise they wished, preceded the gold rush by a year, but it was the sudden rise in population caused by immigration in the 1850s that gave the Australian state councils a sense of independence and authority. New South Wales adopted a constitution

The signature of the Treaty of Paris. Although the Russians were forced to abandon their claims, the treaty failed to prevent further Russian advances in Asia.

precipitates a colony into a nation

The Last of England, by Ford Madox Brown. Emigration from the British Isles made the development of Australia possible.

in November, 1855, and Victoria, South Australia and Tasmania soon followed its example. Queensland was established as a separate self-governing colony in 1859. Western Australia, although recognized as a colony in 1829, was considered to be too thinly populated for self-government until 1890. (At the request of its own settlers it had continued to receive convicts from Britain between 1850 and 1867.)

But even after the adoption of self-government, there remained many limitations imposed by the British government; British troops were stationed in the colonies until 1870, and proposals for a federation were rejected because it was felt that Australia was too large and varied in character to possess

common interests. It was not until the Australian Commonwealth Act was passed in Westminster in 1900 that federation was finally achieved.

The cities of Melbourne and Sydney already had characters of their own by 1860. Each had a university, libraries, theaters, broad gas-lit streets and fashionable suburban villas by the waterside. Their citizens had already shown a passion for sporting contests, and when the first cricket match between Victoria and New South Wales was held in Melbourne in 1856, the state legislature suspended its sitting until after the close of play.

By 1856 settlement had only touched the coastal fringe of a continent almost as large as Europe or the United States. The "outback" was as much of a challenge as the American frontier. The Irish explorer Robert Burke (1820-61), seconded by the English-born William Wills (1834–61), crossed Australia from south to north in 1861 (only to perish on the return journey), and Scottish-born John Stuart (1815–66) trekked from Adelaide to Darwin in the following year. Explorers had led the way; it was hoped that pioneers would follow. The immigrant ships sailed southward from Europe for another thirty years, but the returns were small compared with the North American prairies, and the Australian colonies never again ex-

perienced a change as rapid as they had had in the golden 1850s.

New Zealand

There were of course other colonies apart from Australia and Canada in which British people could satisfy their urge for adventure. Fear of French ambitions in the South Pacific induced the British government to annex the islands of New Zealand in 1840. The Treaty

A Maori war dance; the Maoris accepted British sovereignty in 1840.

of Waitangi (which solemnized the annexation) guaranteed the lands of the Maori chieftains absolutely in return for a formal cession of sovereignty, and most early colonial administrators respected the spirit and the letter of the treaty despite a conflict that lasted from 1843 to 848. The Maoris were willing enough to sell land to white settlers, but they were determined to retain

their independence. During the early 1850s relations between the settlers and the Maoris grew increasingly unfriendly, as the white men tended to look down on the Maoris. In 1860 the second of the Maori Wars broke out, largely because of the attitude of the government after 1856 when New Zealand became self-governing. The normally disunited Maoris elected a king and refused to allow further land sales to the government. The discovery of gold and the obduracy of the colonial authorities added to the difficulties and the Maoris were quickly defeated by British troops. Political and economic difficulties, however, prevented any lasting settlement, and fighting flared up spasmodically until 1870, when the Maoris were at last forced to admit defeat. The Maori Wars discouraged large-scale immigration as well as hastening the process by which the Maoris were deprived of their lands.

A Church of Scotland settlement was begun at Otago in 1854, and two years later the Church of England replied by founding a town, which was suitably named Canterbury. Immigration was slow at first, but the discovery of gold – at Otago in 1861 and at Westland in 1865 – led to an increase in European immigration, and helped to push the number of settlers up to the quarter of a million mark by 1870, but New Zealand never caught the imagination of British immigrants as Australia had done.

Art

As the nineteenth century continued the importance of Romanticism declined steadily. A new school of artistic realism was born. Its first great exponent was Gustave Courbet.

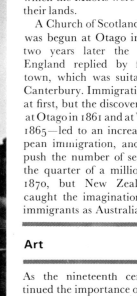

The Victoria Pie and Coffee Rooms at Hill End, New South Wales. Elaborate façades were added to simple one-story buildings to emphasize their importance.

Realism and Revolution 1855

At a time when Classicism—as embodied by Ingres—and Romanticism—as exemplified by Delacroix—were the officially approved schools of art in Paris, along came another as antithetical to both as to the authorities who supported them. In his art—which has been called Realism—as in his politics—which were revolutionary—Gustave Courbet sought to interpret his times as they were. Relying on the power of paint to "translate the customs, the ideas, the appearance" of the times, he forged a style of painting that brilliantly described and antagonized at the same time, and also inspired younger painters to establish a school of painting that came to be called Impressionism.

In the spring and summer of 1855, Napoleon III put on a vast Universal Exhibition in a deliberate attempt to outdo the English and eclipse the success of the Great Exhibition in the Crystal Palace four years before. The centerpiece of the French Exhibition was its display of paintings. There was a roomful of immaculate, calculated works by the master of Classicism, Jean Auguste Dominique Ingres, with his new *Apotheosis of Napoleon* naturally given pride of place. A wall or two was also covered with the canvases of the great Romantic, Eugène Delacroix—one side the old, dark savagery of *Dante and Virgil Crossing the Styx*, painted over thirty years earlier, on the other, the new, wild color and twisting forms of the *Lion Hunt*, the latest picture from Delacroix' studio.

In the rooms beyond, the lesser lights of French painting were on show: the serious pupils of Ingres, with their icy madonnas and painstaking studies "from the life"; the one or two imitators of Delacroix, with scenes of Arab horsemen or reclining nudes; rooms packed with landscapes, the Seine, the Midi, the Roman Campagna; battle scenes, preferably Napoleonic; portraits, preferably official; in the final room, the latest thing from across the Channel —the Pre-Raphaelites, their pictures clustering round Millais' latest work, *The Order of Release*.

This was painting as the powers-that-be wanted, and imagined, it. It was a splendid show, being rich, varied, full of brilliant things. And yet somehow the Universal Exhibition was less than the truth about French painting; it had edged to one side everything that did not quite fit into its picture of art; it had organized a false and comforting consensus, where Classicism and Romanticism fought a dignified, bloodless contest and shook hands at the end of the day. It had frozen French painting at a point some ten or twenty years in the past; it acted, almost, as if innovation in painting had come to an end, and all that was left to the new generation was to consolidate,

imitate and learn from their illustrious forebears.

Perhaps the official view of art is always like this. And equally, perhaps there is always something to spoil the view and disturb the stillness. In 1855 that something was Gustave Courbet, and a style of painting he called Realism. The authorities had not excluded Courbet from the exhibition—that would have been too crude. But they had tried to neutralize his exhibit. They had rejected his two biggest, most ambitious entries. They had chosen work that still allowed the option—if you tried hard, if you were determined to read the signs that way—of seeing Courbet as a painter of the pastoral, of country scenes and country crafts, *The Girl at her Spinning Wheel*, the cliffs and streams of the Jura. It has to be admitted that the officials did not do their job very thoroughly. There were also on show works like *The Meeting*, a bright, big poster of a painting, laid out with the flatness and stiffness of a popular print—Courbet had copied the poses from a cheap peasant woodcut of the Wandering Jew. *The Meeting* was no simple version of the pastoral; it was a portrait of the artist and his patron, confronting each other on the open road—the artist as vagabond, but the artist as *equal*, if not superior, to the man who bought his work. It was an aggressive and ironical painting: plain and straightforward, stripped down to a simple line of three against a blue background; ironically polite, with its humble servant and its raising of hats. If *The Meeting* was "bad"—because it was puzzling, and did not quite fit into any pigeonhole of painting—then for the ordinary spectator in 1855, *The Stone Breakers*, another painting on show, was "worse." Here was the countryside, sure enough, and here were country people. But no longer peasants, and no longer laughing fields. A gloomy, shadowed hillside and, pressed close to us in the foreground, two laborers in thick cloth trousers and torn shirts, their faces hidden or averted, their actions stiff with tiredness.

"Don't be so bourgeois—you must at least admire Courbet"; a Daumier cartoon of 1865 shows how rapidly middle-class taste was changing.

Study of a Man with Pipe, Self-Portrait, by Gustave Courbet. Courbet regarded the final version of this picture as his first Realist painting.

23

The whole picture is filled with the effort and the dreariness of work. The paint is there to give *weight* to stones and picks and wooden shoes, to make the spectator part of the work in hand, to make him feel the ache in the old man's knee as it rests on its mat of ragged straw. If this was Realism, then it was too much for the bourgeoisie. In the Exhibition Complaints Book, they put down their disgust. "The best way to make Courbet stop doing such hideous paintings is to ignore him" wrote one. "So I beg the critics not to talk about him any longer." And another: "Please Mister Courbet, will you mend the shirt and wash the feet of your stone breakers? Signed, a clean and delicate man."

There was worse to come. If the clean and delicate man had made his way out of the exhibition, he would have seen, just a stone's throw from the gates, something that called itself the Pavilion of Realism —a big, crude hut of wood and plaster with a zinc roof. And inside, if he had paid his 50 *centimes*, he would have found himself in the presence of the two great paintings that the officials had rejected—the *Burial at Ornans* and the *Painter's Studio*—and another forty of Courbet's works. Moreover, the catalog contained a manifesto of Realism:

The title of realist has been forced on me, like the title of romantic was forced on the men of 1830. Labels have never given a correct idea of things; if they did, the works themselves would be superfluous.

So instead of arguing about the accuracy of a name that nobody, I hope, is expected to understand very well, I shall just try to explain one or two things and clear up a few misunderstandings.

I have studied the art of the ancients and the moderns, but with no system in mind and with no fixed ideas. I no more wanted to imitate the one than to copy the other; nor was I any more anxious to attain the empty objective of *art for art's sake!*

No! I have simply wished to base upon a thorough knowledge of tradition the reasoned and independent feeling of my own individuality. To know in order to be able to *do*, that was my idea. To be in a position to translate the customs, the ideas, the appearance of my own time, according to my own estimation, to be not only a painter but a man as well; in short, to make a living art—that is my aim.

And further down, as marginal note to the *Painter's Studio*, this parting shot:

The catalog of the Universal Exhibition says I had a teacher of painting: that is false, and I have already fought and corrected the mistake in the newspapers; I did it in 1853.

I have never had any other teachers in painting besides nature and tradition, besides the public and work.

It is, like most things Courbet wrote, a fascinating and untidy hodgepodge of ideas. It is the theorizing of a confident, blundering amateur, a tissue of false starts and half-explained concepts. Few people read

The Stone Breakers, by Courbet. The poverty and exhaustion of the laborers caused anger in an age when it was customary to speak of the dignity of labor.

it in 1855, and those who did tended to laugh. The poet Charles Baudelaire called Courbet a "clumsy Machiavelli," the critic Maxime du Camp dismissed Courbet by saying: "He has put his name and his *bombast* on the fourth page of the papers, in between the ads for *worm-killing pills* and *essence of sarsaparilla*. This is no longer within our province. In our department we are concerned exclusively with art...."

The exhibition itself was a failure. And yet the one-man show of 1855 lived on as a legend and an example. For the young painters of the next generation—the future Impressionists Manet, Pissarro, Monet and Degas for example—Courbet was the master, and 1855 was the beginning of a new epoch in art.

Why did they think so? And what was Courbet's Realism, as it emerges from the pictures and manifesto of 1855? It was, first and foremost, a concrete art. Courbet was a painter of *things*, of actual weight, substance and texture. He wanted an art that was tied to the real world and its various materials. In the cafés, over his eternal pint of German beer, he used to thunder derisively against the "Ideal" in art, and crack jokes, more or less obscene, about "painters of angels." "What do *those* look like? I've never had the luck to see one in the flesh." As far as Courbet was concerned, both the Classicist Ingres and the Romantic Delacroix were painters of angels. They were both too preoccupied with the Ideal; the contest between them was a false contest, and the antagonist of both was Realism.

But Realism did not just mean vulgar materialism. It was not an instruction simply to "copy nature" or "stick to the facts"—those were simplifications that later, lesser artists made. Another look at the manifesto, or at the *Painter's Studio*, will show that Courbet's ambitions were almost always more complex than those slogans imply.

The manifesto talks about "translating" the time, that is, the time according to one man's estimation. Thus interpretation comes first, followed by representation. And what the painter "translates" is not simply appearances, but ideas and customs as well. The "teachers" of a Realist painter are not only nature and hard work but also tradition, freely and expertly interpreted, and, even more ambitiously, the public itself. A Realist keeps up a permanent dialog with his time and with his audience. His patrons and his public are part of what enables him to paint. And the aim of the Realist, the end product of all this complex juggling of intentions, is "the reasoned and independent feeling of my own individuality."

A look at the *Painter's Studio* makes clear the scope of Courbet's Realism. He described the picture as a "real allegory," an allegory of the seven great years in his artistic life from 1848 to 1855. And, indeed, the subject of the picture is the painter himself, showing off his Assyrian profile in the center, putting the last touches to a landscape of the Jura. But it is typical of Courbet that a self-portrait should take on these colossal dimensions, twenty feet long, twelve feet high. And that the painter's studio should be crammed with his subject, with his critics, his friends, his models, his enemies and his patrons. On the left are the various characters that Courbet had painted or aimed to paint, a gallery of

social types—rabbi, beggar-woman, huntsman, hired mourner, peddlar of cheap textiles, clown. On the right are Courbet's associates, friends and buyers—anarchist Proudhon in the background, poet Baudelaire reading his book at the right, anonymous lady in her fashionable cashmere shawl.

If ever a painting tried to put down the "customs, ideas and appearance" of an age, it was this one. And yet in the end it is a puzzling, ambiguous work. The painter is hemmed in by other people, and yet nobody really looks at what he is painting. Nobody except the little peasant boy and the marvelous nude model whom Courbet adapted from a photograph. It is as if his public, when it came down to it, was as small and as strange as this. And the figures themselves—the intellectuals in the gloomy background, the various grimacing performers on the left—are somehow neutralized, almost absorbed, by the great empty wash of paint above them; as if, even for the Realist, the world disappeared in front of the easel, and the picture became its own subject.

The *Painter's Studio* is an ambiguous picture. It changes form as we look at it. At one moment it is densely descriptive, packed with social detail; at another, curiously empty, a picture in praise of pigment itself. And those, precisely, were the ambiguities of Realism.

That the Realists were socially and politically committed there is no doubt. A few years before,

Courbet had called himself "not only a Socialist, but also a democrat and a Republican: in a word, a supporter of the whole Revolution, and above all a Realist, that is to say a sincere friend of the real truth." Courbet and his friends went on talking of Realism and Revolution in the same breath; they went on believing that the time had come for a new art, addressed to a new public—no longer the middle-class connoisseurs but the mass public of the city and the countryside. The People would be the subject and the public of Realism. It was time, wrote Courbet in 1850, to take art into the streets: "My sympathies are with the people, I must speak to them directly, take my science from them and they must provide me with a living."

Hence his inclusion in *The Meeting* of a quotation from a cheap print produced for farmhouse dining rooms. Hence the various Realist almanacs, produced in the 1850s in the hope that peasants would read them. Hence Courbet's friendship with the anarchist, Proudhon, or the revolutionary, Jules Vallès. The end of that road was real revolution—the Paris Commune of 1871, in which Courbet was deeply involved and for which he paid with imprisonment and exile.

Realist politics were erratic; in the end, perhaps, they were disastrous. But they were essential to the movement, and especially to Courbet's art. His greatest moments as a painter came when his

Above The Meeting, by Courbet.

Opposite above The *Painter's Studio.* Of all Courbet's works this picture exemplifies best the ambiguities of Realism.

Opposite below Burial at Ornans, by Courbet. Together with the *Painter's Studio* it was first shown at Courbet's Pavilion of Realism outside the Exhibition of 1855.

unparalleled natural gifts as a painter, his sheer physical involvement with paint, were meshed with a complex political concern. This was Courbet's legacy to the generation that followed. Somehow or other, for the Impressionists in the 1860s and 1870s, paint still had to translate the customs, ideas and appearance of the times. Everyone dreamed of a new *Burial at Ornans*, a new *Meeting*—pictures that showed the public what they looked like, pictures that described and antagonized at the same time. That was most likely Manet's aim in the *Luncheon on the Grass* or the *Olympia*, or in the direct muck-raking reportage of his *Execution of Emperor Maximilian*. That was Monet's aim, when he painted the new, open, shifting life of the boulevards, or stalked off to that latest bourgeois invention, the seaside resort. That was Renoir's intention, when he painted his fellow-Impressionist Sisley—a portrait of the artist in full bourgeois uniform, with his doting, obedient wife on his arm.

Like Courbet himself, the Impressionists were of two minds about their art. On the one hand they were the most self-conscious of aesthetes, bound up in the business of painting, wanting a world of undefiled visual pleasure. On the other, they were drunk on "modernity," haunting the *café-concerts* and the brothels, copying fashion plates from the magazines, putting up their easels in the Gare St. Lazare or the Folies Bergère. They began as Realists, and though their politics were never as openly provocative as Courbet's, their involvement with the social life of Paris was just as close, perhaps closer for a while. And if eventually they abandoned Realism —becoming obsessed with worlds of pure vision, lily ponds, ballet dancers, haystacks in dazzling sun, with so many pretexts for paint itself—that was partly because Realism itself had always been an unstable synthesis. The faces of the mourners in Courbet's *Burial at Ornans* are almost sculpted from paint, dense, personal, a little grotesque; but below the faces is a sea of black, in which the color of mourning takes on its own life, and pigment swallows up particulars.

Realism was always like that, always veering between anecdote and pure improvisation. For a while at least, Courbet managed to combine the two, and this made him a giant figure for the artists who succeeded him. Pictures like the *Burial at*

Right Apotheosis of Napoleon, by Ingres. Courbet consciously rejected Ingres' academic approach.

Opposite above The Two Friends, by Courbet.

Opposite below Proudhon and his Children, by Courbet.

Ornans, or the great blowsy females of his *Young Women on the Banks of the Seine*, remained as touchstones of art, as lessons and reproaches. They were completely modern, rigorously tuned to the exact flounce of a petticoat that year, the precise turn of a cravat. And they were completely individual, *tours de force* of personal gesture in paint. Few painters after Courbet could do both things at once; but because Courbet had existed, they continued to try.

That was why artists looked back to the exhibition of 1855 with such affection. And that is why the Manifesto of Realism, for all its ragged edges, is a masterpiece of sorts. It is not a measured, or even a very attractive piece of writing. It is conceited, cocksure, a little pedantic; its ambitions are enormous, almost lunatic in scope. But they *worked*. The pictures themselves are proof of that. The *Painter's Studio* and the *Burial at Ornans* achieve what the manifesto claims, and avoid ending up as the hopeless, pretentious story-pictures we might have feared. These paintings are the evidence of Realism; the manifesto tells us a little of the complex intelligence that invented them.　　T. J. CLARK

Photography provides an alternative to

Despite their energy, Courbet's attacks on the orthodoxy of contemporary art did not have an instantly shattering effect. The influence of Romanticism lived on. The Gothic revival in architecture, for example, had started in part as a Romantic protest against the utilitarianism, which many found boring, of much contemporary building. Its leading exponent, Augustus Welby Northmore Pugin (1812–52), had a genuine, if emotional, feel for the buildings of the Middle Ages. Under the influence of Eugène Emmanuel Viollet-le-Duc (1844–79) in France, and of the Cambridge Camden Society in England, whose leading light was John Mason Neale (1815–66), Gothic architecture—particularly in the early English style—quickly became accepted as

Barcelona apartment block by Gaudi.

the only Christian style for church building, and was also widely used for domestic and municipal buildings. Gradually, however, large-scale architecture grew more eclectic in its inspiration, and toward the end of the century a new grand style, Baroque in its influence, came into fashion in Europe. The huge monument to Victor Emmanuel II, which was begun in Rome in 1884, and the Cathedral in Berlin, begun a decade later, typify the grandiose pretentions of nationalist European states at the end of the century. There were, however, a few more individual talents, such as Charles Rennie Mackintosh (1868–1928) in Glasgow and the eccentric Antonio Gaudi Y Cornet (1882–1926) in Barcelona.

In painting, the decline of Romanticism was somewhat more rapid, and was apparent in the

An 1845 photograph taken outside Fox Talbot's photographic studio.

work of the most notable pupil of Jacques Louis David (1748–1825), Jean Auguste Dominique Ingres (1780–1867), who developed the Neoclassicism of his master as a style in total opposition to Romantic art. Ingres' influence grew steadily, but neither his ideas nor his art—except for his portraits, which are his finest work—showed any development, and he became a resolute, and, at an official level, successful enemy of all that was novel.

In England, after the death of John Constable in 1837, the Pre-Raphaelites reigned supreme. Founded in 1848, the Pre-Raphaelite Brotherhood sought to bring painting and literature closer together. The original brotherhood, formed around Dante Gabriel Rossetti (1828–82), William Holman Hunt (1827–1910) and John Everett Millais (1829–96), dissolved in 1851. It was replaced by a new brotherhood, whose principal members were William Morris (1834–96) and Edward Burne-Jones (1833–98). However, despite the beauty of much of the work of the Pre-Raphaelites, their main impact was on graphic design and pottery rather than on painting. Elsewhere, with the exception of the talents of a few individuals, of whom the landscape painter Jean Baptiste Camille Corot (1796–1875) was the most notable, the mid-nineteenth century lacked artists of outstanding ability.

Partly as a result of the energy of Ingres' opposition, painting went through a period of self-doubt and undirectedness. Neoclassicism and Romanticism were dead, but no one knew what they should be

replaced by. This problem was greatly exacerbated by the birth of "photography," a word coined in 1839 which rapidly replaced "daguerrotype" in popular use. Due to important improvements in photographic papers made in 1840 by William Henry Fox Talbot (1800–77), to the introduction of sensitized glass plates by Sir John Herschell (1792–1871) two years later and to a steady improvement in lenses and shutter mechanisms, photography rapidly caught the public imagination. The phrase, "From today, painting is dead," expressed a popular point of view. In the event it was wrong-minded; what was really needed was that painting should take a new direction.

The Impressionists

The new direction that painting found was based on a move away

from the Realism of Courbet. "Impressionism" was coined as a term of derision for the techniques used by Claude Monet (1840–1926) in his painting *Impression: Sunrise*, which showed the play of sunlight on water. Monet's picture was exhibited in 1874 at the first

Detail from Monet's *Impression: Sunrise*.

Impressionist show, which included works by Pierre Renoir (1841–1919), Camille Pissarro (1830–1903), Edgar Degas (1834–1917) and Alfred Sisley (1839–99). The Impressionists tried above all

Farmhouse in a Wheatfield near Arles, by Van Gogh.

to achieve a greater naturalism by analyzing tone and color in order to render the tone of light on the surface of objects. Thus they rejected traditional methods of composition and drawing, and their work initially incurred great hostility from the public. The early technical devices used were later crystallized by the neo-Impressionists, of whom the most influential was Georges Seurat (1859–91), into a quasi-scientific method of applying paint. With the Impressionists, painting had found a new direction, and the post-Impressionists, such as Vincent van Gogh (1853–90), Paul Gauguin (1848–1903) and Paul Cézanne (1839–1906), owed much to Impressionism, although their work developed in a more purely artistic and anti-naturalist direction.

Art in America

Although the United States had won its political independence in 1776, its artistic tradition remained firmly European well into the nineteenth century. The more talented American painters—men such as John Singleton Copley (1738–1815) and Benjamin West (1738–1820) were so firmly European in their outlook that they forsook their native land to live in Europe. Not that there were many American artists of ability—the idea of an American artist was so unnatural that when West was in Rome he was mistaken for a Red Indian by a blind cardinal to whom he had been presented. West did, however, win acceptance and respectability in England and became President of the Royal Academy. Washington Allston (1779–1843) was the first American painter of distinction to remain in America, but even he had traveled extensively in Europe. Nor was American art helped by the need that Americans felt to provide themselves with an heroic past. It drew painters like John Vanderlyn (1775–1852) and John Trumbull (1756–1843) into desperate competition for commissions for historical paintings at the federal and state capitals—a temptation that even Allston could not resist.

John James Audubon (1785–1851), perhaps the most American of artists in his choice of subject matter and his individualism, was a Frenchman and only settled in the United States at the age of twenty-

A Rocky Mountain at Sunset, by Benjamin West.

six. He did, however, adjust to the way of life of a settler in the wilds of Kentucky, and became a painter almost incidentally after the disastrous failure of several supposedly money-making ventures. His keen observation and outstanding draftsmanship brought him a wide popularity in the United States. The American market for painting (other than portraits) was, however, small, and Audubon's bird pictures were published and sold in Britain.

Like Audubon, several of the painters of the Hudson River School, most notably Thomas Cole (1801–48), were Europeans, mainly from Britain. Love of the American landscape, already present in Allston's work, and implicit in much of Audubon's, was made explicit in the paintings of the Hudson River artists. It struck a deep chord, and many minor works depicting canyons, rivers and mountains in all parts of the United States survive, although their painters have long been forgotten.

Many other aspects of contemporary American life, including scenes of frontier life in Missouri by George Caleb Bingham (1811–79) and Maine fishermen by Winslow Homer (1836–1910), were portrayed. Yet these artists were essentially primitives compared with the small group of American painters—notably James McNeill Whistler (1834–1903), John Singer Sargent (1856–1925), and Mary Cassatt (1845–1926)—who had a real impact internationally. All of these were essentially Europeanized in the same way as was America's outstanding nineteenth-century novelist, Henry James. Although America had succeeded in evolving a native artistic tradition, this tradition only became part of the cultural mainstream after 1913. This was the year the famous Armory Show (held in the 69th Regiment Armory in New York City) introduced modern art to the general public.

The emigrants

The small place that art held in America was due in part to its irrelevance to a frontier society. In part it was also due to America's being largely an immigrant society.

In the European countryside were tens of thousands of poor and ill-educated people who instinctively felt that only in new lands could they achieve material betterment. Although emigration from Europe had been growing steadily throughout the nineteenth century, it was only in the years after the 1848 revolutions—and the great famine in Ireland two years earlier—that it reached epidemic proportions. The stream of emigrants from Britain, for example, reached a higher level in the 1850s than it had during any previous decade, and it flowed little less strongly from other, poorer West European countries. Most settlers went to North America, a continent whose people were also on the move westward. Strangely, the movement into the United States was larger, even from Britain, than it was into Canada, where as late as 1870 Winnipeg was no more than a small outpost with a few hundred inhabitants. During the 1850s great numbers of English-speaking immigrants settled in California and Australia. In each case the

main attraction to settlers as well as those with an adventurous approach was the quest for gold.

As a result, Canada, which earlier in the century had benefited more than any other British colony from immigration, rapidly lost its attraction. This did not, however, prevent continued exploration and colonization of the western regions of the country. Other European colonies were much less successful in attracting immigrants. Neither the West Indies nor South Africa were able to attract many settlers during these years. The abolition by Great Britain of all sugar duties (by a free-trade government which held power from 1846 to 1852) was a severe blow to the West Indian planters who were largely dependent on the British market. The islands, which had been such a source of wealth in the previous century, offered no reward for the surplus working population of the home country. Cape Colony (later to become South Africa) was also unpopular, partly because government-sponsored emigrants from Britain in the 1820s had found farming conditions very difficult. The proud independence of the original Dutch settlers, the Boers, also did not make for unity. (Indeed, in order to free themselves from British restraint, some 10,000 Boers migrated northward between 1835 and 1837 in what is known as the Great Trek, seriously depopulating the Cape Colony.) Furthermore, the fighting qualities of the native Kaffirs hampered expansion. Nor did poor transport facilities help; it was not until 1885 that the railroad was open as far as Kimberley, five hundred miles north of Cape Town. During the economic depression of 1841 more than 38,000 emigrants left Britain for Canada or Australasia; only 150 departed for Cape Colony.

There remained the mysterious appeal of India. The shadow of political authority still rested with the East India Company, but a succession of governors-general had modernized the Indian states and had begun to prepare the way for Indians to assist in administering their homeland. The British ruling classes were prouder of the guardianship that they believed they were exercising in India than they were of the newer colonial settlements. But the events of 1857 were to shatter their complacent assumptions.

1857

Mutiny in India

During the first half of the nineteenth century, the enormous British mercantile combine known as the East India Company forced a program of sweeping reforms upon the inhabitants of the Indian subcontinent. British insistence upon legal and social equality gravely threatened India's centuries-old caste system and stirred deep resentment among upper-class Moslems and Hindus alike. In May of 1857, that welling unrest resulted in a series of Bengal Army mutinies. Those risings were led by native troops (known as sepoys), who were primarily upper-caste Hindus—members of the class that was most threatened by British reforms. The rebellions were ultimately suppressed, but not before the stunned British had been forced to acknowledge that a kingdom won by the sword could be lost by the sword. Englishmen in all parts of the world began to reconsider the relevance of their reforming zeal.

Lord Lawrence, ruler of the Punjab during the Indian Mutiny, later Viceroy of India.

Opposite British troops storming the batteries at Badle-Serai.

The year 1857 began badly for the Bengal Army of the East India Company. There was trouble with the native troops, or sepoys, in February and again at the beginning of May. These disturbances were summarily dealt with, but on May 10, the sepoys quartered at the great cantonment of Meerut revolted, murdered their officers and headed for Delhi, home of the titular Emperor, Bahadur Shah. An octogenarian pensioner of the East India Company, Bahadur Shah was a bad poet and a mystic who believed that he could change himself into a gnat in order to visit faraway places incognito. Moreover, he was a descendant of the Moguls, and for two hundred years—from the middle of the sixteenth century to the middle of the eighteenth—the Moguls had dominated the land as well as the imagination of India. (The East India Company itself had sheltered its power in Northern India under a Mogul grant.) On May 12 the mutineers proclaimed the terrified Bahadur Shah Emperor of India. The mutiny had become a rebellion.

Fortunately for the British, the mutiny spread slowly. There was no concerted uprising; instead, garrisons mutinied at different times, some not until the revolt had almost been crushed. The sporadic nature of the mutiny gave the East India Company two advantages. First, trouble never spread beyond the Bengal Army. The Bombay and Madras armies stayed substantially loyal, and so did the forces that had recently been recruited in the Punjab. Second, except for the Bengal Army's home country, the Hindi-speaking area of the United Provinces and Central India, the Company was able to suppress the mutinies as they arose. In such key cities as Lahore, Peshawar, Karachi and Barrackpore, the sepoys were successfully disarmed.

The mutineers, however, captured Delhi in May. By the end of June Cawnpore had fallen, and the city's capitulation was followed by the infamous massacre of the entire British garrison there, including women and children. The siege of Lucknow began at the end of June. By the beginning of October, 1857, Delhi had been recaptured from the mutineers and thoroughly sacked, but the rebels controlled the entire Ganges Valley except for Bengal and a large part of Central India. Roughly 130,000 mutineers had been joined by several princes and great landlords. The princes were mostly dispossessed; often, as in the case of the most famous of them all, the Rani of Jhansi, they revolted under pressure from the mutineers rather than of their own free will. The landlords were heavily concentrated in Oudh, the eastern half of the United Provinces, where the mutiny had wide popular support.

October marked the high point of the mutineers' success. During the next nine months the British recaptured the rebel-held area bit by bit. In December, at the second Battle of Cawnpore, the East India Company won back much of the central United Provinces. The relief of Saugor in February restored a large part of Central India, and the recapture of Lucknow in March and of Azimgarh in April returned the eastern United Provinces to the Company's domination. When Jhansi fell in April and Bareilly in May, the Company's authority was restored in the western United Provinces as well.

The mutiny was substantially over. There was a last flare-up at Gwalior in June, 1858; after that, only the mopping-up of guerrillas remained. That, too, was finished by the end of 1858, though the last embers did not flicker out until the rebels' great leader, Tantia Topi, was executed in April, 1859.

The roots of the Sepoy Rebellion lay in the changes that had taken place in India during the preceding thirty years. In 1818, with the final defeat of the Mahrattas—Hindu warriors who had replaced the Moguls as the great power in India—the British had become the unquestioned lords of India. From the 1820s onward they had felt free to reform Indian society according to their own ideals, and at an ever-increasing pace.

Indian cavalry attacking
British infantry during
the mutiny.

The reforms were many. Perhaps the first that really alarmed the Indians who retained their original customs was the Charter of 1813, which allowed missionaries unrestricted entry. The missionaries lost no time in proselytizing, and their often unrestrained attacks on Hinduism and Islam caused widespread and increasing offense. They also established many schools and colleges, and they did much to introduce social reforms. Ram Mohan Roy indeed traveled all the way to Westminster to press for reforms, defying the old Hindu prohibition against crossing the black water.

Soon the far-reaching reforms began. Suttee (the burning alive of a widow with her husband's corpse), thuggee (human sacrific to the Goddess Kali) and female infanticide were all banned. Hindu widows were allowed to remarry (child marriage and the high mortality rate produced many young widows condemned to a life of hardship). Hindu converts to Christianity were given the right to inherit family property.

The suspicion began to spread among Indians that the British intended to Christianize them. In the literal sense, this was untrue. Occasionally a government official or an army officer would prove to be a zealous evangelist; but for the most part the government was uninterested, even hostile, toward such activities. From the early 1830s on, however, the British did begin the Westernization of India. As Thomas Macaulay, the Whig historian who was for a time a member of the Indian Governor-General's Council, told the British House of Commons in 1833:

> We must do our best to form a class of persons Indian in Blood and colour, but English in taste, in opinions, in morals, and in intellect. . . . It may be that by good government we may educate our subjects into a capacity for better government . . . that they may, in some future age, demand European institutions. . . . Whenever it comes, it will be the proudest day in English history. To have found a great people sunk in the lowest depths of slavery and superstitions, to have so ruled them as to have made them desirous and capable of all the privileges of citizenship, would indeed be a title of glory all our own.

Macaulay's words were truly prophetic: those who rule India today are the heirs of his policy, but at the time his words were a threat to many educated Indians. The Persian and Sanskrit that had given them their position would no longer suffice for their sons. The power that they had been accustomed to would in future go to Englishmen and the *babus* (clerks) who knew English.

The British insistence on equality threatened the Indians even more severely. Individual British

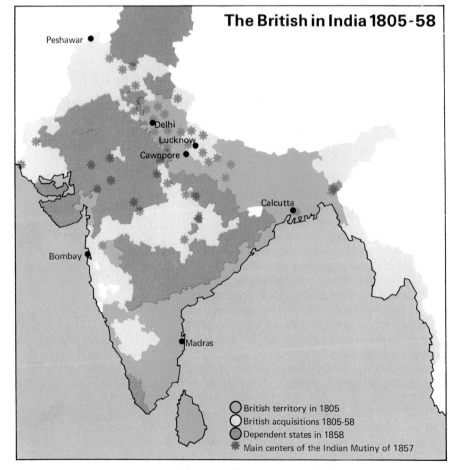

The British in India 1805-58

Peshawar

Delhi
Lucknow
Cawnpore

Calcutta

Bombay

Madras

○ British territory in 1805
○ British acquisitions 1805-58
○ Dependent states in 1858
✳ Main centers of the Indian Mutiny of 1857

officials were frequently great respecters of rank and ancient lineage, but the British government did insist upon certain qualifications before a man could get a job. More significantly, British law made all men equal in the courts: a Brahmin could be hung as easily as an Untouchable, the testimony of an unbeliever was worth as much as that of a true believer (a Moslem), and the greatest feudal noble could be made a defendant—or even an accused— by the lowliest of his tenants. In the new railway trains an Untouchable could sit next to a Brahmin for the price of a ticket.

But it was Governor-General Dalhousie's policy of annexation, rather than the imposition of British law, that gave teeth to frustration. After Dalhousie arrived in 1848, he lost no time in extending the Company's empire. He annexed the Punjab beyond the Sutlej, took over the state of Oudh (whose kings had always been totally loyal to the Company), annexed princely states whose rulers died without natural heirs, and dispossessed thousands of semi-feudal landlords, especially in the Deccan and in Oudh, who could not show good title to their land. Dalhousie's motive was to protect the peasant. He saw the prince and the landlord as oppressors and the British official as a liberator—and he had plenty of evidence to support his view, especially in Oudh. In 1854 the British Governor in Lucknow, the capital of Oudh, reported on:

. . . the vile life of the King, the misery of the unprotected cultivators, 78 of whose villages are plundered or burnt each year, the inhabitants tortured, slain or sold into slavery. In upholding the sovereign power of this effete, incapable dynasty, we do so at the cost of 5 million people.

Dalhousie vainly warned the King of Oudh. The King and his feudal nobles, the Talukdars, took no heed. In 1856, therefore, Dalhousie acted, informing the Court of Directors in London: "In humble reliance on the blessing of the Almighty (for millions of His creatures will draw happiness from the change), I approach the execution of this duty [the annexation of Oudh] gravely . . . but calmly and altogether without doubt." Nor did Dalhousie act without realizing the possible consequences of his actions:

Insurrection may rise like an exhalation from the earth, and cruel violence, worse than all the excesses of war, may be suddenly committed by men who to the very day on which they broke out in their frenzy of blood have been regarded as a harmless and timid race.

The British threat to the old society of India was particularly upsetting for the sepoys of the Bengal Army. They came, by and large, from Oudh, and they were frequently upper-caste Hindus or Moslems of good family. Dalhousie's reforms benefited their tenants and the poor and seemed to endanger the sepoys and their relatives. Further, a considerable number of them felt loyalty for the traditional royal house of Oudh, despite the weakness and debauchery of successive rulers. Many sepoys had

A rare contemporary photograph showing the damaged palace at Lucknow, where a small British garrison and some loyal sepoys held out until reinforcements arrived from Cawnpore.

An English family on the point of death. Many women and children were murdered during the Indian Mutiny.

The Marquess of Dalhousie, Governor-General of India during the Indian Mutiny.

Right A painting by an unknown Indian artist, thought to show Wajid Ali Shah embracing the Governor-General, Lord Hardinge, on his visit to Lucknow.

Illuminations at Peshawar celebrating the visit of Canning, the first Viceroy. As a result of the Mutiny India passed from the East India Company to the British Crown.

relatives among the courtiers—court retainers whom Dalhousie's annexation of Oudh had left jobless.

To those troubles were added more immediate problems in the Bengal Army itself. Pay was in arrears. Some British officers and noncommissioned officers (NCOs) displayed an intolerable racial arrogance toward their men. Many were ignorant of the feelings and even the religious beliefs of the sepoys—and it was that atmosphere that made the Affair of the Greased Cartridge so important.

In 1856 the Enfield rifle was introduced into India. It required a new cartridge that had to be bitten open before loading. Those cartridges were heavily greased. The rumor spread that the grease was made of pig and beef fat. But Moslems will not eat meat from pigs, and cows are sacred to Hindus. The rumor was therefore profoundly upsetting to the sepoys, whose position in their home villages would be destroyed if it were true. In truth, the grease was probably mutton fat, but the government was slow and hesitant about making the truth clear. The British Commander-in-Chief, for instance, took no action against an NCO of his own guard who taunted some junior NCOs with having lost caste from biting these cartridges. Once the mutiny had started, it was too late. As John Lawrence, himself later Viceroy, put it:

The misfortune of the present state of affairs is this— each step we take for our own security is a blow against the regular Sepoy. He feels this, and on his side takes a further step, and so we go on, until we disband or destroy them, or they mutiny and kill their officers.

Without the sepoys there would have been no mutiny. The motives of others outside the Bengal Army were mixed; they probably would not have taken the initiative to create a rebellion by themselves. The Nana Sahib himself, the villain of Cawnpore, the murderer of British women and children, was probably coerced by the mutineers into rebellion; he may not even have ordered the murders. The landlords of Oudh were moved by a mixture of patriotism, resentment over villages lost for lack of title, their loyalty to the deposed royal house and a general love of anarchy. The peasantry of Oudh followed their local nobles as they had always done. The Mogul princes snatched at a chance to restore the glory of their house.

It was all much too muddled and local. Above all,

it was too much an army mutiny to be called a war of independence. The men who took up arms against the British were not forerunners of Gandhi and Nehru who were striving for a free, united India. They were backward-looking members of a hierarchical society who were fighting for the privileges and the traditions that the reforms of the East India Company had begun to threaten. Yet so great was the gulf that the mutiny created between Indians and Britons in northern India that for two generations men like Nehru and Maulana Azad thought of it as a great national revolt against foreign rule.

The gulf between the races was caused by the very nature of the war. British officers had been murdered unawares; many thereafter found themselves totally unable to trust Indians. The artillery had been vital in intimidating and disarming mutinous regiments; the artillery thereafter was kept in British hands. The sepoys had been Brahmins and Moslems; for nearly fifty years the British in the north nurtured a suspicion of Brahmins and still more of Moslems. Indians had murdered British women and children; thereafter, in Northern India, the idea of Indian treachery lingered in many minds.

But the atrocities were not confined to one side. Colonel Neill and his men behaved little better than the Nana Sahib and his:

They [the British] were hunting down criminals of all kinds and hanging them up with as little compunction as though they had been pariah-dogs or jackals or vermin of a baser kind. . . . Volunteer hanging parties went out into the districts, and amateur executioners were not wanting to the occasion. One gentleman boasted of the number he had finished off quite "in an artistic manner," with mango-trees for gibbets and elephants for drops, the victims of this wild justice being strung up, as though for pastime, in the "form of a figure of eight."

And a British clergyman records having seen

. . . a row of gallowses, on which the energetic colonel was hanging mutineer after mutineer. . . . On one occasion, some young boys, who perhaps in mere sport had flaunted tom-toms, were tried and sentenced to death.

Above all, the mutiny was a shocking reminder to the British that they had won India by the sword

Mutineers Surprised by the 9th Lancers. A drawing from the book *Campaign in India 1857–58* which was dedicated to Queen Victoria.

and could lose it by the sword. After the mutiny, even in the halcyon days of the 1880s and 1890s, British confidence in their own permanence was never complete. The suspicion always lingered that the great early administrators had been right, that British rule was only for a time, though perhaps for quite a long time.

The most disastrous result was social. Relationships between Indians and Englishmen had been intimate in the early days when Indians were potentates and Englishmen had Indian mistresses. They had weakened considerably in the generation before the mutiny. In Northern India they weakened further in the half century after. Clubs were often for white men only, and British social life went on largely within the British community. The Briton knew his soldiers or the peasants of his district or his policemen. He talked to his servants and his clerks, and he chatted with the great men of the district when they came to call or to ask a favor. But rarely again in Northern India did Britons relax in Indian company to the extent that they had at one time when the officers of Cawnpore had played billiards with the Nana Sahib.

The mutiny had more material consequences too. The first was the abolition of the East India Company in August, 1858, followed on November 1 by Queen Victoria's proclamation announcing the transfer of India's affairs to the crown and offering a full amnesty to her Indian subjects. The Bengal Army was disbanded and the native contingent in the Indian Army was reduced. Moreover, the British contingent was raised in such a manner as to bring the premutiny ratio of one Briton to six Indians up to one Briton to two Indians. Indians were also debarred from the artillery.

There were rewards for those who had remained loyal and punishments for those who had revolted. The new regiments that had been raised in the Punjab were retained, and landlords who had helped refugees were given extra villages. The Sikhs, who had swarmed to the British colors, were favored; the Moslems of the United Provinces were suspect for a generation. Bengal, Bombay, Madras, the Punjab progressed socially and economically; the Hindi-speaking areas, the mainspring of the revolt, remained backward.

For the British, the mutiny was a lesson on the dangers of reforming zeal. The new government of the Queen showed none of the radicalism of Lord Dalhousie. Adopted heirs were recognized; annexation of princely states was terminated, and the British Viceroy was very slow to interfere even with the most grievous misgovernment. The Talukdars of Oudh were guaranteed their rights, and religion was left untouched. (Untouchability went on, and child marriage was not stopped until Indian opinion itself demanded legislation). The British government enforced law and order, built railways and public works and defended the frontiers. It no longer tried to change Indian society, except by the slow and indirect method of Western-style education, and there were some who criticized even that.

Such caution meant that when the demand for social reform did arise in India, the leaders of it more and more joined the parties that were asking for self-government. Yet they were all men whose minds had been formed by British-style education. The true victory of the British over the mutiny was that the leaders of the independence movement that followed were nearly all reformers. Not one was descended from a rebel of 1857. TAYA ZINKIN

The Victorian novel

The excesses of the Indian Mutiny shocked English society. They disturbed the calm complacency of mid-Victorian London and temporarily discredited the patronizing assumption that British sovereignty universally bestowed beneficent rule. There was a startling contrast between the news from India and the sedate tone of government in Westminster. Only a few months earlier, members of the House of Commons had fulminated against commanding officers who permitted regimental bands to give concerts in the royal parks on Sunday afternoons, an early display of the Sabbatarianism that was to become a notable feature of late Victorian England. Then in November, 1857, those members read in their newspapers how the women and children of Lucknow had caught the distant sound of marching drums and had realized that relief was at hand; *that* regimental band had also been playing on a Sunday. The Queen herself wrote of "the horrors of shame and every outrage" of Cawnpore, although she felt that detailed accounts of the tragedy should have been suppressed to spare the victims' relatives the pain of knowledge.

There was, indeed, a difference between the reports from Delhi and the normal reading matter of the English middle classes. The year of the mutiny saw the publication of Anthony Trollope's *Barchester Towers*, and George Borrow's *The Romany Rye*, the former a chronicle of ecclesiastical politics in a provincial city, the latter a vivid evocation of vagabond life. The younger generation could be excited by Robert Michael Ballantyne's *Coral Island* or uplifted by the

The most influential of Victorian art critics, John Ruskin.

didactic morality of Thomas Hughes' *Tom Brown's School Days* or the novels of Charlotte M. Yonge. Readers who preferred their fiction in monthly installments (and there were at that time many thousands of serialized novels being published in Britain and the United States) had a chance to finish *Little Dorrit* by Charles Dickens, to begin *The Virginians* by William Makepeace Thackeray and to complete *Scenes of Clerical Life* by a highly praised young novelist who called herself George Eliot. Alfred, Lord Tennyson, Poet Laureate since 1850, was turning his muse to Arthurian legend and was momentarily less in favor than Matthew Arnold, who had been elected Professor of Poetry at Oxford. John Ruskin, who had surprised his readers in 1856 by ending Volume III of *Modern Painters* with a digression on the Crimean War, was puzzling earnest listeners in Manchester with lectures on "The Political Economy of the Arts." The cultural taste of the decade was certainly eclectic, although it was perhaps a little amateur in its enthusiasm and disapprobation. It was also strangely homemade. At both the beginning and end of the century, the English mind was open to easy dominance by Continental ideas, but in the second half of the 1850s it was very insular.

Enter the tourist

During the 1850s and 1860s the middle classes for the first time began to be able to afford foreign travel. In 1855, Thomas Cook—who had been organizing railway excursions in the Midlands for ten years—had the enterprise to arrange a special trip to Paris. Soon Cook's Tours were conveying English visitors to Switzerland and Italy as well as France. Leisure travel became an industry before 1870 and grew rapidly in the following two decades, especially after the introduction of sleeping cars—an American innovation—in 1873. Foreign travel, which had been the privilege of the very rich, the exile and the mercenary soldier, was now available to a larger middle-class market. With the birth of the tourist, the Grand Tour took on a new meaning.

The English were the most numerous and determined of foreign tourists (although Germans,

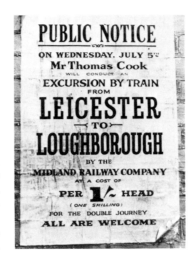

The first advertisement for Cook's Tours—the beginning of organized tourism.

complete with the loftily patronizing guidebooks of Karl Baedeker, flocked to Venice, Florence and Paris). It is probable that travel of this nature merely confirmed established national prejudice, but it did at least represent a change in social habit.

In general, the French saw no need to leave their native land, unless, like Victor Hugo, their political conscience forced them into exile. As in earlier centuries, a small number of French critics did travel, and their astringent comments on neighboring countries have rare value. Hippolyte Taine, for example, was in England from 1861 to 1862; and although his conclusion that English women had long teeth because they persisted in eating too much meat and long feet because they tramped for miles across rain-sodden fields may have lacked generosity, his observation of the social distinctions separating the propertied classes from the laborers helped to explain why Karl Marx found London such an ideal center for studying capitalism.

Taine's London

Taine noted the five miles of prosperous houses that covered the hills of south London; the iron resolution of the businessmen with perpendicular black hats and rolled umbrellas who arrived each morning at the railway terminals; and the massive Italianate squares of London's West End. He contrasted this repository of wealth with squalid alleys "in the shade of the monumental streets," where "pale

children nestled on mud-stained stairs." And he noted the mean rows of gray houses in the liquid fog of "dockland," an area as large as many Continental cities where the "submerged tenth" of the population hid their lives in despairing shame.

No doubt Taine was overly harsh; working-class districts were as much a part of the Industrial Age as the steam engine, and brutality and degradation were present in the Parisian slums as much as in those of London (as the sociological novels of Emile Zola record). The mortality rate was actually higher in the poorer parts of Berlin than in similar areas of London, Birmingham or Liverpool. The extraordinary feature of mid-Victorian London was the size of each stratum of society. The commercial aristocracy could be numbered in thousands, rather than in hundreds (as it was in New York, Baltimore and Boston during America's Gilded Age), and by 1861 the chronically poor in London

Hippolyte Taine, the first writer to examine the structure of London society.

were reckoned at a quarter of a million.

Until the last quarter of the century, there was a lamentable failure to provide an adequate water supply for London or to institute proper drainage. Consequently, the stench from the Thames became so bad by the summer of 1858 that the House of Commons was almost uninhabitable. England, like most of Western Europe, had been ravaged by an epidemic of cholera in 1831–33, but it was not until the disease returned on a large scale in 1865–66 that a royal commission was established to discover "the requirements necessary for civilized social life." (Parliament accepted the responsibility for educating the local authorities in public health during the next decade.) Yet, paradoxically, the Victorians always accepted the need for tidiness and cleanliness. In one of his lighter moments, the Prussian historian Heinrich von Treitschke (1834–96) declared, "The English think that Soap is Civilization." And there was justice in his dictum, for Victorian cleanliness—like the godliness that it proverbially stood next 'to—was considered an outward sign of an inner respectability.

Steel and steam

Many of the inventions of the earlier part of the century had come not from the minds of distinguished scientists but from the practical application of natural ingenuity by mechanics and artisans. After about 1850, however, technical progress became more complex. The spread of railways across continents required cooperation between men who could build tunnels and bridges, lay telegraphic wires along the track and understand the stresses and strains of the new processes of making steel. Similarly the application of the dynamo to generate electricity depended on adapting the researches of the physicist to the mass demands of the factory system.

The second stage of the Industrial Revolution was far less dramatic in its immediate impact and far more specialized than the first stage had been, but its effects were even more far reaching. The globe itself was rapidly encompassed by technology, and the laying

An early clipper. During the 1850s coal-burning steamships dealt a death blow to the graceful clippers.

of the first durable and successful cable for the electric telegraph under the Atlantic in 1866 marked the dawn of a new age in communications.

It would, however, be a mistake to antedate the triumph of steam and steel. British shipyards built more vessels in the 1860s and 1870s than ever before, easily outstripping the combined output of the other European powers. But although a few steel ships were launched in the 1860s, most vessels were made of iron—which was far cheaper—until the middle of the 1880s. Many ships of the period were composites of wood resting on an iron frame (the famous Cutty Sark was built in this way in 1869). The earliest British steamship lines, the Peninsular and Orient and the Cunard companies, had begun their services in 1839 and 1840 respectively. But it was not until 1883 that the registered tonnage of British steamships was greater than that of British sailing ships. Significantly that change coincided with the Cunard Line's introduction of the first all-steel transatlantic liners (which were illuminated by incandescent electric light and were powered by ever-improving engines).

Before the revolution in shipping was complete, sail momentarily reached the acme of perfection. The loveliest and fastest ships in the world were the Yankee clippers of the 1850s—long, narrow, tall-masted vessels with gracefully curved concave bows and an enormous spread of sail, whose foremost designer-builders were Donald McKay in Boston and William Webb in New York. In

1854 one of these beautiful vessels sailed 465 nautical miles in a single day's run—an average speed of over twenty knots—and another crossed from Boston to Liverpool in the record time of twelve days and six hours. The preeminence of the clipper ships was, however, short-lived. Iron, screw-driven steamers forced them off the Atlantic run at the end of the 1850s, and a decade later the oceanic sailing ships of all countries suffered a fatal blow when the opening of the Suez Canal destroyed the need for crossings to Australia and the Orient from Europe and the west coast of the United States by way of the dangerous Cape Horn. The future was with steam but for some ten years the majesty of the clippers reigned supreme.

Scientific discoveries

But it was not only at sea that the age of steam and steel made its presence felt. The middle years of the nineteenth century saw a new spirit of scientific enquiry. Michael Faraday (1791–1867) had made possible the harnessing of electricity by his formulation of the principles of electromagnetic induction in 1841 and his discovery of diamagnetism in 1845. James Joule (1819–89) had informed the British Association in the same year that he had established the primary facts of the conservation of energy and had formulated the first law of thermodynamics. The second law of thermodynamics (on which most developments in physical chemistry and engineering have subsequently been based) had been first pro-

pounded by the French physicist Sadi Carnot (1796–1832) in a paper discovered in 1838, after his death. Its importance, however, only came to be fully realized following the work of Rudolph Clausius (1822–88) in Germany in 1850 and William Thomson (1824–1907), Baron Kelvin, in England in 1853.

Indeed scientific progress was international in scope. The work of the German Hermann von Helmholtz (1821–94) complemented that of Joule and Kelvin, and Italy's Alessandro Volta (1745–1827), France's André Marie Ampère (1775–1836) and Germany's Georg Ohm (1787–1854) were at least as much the fathers of electricity as was Faraday.

Sir Charles Lyell, the geologist who challenged the chronological assumptions of the Old Testament.

Other disciplines were also beginning to come under scrutiny. The geological studies of Sir Charles Lyell (1797–1875) challenged the chronological assumptions of the Old Testament, and the cell theory of living organisms, formulated in 1838 by Matthias Schleiden (1804–81), revolutionized the field of biology. As yet, however, the educated public had taken little notice of these developments in science. Lyell, who was a pillar of polite society, advanced his theories with an air of apology, and Joule's important address to the British Association for the Advancement of Science was hardly reported. By the time the British Association met in Oxford in 1861 all that had changed, for two years before Charles Darwin (1809–82) had published *The Origin of Species*. Science stood confidently arraigned at the bar of public opinion.

Ape or Angel?

*The "most dangerous man in England"—at least in the year 1859—was a gentle and retiring
invalid named Charles Darwin. The middle-aged naturalist earned that epithet with the
publication of a single volume of scientific speculation,* **The Origin of Species.** *That work,
which was based on data collected over a period of many years, suggested that "natural selection,"
rather than God's Will, dictated which species survived and flourished, and which became extinct.
Most significantly of all, Darwin's treatise implied that man himself was subject to the same
laws of necessary adaptation—what Darwin called "survival of the fittest"—which affected the
finches that the biologist had observed in the Galapagos archipelago in the 1830s.
In denying* **Genesis** *and advocating evolution, Darwin sparked a heated debate among world
scholars. Many rejected Darwin's "monkey theory," but ultimately none could refute it.*

Charles Darwin's diary for late July and early August, 1858, contains the laconic entry: "Began abstract of species book." Like everything about Darwin, except the sweep of his scientific imagination, that casual note was unpretentious and matter-of-fact. One could scarcely have guessed—indeed, Darwin himself did not yet know—that after twenty years of patient preparation he had begun work on a book that was permanently to revolutionize man's attitude toward the natural world as perhaps no other work had ever done. For the book to which Darwin referred was *On the Origin of Species by Means of Natural Selection, or the Preservation of Favoured Races in the Struggle for Life,* a colossal milestone in the history of man's understanding of nature. Its publication was to earn Darwin both enduring fame and temporary vilification as "the most dangerous man in England."

There could hardly have been a less likely person for such denunciation than Darwin, who was a gentle invalid with the tastes of an English country gentleman and a devoted husband and father who impressed his acquaintants with his almost child-like simplicity and goodness. Certainly no such suspicion can have crossed the minds of the other middle-class guests at the King's Head Hotel on the Isle of Wight, where Darwin and his family were staying when he began the book that was ultimately to win its author a resting place alongside Sir Isaac Newton in Westminster Abbey. Yet "Darwinism" was subsequently to become virtually synonymous with militant atheism, callousness and aggression.

All but a very few of Darwin's scientific colleagues would have been astonished to discover that the modest, rather inarticulate, somewhat plodding naturalist was the greatest scientific genius of their century—and the greatest English scientist since Newton. Darwin was known as the author of an entertaining and informative scientific travel journal, *The Voyage of the Beagle,* as an able geologist with a touch of originality, and as an unrivaled authority on barnacles (which he had spent eight years studying). Only a chosen few knew that the patient, laborious, genuinely humble man of science was, in scientific terms, a revolutionary—and was so, moreover, in an area that touched the tenderest religious and moral feelings of the Victorian world, the question of the origin of species.

More accurately, only a few had known of Darwin's genius prior to July, 1858. And the rest might never have known, but for an event that occurred on June 18 of that year—an event that was to force Darwin out of his long secretiveness. On that date Darwin received a paper from a young naturalist in the East Indies, Alfred Russel Wallace, that showed that Wallace had hit independently on the key idea of Darwin's own work. Horrified at the prospect of a squalid controversy over precedence, Darwin called in leading men of science to arbitrate —and Wallace's paper was read (together with one Darwin had written in 1844) to a meeting of the Linnean Society in London on July 1. Darwin had declared himself at last.

Curiously, the papers written by Darwin and Wallace produced little stir in the skeptical atmosphere of a learned society. Speculation on the origin of species was not uncommon; the question was whether Darwin's theory would prove the key to the problem. Darwin's supporting evidence, accumulated during years of research, was the basis for the "species book" that he began to write in late July of 1858 while his family enjoyed their South Coast holiday.

On April 5, 1859, Darwin sent the first three chapters of that book to his publisher, John Murray. Murray was somewhat doubtful. What would "natural selection" mean to the public? Why was the book called an "abstract"? Would it sell? One of his advisers suggested that Darwin publish only the part of the work that dealt with pigeons and include a brief statement of his theory with it. Modest though he was, Darwin fortunately objected

ON

THE ORIGIN OF SPECIE:

BY MEANS OF NATURAL SELECTION,

OR THE

PRESERVATION OF FAVOURED RACES IN THE STRUGGLE
FOR LIFE.

By CHARLES DARWIN, M.A.,

FELLOW OF THE ROYAL, GEOLOGICAL, LINNÆAN, ETC., SOCIETIES;
AUTHOR OF 'JOURNAL OF RESEARCHES DURING H. M. S. BEAGLE'S VOYAGE
ROUND THE WORLD.'

LONDON:
JOHN MURRAY, ALBEMARLE STREET.
1859.

The title-page of the first
edition of *The Origin of
Species.*

Opposite Charles Darwin
"the most dangerous man in
England."

Right Down House, Kent, where Darwin lived for many years.

Opposite Charles Darwin in 1840.

Canon Charles Kingsley, Regius Professor of History at Cambridge. He was one of Darwin's earliest supporters.

to the proposal. Murray's doubts about whether the book would sell proved unfounded. He printed 1,250 copies, and published the book in November 1859. A second edition was called for immediately.

Years earlier, when he had first revealed his secret to his friend, the botanist Joseph Hooker, Darwin had written that his admitting to a belief in evolution, or "transmutation" as it was then called, was "like confessing a murder." The immediate reaction to *The Origin of Species* showed that Darwin's apprehensions were well founded. The book raised a storm of controversy from which Darwin held aloof as far as he could. He had tried, he said, to ensure that his book was "not more *un-*orthodox than the subject makes inevitable. I do not bring in any discussion about Genesis," he added, but his disclaimer was in vain. Darwin's theory was passionately denounced by orthodox believers. A distinguished scientist to whom Darwin had sent a copy of the book wrote back that he had found it "grievously mischievous" and that it had greatly shocked his moral sense. One journal observed that the book was "subversive of the foundation of both religion and morality."

The subversiveness of the book did not lie simply—or even mainly—in the fact that it contradicted the literal word of the book of Genesis, although there were some to whom that fact alone was affront enough. Orthodox, educated opinion had recently learned to interpret at least some of the Bible's statements about the creation in a figurative way. The science of geology, for example, had

revealed that the formation of the earth's crust was a matter of millions of years rather than six days. "Days" had subsequently been interpreted as symbolizing epochs of enormous duration. It is even possible that the idea of evolution as a scientific interpretation of God's command to "let the earth bring forth the living creature after his kind, cattle and creeping things and beasts of the earth," might have been accepted without too much anguish. The crucial row arose over a creature who was not discussed at all in *The Origin of Species* (although Darwin was to do him full justice in later works): that creature was man.

The new geology had not yet ventured any observations about man. The earth itself might be unimaginably old, and the evidence locked in the earth might suggest that whole species had arisen and then become extinct. But man was still taken to be a creature whose story spanned only some six thousand years. Adam was a still plausible ancestor for such a species, and knowledge of man's early history was still based largely on the Old Testament. To see mankind as a product of evolution from lower animal and amphibian species—as cousin to the apes and descended from them—seemed a shocking debasement of human nature. *That* concept was what made "Darwinism" subversive. Critics called Darwinism "the monkey theory," a low, materialistic doctrine which asserted that "there is no God, and the ape is our Adam."

Darwin's theory soon won distinguished converts among leading scientists who were impressed by the

Darwin and his Precursors

1721
Charles de Montesquieu conceives of the possibility of change in species

1753
Denis Diderot sees possibility of common ancestor for all living bodies

1760
Carl Linnaeus doubts the unchangeability of organisms

1785
James Hutton attacks traditional biblical chronology and the idea of a universal flood

1794
Erasmus Darwin propounds an early theory of evolution

1809
Jean Baptiste de Lamarck helps make evolutionary ideas respectable

1817
William Smith's *Stratigraphical System of Organized Fossils* throws doubts on the biblical concept of creation

1830
Sir Charles Lyell's *Principles of Geology* opposes ideas of catastrophe in pre-history

1844
Robert Chambers in his anonymous *Vestiges of the Natural History of Creation* advocates a crude — and unpopular — theory of evolution

1858
Darwin and Wallace publish short articles on evolution and natural selection

1859
Publication of *The Origin of Species*

The Beagle, on which Darwin made an important voyage of discovery to South America.

ingenuity of his arguments and the sheer weight of the evidence that supported them. However, not even Darwin's closest friends were easily won over. The belief that each species was fixed for all time, exactly as it had issued from the hands of God (if not on the sixth day of the Creation, at least at some distinct point in time), was still the orthodox belief in 1859, not only among the laity but also in the scientific community. That belief had occasionally been challenged, it is true. In 1844, for example, *Vestiges of the Natural History of Creation* had caused a sensation when it was published anonymously by the Scottish publisher Robert Chambers. Like many such "challenges," *Vestiges* was scientifically disreputable, and it served to discredit rather than further the concept of evolution.

Darwin could sympathize with the attitude of those who doubted evolution on scientific grounds (he too regarded *Vestiges* as rubbish). He had come to the idea of evolution—against the weight of

scientific opinion and against his own earlier acceptance of the "fixity" of species—with some difficulty, and his acceptance of that radical view had come only after a voyage around the world. Darwin's interest in evolution had first been aroused in the late 1830s while he was traveling around South America as ship's naturalist aboard the naval survey ship H.M.S. *Beagle*. He had been struck then by the close resemblances between species in the same area and by their similarity to extinct species of the area, which suggested that they had come from a common stock and had become distinct species only in the course of time and as they spread outward. Why should species be so distributed if each were the result of a unique, divine creation?

Darwin did not invent the doctrine of evolution. The idea had been considered by the ancient Greeks, and it had been toyed with by the thinkers of the eighteenth-century Enlightenment. It was only in the nineteenth century, however, that men's

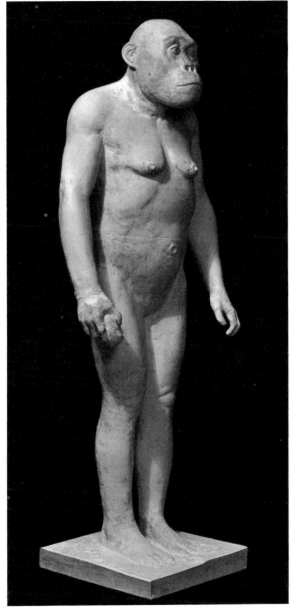

understanding of the fossil record of the successive forms of life became adequate to support a theory of evolution, just as it was only in the nineteenth century that the new, drastically revised estimates of the age of the earth allowed sufficient time for biological evolution. It would have been utterly incredible to suppose that life had developed its complex and varied forms in a mere six thousand years (the long-accepted estimate of the earth's duration). Moreover, the fact that much of that six-thousand-year period was recorded history and contained no historical record of dramatic biological transformations added to its implausibility.

More significantly, the idea of evolution was congenial to the belief in progress so characteristic of the period. It also appealed to many people because it seemed more truly scientific than the theory of special creations. Ever since the seventeenth century, physicists and chemists had refused to concede that God's intervention was a direct cause of physical occurrences, but biologists were still obliged, in explaining the origin of living species, to speak, as Darwin said, as though "elemental atoms have been commanded suddenly to flash into living tissues." If it could be established that the species had emerged gradually, in accordance with the operation of a natural law of organic development, then biology too could dispense with the need to invoke sudden and incalculable Divine Intervention to explain its subject matter.

But what law of development could explain evolution? The inadequacy of pre-Darwinian explanations was largely responsible for the skepticism about evolution that was felt by scientists, and that theoretic shortcoming was coupled with the fact that the fossil record of the earth's history was too fragmentary to prove whether life had developed from the simplest beginnings through successively more complex forms. Evolutionist doctrines had been reduced to the level of sheer guesswork. The

45

Above Bishop Wilberforce of Oxford, most energetic of the anti-Darwinians.

Right John Murray, the publisher of *The Origin of the Species*.

(among them Chambers' belief that a whole new species could arise from a single monstrous birth). After a superficial reading of Darwin's work his publisher, John Murray, seems to have thought that *The Origin of Species* was a reworking of Chambers' *Vestiges*, for he declared that Darwin's theory was "as absurd as though one should contemplate a fruitful union between a poker and a rabbit."

A plausible explanation of evolution was one of Darwin's two great achievements; the other was the almost infinite pains and the very remarkable success with which he anticipated objections to his theory and vindicated it through numerous references to a vast compendium of natural observations. He thus set evolutionary theory on a completely new path. From this point on, testable theory replaced wild guesswork in accounting for the variety of living things.

In his autobiography Darwin declared that he owed his discovery of the mechanism of evolution to the economist Thomas Malthus, whose work he read shortly after his return from the voyage of the *Beagle*. At the time his mind was full of the puzzling evidence for evolution he had encountered in South America. Malthus had pointed to the discrepancy between the capacity of populations to expand and their limited food supply; Darwin applied Malthus' theory to the problem of species that so preoccupied him. Populations were kept down by restrictions on their food supply. But which elements in the population survived and left offspring? In a natural state, those best adapted to their environment survived, Darwin answered. That was the law of "natural selection." It led to the formation of new species through the commonly observed and apparently random variations that

noted nineteenth-century evolutionist and zoologist J.B. de Lamarck had held that creatures acquired new organs to satisfy new needs and then passed these modifications on to their offspring in the next generation. There was no evidence for Lamarck's speculation, and Darwin himself held that the Frenchman's theory was nonsense.

Like virtually all nineteenth-century biologists, Darwin did believe that attributes acquired in an animal's lifetime could be passed on to the next generation—a belief no longer accepted by scientists. He did not subscribe to several of the less appealing contemporary explanations of evolution

occurred in offspring. *Some* of these variations conferred an advantage on their possessors; those fortunate few had been "selected" by nature for survival and perpetuation just as a dog breeder selects the variations he wishes to encourage. Darwin wrote:

Owing to this struggle for life, any variation, however slight, if it can be in any degree profitable to an individual of any species, in its infinitely complex relations to other organic beings and to external nature, will tend to the preservation of that individual, and will generally be inherited by its offspring.

The concept of natural selection was Darwin's greatest contribution to evolutionary theory, but it was also the point at which Darwin's theory most rudely shattered traditional notions of God and nature. Evolution would have been a less revolutionary doctrine had it merely asserted a development of living forms, in the general direction of greater complexity and specialization, while accounting for this development in terms of an overall cosmic purpose. Darwin, however, would have none of such purposeful evolution. "Never use the words higher and lower," he wrote in his copy of *Vestiges of the Natural History of Creation*. Nature was not purposeful. So far as science could tell, man was not the result of some long-prepared cosmic plan. Natural selection was simply the result of scarcity working upon blind chance—the occurrence of chance variations in offspring. It would select *anything* if it was better adapted to the environment than its competitors. Within the realm of Darwinian theory, science and emotion were obliged to part company; man's sense of purpose could not be projected into nature, and man himself appeared to be the random product of a blindly struggling nature.

Theologians quickly came to terms with the Darwinian world. Charles Kingsley, a novelist and theologian who was one of the earliest to accept Darwin's theory, wrote to him:

I have gradually learnt to see that it is just as noble a conception of the Deity to believe that He created primal forms capable of self-development as to believe that He required a fresh intervention to fill the [voids] which He himself had made.

Humanists like Sir Julian Huxley, himself the grandson of Darwin's great champion T. H. Huxley, have found excitement in the idea that in man evolution has produced, albeit blindly, a creature capable of purposive control of his environment and of his destiny as a species. Nevertheless, it seems unlikely that anyone now can ever feel quite the same sense of community with the natural world as when nature's ends were thought of as divinely attuned to those of men, and Adam, quickened into life by the finger of God Himself, was little more than a great-grandfather. Twentieth-century thought, and doctrines like existentialism and logical positivism, presuppose the purposelessness of the physical world to an extent that would have been almost unthinkable in the early nineteenth century.

Some, it is true, have found positive inspiration in the idea of a struggle for existence. To some war became "a biological necessity"; the law of competition in business was "the survival of the fittest." Marx announced that *The Origin of Species* provided "a basis in natural science for the class-struggle in history," and Darwinian ideas formed an integral part of Hitler's doctrine of racial superiority. Such uses of Darwinism have diminished in recent years, for the problems of human society are too complex and their solution too much a matter of human preference to be resolved by a simple formula like the survival of the fittest. Societies themselves do whatever selecting is done on grounds quite different from nature's.

One subsequent development in which Darwin would undoubtedly have rejoiced has been the development of the science of genetics. To Darwin the causes of the mutations on which his theory rested remained a mystery. Genetics has now begun to penetrate the mystery, and modern biology rests equally on Mendelian genetics and Darwinian evolution by natural selection.   J. W. BURROW

Above Erasmus Darwin, grandfather of Charles Darwin and precursor of much of his thinking.

Above left Wallace, one of Darwin's contemporaries, who independently came to similar conclusions to those of Darwin.

Far left A cartoon entitled *The Lion of the Season* published in *Punch* during the controversy that followed the publication of Darwin's book. The alarmed flunkey exclaims "Mr. G-g-g-o-o-o-rilla" as the guest enters.

Apes or angels?

In November, 1864, Benjamin Disraeli, one of the most gifted of British parliamentary debaters, summarized the Darwinian controversy in a speech at Oxford. "Is Man an ape or an angel?" he asked, adding, "I, my lord, I am on the side of the angels." So, indeed, were most men and women in the Western world. Popular pride in progress and achievement rejected the "new-fangled theories" that traced descent from the primitive anthropoids. Familiar concepts of Divine Revelation had a comforting reassurance that made

Herbert Spencer, who built a reputation as the greatest exponent of Darwinism as a social philosophy.

belief in evolution appear not merely blasphemous but amoral. The possibility of reconciling Genesis and genetics overtaxed conventional minds.

But Darwinism could not be dismissed in a slick Disraelian phrase. It provided a powerful reinforcement for thinkers who were already seeking to explain natural phenomena in materialistic terms. Historical analysts and social theorists had sought tentative scientific rules of causation for many years, and they were delighted when Darwin was able to show that a synthesis of inquiry could produce an intellectually satisfactory means of speculation. It is hardly surprising that the Father of Communism,

Louis Pasteur, who made great contributions to bacteriological science.

Karl Marx (1818–83), offered to dedicate *Das Kapital* to Darwin in admiration for his researches on biology (an honor that Darwin hastily, but politely, declined), for Marx believed—with some justice —that he was doing for the new discipline of sociology what Darwin had done for biology.

The principle of evolution was gradually extended to other spheres. Darwin's cousin, Sir Francis Galton (1822–1911), ap-

plied it to psychological analysis of the relationship between heredity and ability in 1869; Sir Edward Tylor (1832–1917) applied it to anthropology in 1871; and Walter Bagehot (1826–77) extended it to the growth of political institutions and customs in 1873. The greatest exponent of Darwinism as a social philosophy was Herbert Spencer (1820–1903), whose *Programme of a System of Synthetic Philosophy* was announced in 1860, when its author was forty years old. In the United States, Spencer's impact on educational thought was more direct than Darwin's whose theories continued to arouse virulent hostility in the Bible Belt areas right into the twentieth century. Between them, Darwin and Spencer dominated late Victorian thought as completely as Francis Bacon and René Descartes had dominated that of the late sixteenth and seventeenth centuries.

Yet if the scientific age had found its prophet in Darwin, it was to gain its most revered figures from the field of medicine. Joseph Lister (1827–1912) in England, Louis Pasteur (1825–95) in France, and Robert Koch (1843–1910) in Germany advanced the study of antiseptics and the isolation and identification of dangerous viruses in the last third of the century.

During that same period the science of bacteriology and the introduction of preventive inoculation grew out of the work that Pasteur was doing in Paris.

Public education comes of age

Herbert Spencer—who was considerably more optimistic than many of his contemporaries— believed in the ultimate inevitability of human perfection, and yet he saw the good life as attainable only through technological improvement. He therefore urged that science, rather than classical studies, form the basis of education. His theories were ahead of their time in England where "public schools"—those exclusive, private institutions where "muscular Christians" imparted the grace of Homer and the wisdom of Cicero to the future rulers of the British Empire with numerous strokes of the birch—were reaching their zenith in the 1860s.

Secondary education in Germany and France, on the other hand, was already coming to terms with the new applied sciences, and American academies had always offered a broader curriculum than the English public schools. There were some six

The Cow Pock, or the wonderful effects of the New Inoculation, a cartoon by James Gillray.

The Last In, by William Mulready. The teacher at a village school bows ironically in greeting a latecomer. Primary education spread rapidly in the second half of the nineteenth century.

thousand academies—almost all of them private institutions controlled by boards of trustees—in the United States on the eve of the Civil War, and the comprehensive educational tradition of Jefferson and Benjamin Franklin still survived in the more prosperous communities of the rapidly expanding American nation.

The Risorgimento

Although the failure of nationalist revolution in 1848 had left Austria in an apparently invincible situation in Italy, the reality was very different. The harsh reaction against liberalism on the part of the Austrian government and of the supposedly independent governments elsewhere in Italy proved to be counterproductive; torture, imprisonment, exile and execution merely united public opinion throughout Italy against repressive government, while the withdrawal of even the shadow of parliamentary representation brought disapproval from Britain and France.

The only Italian state in which the government did not withdraw the constitution was Piedmont, which encompassed both Piedmont and Sardinia. Piedmont alone among the states of Italy retained a European as opposed to a purely local importance. Under the guidance of Prime Minister Count Camillo di Cavour (1810–61), King Victor Emmanuel II sought to increase his country's status as an influential European power. In 1855 Piedmont entered the Crimean War as an ally of France and Britain. Piedmontese troops participated in the Battle of Chernaya in the fall of that year and acquitted themselves well. But Cavour's aim in sending his troops to fight the Russians was no less Italian than European. "Out of this mud, Italy will be made," a Piedmontese soldier is alleged to have said at Chernaya—and in a real sense he was to be proved right. At the Congress of Paris Cavour placed the Italian Question on the agenda of Europe.

What Cavour sought to achieve was a state that would unite all

Italians. It would be a monarchy under the House of Sardinia, but its government would be liberal and would devote itself to social improvement and economic advance. In Piedmont he set an example of the way in which he thought that Italy should be developed: he built railroads and enlarged the port of Genoa; he started extensive irrigation schemes; and he made the government's fiscal system more efficient. His methods won him widespread support among those who sought to unify Italy. His commonsense approach and his determination to get things done were contrasted both with the almost-mystical imaginings of utopians like Giuseppe Mazzini (1805–72) and with the capable but often rash actions of Giuseppe Garibaldi (1807–82). Indeed Garibaldi, who had been a republican, saw how able Cavour was, and pledged his support to the House of Sardinia. He went on to found the Italian National Association, dedicated to working for a united Italy under Victor Emmanuel II.

But without the support of foreign troops the Piedmontese army and those who wanted unification would not have been able to overthrow the forces of reaction in Italy. The Austrian army, unpopular though it was, was firmly in military control, and most of the natural Italian leaders were either exiled or in prison. The papacy under Pius IX had retreated into an illiberalism that was worthy of his reactionary southern neighbor, King Ferdinand II of Naples and Sicily. Ferdinand, who was known as "Bomba" because of the enthusiasm with which he had used his heaviest cannon to crush the rebels in 1848, was the most unpopular monarch in Italy. He had reacted to the 1848 Revolution by trebling the size of his army.

But none of the reactionary regimes was secure. The Austrians knew that they were hated by most of their subjects. The papal government, beset by financial difficulties, was unable to rule efficiently. Naples was in a still weaker position; Bomba's huge army was almost untrained and its loyalty was far from certain. In addition the size of the army put an intolerable strain on the country's already weak economy. The King's unexpected death in 1859 at the age of forty-nine left his young son, Francis II, who lacked even his

The champions of Italy cut the claws of the Austrian bear.

father's meager abilities, to govern his discontented kingdom. In the north, the second war of independence had increased the area under Piedmontese control, and Giuseppe Garibaldi invaded the Neopolitan kingdom.

The Emergence of Italy 1860

The bitter struggle in the Crimea had reached a virtual stalemate by 1855, when Sardinia's shrewd Prime Minister, Count Camillo Benso di Cavour, dispatched a 15,000-man army to aid the French and British. Indeed, hostilities ceased little more than a year later—but by that time the Prime Minister's move had earned his tiny kingdom a hearing at the peace congress in Paris and had netted Sardinia a powerful ally in Napoleon III. As Parma, Modena, Romagna and Tuscany voted for unity with Sardinia, rebellion broke out in the south. Giuseppe Garibaldi and his Thousand Red Shirts sailed to Sicily to aid the rebels and defeated the Bourbons in the name of Victor Emmanuel II, King of Sardinia. Within a year Victor Emmanuel was proclaimed King of Italy.

The *Risorgimento*, the name given to the Italian unification movement, was largely the achievement of three men: Giuseppe Mazzini, Giuseppe Garibaldi and Count Camillo Benso di Cavour. Of the three, only Cavour, the head of the Sardinian government, had the means at his disposal to achieve the aims that had long been voiced so passionately by Italian patriots. Aspirations of independence had naturally found expression in the works of Machiavelli, Alfieri and Ugo Foscolo. But not until the 1830s were those aspirations consciously directed toward national unity.

Mazzini promoted a unification movement in the 1830s and encouraged insurrections against Austrian rule, but the Republic of Rome that his movement established was suppressed by the French in 1849. In the previous year, King Charles Albert of Sardinia (Piedmont) granted his kingdom a constitution and declared war on Austria. He was defeated at the battles of Custoza and Novara and abdicated in 1849 in favor of his son, Victor Emmanuel II. The young King invited Cavour to join the government—first as Minister of Agriculture and Commerce, later as Minister of Finance, and finally in October, 1852, as Prime Minister—despite the fact that he strongly disliked him.

Cavour's political genius was soon revealed: he introduced social and economic reforms to Sardinia (in order to win French and British sympathy) and then—in his first daring act of diplomacy—he persuaded his King to send a small contingent of 15,000 men to the Crimea to fight with the allied armies against tsarist Russia in 1855.

Cavour's bold move demonstrated Piedmont's solidarity with the Western powers, and when hostilities ended in the Crimea and a diplomatic congress was convened in Paris to draw up the terms of the peace treaty, Cavour took part in those peace talks. He was careful to adopt a reserved and modest attitude toward the great powers. Cavour's primary objective was to gain the sympathies, through informal private meetings, of ministers who

had already been shocked by the little they knew about the triumphant antiliberal forces in most of the Italian states, above all in Rome. The Emperor Napoleon III listened sympathetically; the British Minister, Lord Clarendon, and Count Walewski, the French president of the congress, condemned the reactionary policies of both the Papal States and the Kingdom of the Two Sicilies (as Naples and Sicily were called at the time). Cavour, for his part, pointed out that the revolutionary upheavals in the Italian peninsula, fostered by the stupidity and blind indifference of absolutist rulers, were a potential danger not only to the Kingdom of Sardinia but to the peace of Europe as a whole. The congress ended stormily with the majority of the delegates expressing themselves clearly in favor of Italian reforms in spite of Austria's determined opposition. From then on, Europe could no longer ignore the Italian problem.

Cavour returned home in triumph. He had already persuaded the French Emperor that war against Austria was the only way to achieve the aims voiced so persistently by the Italian people. He then informed the Sardinian Parliament that he and the Austrian delegates to the peace congress in Paris had parted company "with the firm conviction that they were further away than ever from finding some form of compromise between the policies of the two countries, and that the principles upheld by each country were irreconcilable."

In the eyes of Italian liberals, the leader of the Piedmontese government had now become the champion of what was to be, from that time on, a national cause. Cavour's future success depended on two conditions: first, that a military alliance be formed with France, and second, that Austria be provoked into declaring war on Piedmont (so that the latter would not appear to be the aggressor in the eyes of the world).

On July 21, 1858, Cavour and Napoleon III reached a secret verbal agreement that France would come to the aid of Sardinia if Austria attacked

Pope Piux IX, whose early liberalism was translated into bigoted reaction after the revolutions of 1848 had threatened the Papal States. His determined opposition to the movement for Italian unity was almost successful.

Opposite Garibaldi looking over the city of Capua.

Count Cavour, Prime Minister of the Kingdom of Sardinia, and architect of the *Risorgimento*.

Cavour's homeland. War between the Franco-Sardinian alliance and Austria seemed inevitable. The latter no longer made any secret of its military buildup along the Piedmontese frontier, while on the other side, a marriage between Princess Clotilda, eldest daughter of the King of Sardinia, and Prince Jerome Napoleon, the Emperor's cousin, united the two dynasties. French clerics, who wielded great influence at the court in the Tuileries, were strongly opposed to a conflict that might lead to the end of the temporal power of the papacy. But on April 23, 1859, Austria sent an ultimatum to Piedmont enjoining her to disarm within three days. As a result of that ultimatum, tantamount to a declaration of war, hostilities finally broke out.

Austrian troops crossed the Ticino, on the frontier of Austrian Lombardy, into Piedmont. The French immediately intervened: Napoleon III landed at Genoa on May 12, and his army of 120,000 joined forces with a Piedmontese army of some 60,000 men. The first attack—and the first victory of the Franco-Piedmontese forces—took place near the small village of Montebello. It was carried out with such spirit that the Austrian general mistakenly thought the enemy was making a frontal attack and hurriedly withdrew his soldiers to the south. A second confrontation took place at the village of Magenta, which the French soldiers occupied with difficulty, house by house, on June 4. Four days later, King Victor Emmanuel and Napoleon III made a triumphal entry into Milan.

The next great battle began on the morning of June 24, on the hills south of Lake Garda, where the Franco-Piedmontese forces were suddenly confronted by the massed Austrian army. The terrible battle that followed was waged violently and relentlessly throughout the day along a seven-mile front. Fighting was fiercest around the villages of Solferino—which was finally occupied by the French late in the evening—and San Martino, which a Piedmontese army led by King Victor Emmanuel gained and lost four times before re-occupying it for a fifth time at about six o'clock in the evening. The Austrian troops were forced to retreat during a terrific storm to the fortress of Peschiera. The losses suffered in the course of the day's fighting totaled 25,000 killed or wounded.

The whole of Italy waited breathlessly for the liberation of Venetia, for according to the agreement drafted at Plombières and ratified at Turin, that region, together with Lombardy and Piedmont, was to form part of the independent kingdom of northern Italy. To the Italians' considerable surprise, the news suddenly came through that the Austrian and French emperors had met at Villafranca di Verona on July 8—without the knowledge of Victor Emmanuel—and had signed an armistice. Lombardy was to be ceded to Napoleon III, who, in turn, would hand it over to Piedmont. The other Italian states were to form a federation presided over by the Pope, while Venetia, although belonging to the federation, would continue to be an Austrian possession.

The Italian people were profoundly disillusioned when they heard the news, and Napoleon's popularity on the peninsula evaporated overnight. Cavour tried desperately to enlist the help of the army, bitterly reproached his King for having accepted such terms and handed in his resignation. Victor Emmanuel had realized more clearly than Cavour, however, that it would be unwise to sever relations with an ally to whom he already owed so much.

Napoleon III's decision had been determined by a number of factors. The first was a simple question of humanity, for he had been profoundly moved by the horrifying sight of the battlefield at Solferino piled high with corpses, and he was afraid that the battles to follow might be even more bloody and violent. (The Prussian government had indicated that it might invade France if French victories against the Austrians continued.) Equally serious was the growing unrest among clerical circles in France itself. Finally, Napoleon III was reluctant to see Italy expand beyond the frontiers already defined by his uncle when he had created the Kingdom of Italy for his stepson, Eugène de Beauharnais.

The peace treaty that was concluded at Zurich on November 10, 1859, envisaged a confederation of Italian states under their former rulers. In actual fact, however, the dispossessed rulers had no chance whatsoever of recovering their states by force. The whole of central Italy longed to be united with Piedmont, and plebiscites held in 1860 in Parma, Modena, Tuscany and the Papal States of Bologna and Romagna approved such a union. Yet the uninspired, timid Sardinian government that had replaced Cavour lacked the necessary authority

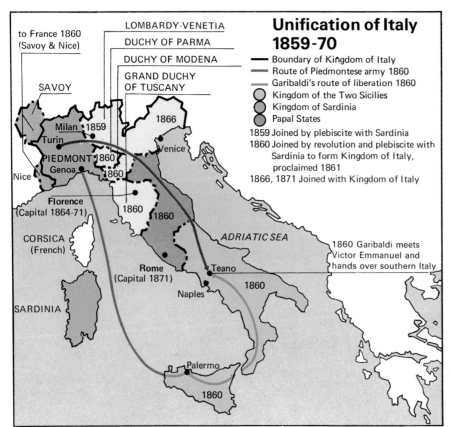

Unification of Italy 1859-70

LOMBARDY-VENETIA
DUCHY OF PARMA
DUCHY OF MODENA
GRAND DUCHY OF TUSCANY

to France 1860 (Savoy & Nice)
SAVOY
Milan 1859
Turin
PIEDMONT 1860
Nice
Genoa 1860
1866
Venice
Florence (Capital 1864-71)
1860
1860
CORSICA (French)
ADRIATIC SEA
SARDINIA
Rome (Capital 1871)
Teano
1860
Naples
1860
Palermo
1860

— Boundary of Kingdom of Italy
— Route of Piedmontese army 1860
— Garibaldi's route of liberation 1860
○ Kingdom of the Two Sicilies
○ Kingdom of Sardinia
○ Papal States
1859 Joined by plebiscite with Sardinia
1860 Joined by revolution and plebiscite with Sardinia to form Kingdom of Italy, proclaimed 1861
1866, 1871 Joined with Kingdom of Italy

1860 Garibaldi meets Victor Emmanuel and hands over southern Italy

and initiative to take advantage of the situation and press for union. The King, realizing the dilemma, overcame his personal resentment toward Cavour and recalled him on January 20, 1860.

The movement for national unity had found a leader once again. Cavour had little difficulty in making Napoleon III realize that it was impossible for him to oppose the Italian people's desire for union with Piedmont, since Napoleon himself had been elected to power by popular vote. As a reward for recognizing the plebiscites in Italy, France was given Savoy on March 24, 1860, as well as the county of Nice—which, as Cavour was quick to point out in the Sardinian Parliament, was really far more Provençal than Italian in character.

After northern Italy and Tuscany were united, few difficulties arose in integrating populations that differed widely in character and traditions. The Hapsburgs had been infinitely superior to the popes and the Spanish Bourbon dynasty in the art of government, and since the eighteenth century they had carried out beneficial reforms in northern Italy, specifically in Milan and Florence. Enormous cultural, economic and even religious differences existed between northern and southern Italy.

Nonetheless, even though rebellion broke out in the spring of 1860 in the Kingdom of the Two Sicilies, it was morally out of the question for Piedmont to launch an attack on the Kingdom of Naples or on the Papal States (which were openly protected by France). Cavour could and did encourage Garibaldi to aid the rebels, however, and the National Society, a large patriotic association, supplied him with arms and money. Cavour secretly allowed volunteers to seize two ships in the port of Genoa, and those vessels were used to transport roughly one thousand volunteers (known as Red Shirts) to Sicily. They arrived off the port of Marsala on May 11, and four days later they came face to face with Bourbon troops at Calatafini. The

enemy was in an advantageous position on a steep, terraced hillside, but the Garibaldini, who were inferior in numbers and arms, attacked with such ferocity and bravery that they finally won. Garibaldi had already publicly proclaimed himself dictator of Sicily in the name of King Victor Emmanuel. The Bourbon government, for its part, inundated the chancelleries of Europe with protests against the perfidy of the Piedmontese government.

Within the space of a few days, Garibaldi's army was reinforced by local volunteers who had flocked to join it from all parts of the island. The army then set off to conquer Palermo. On May 27, after cunningly drawing the main force of the garrison out of Palermo and into the interior of the island, Garibaldi's finest men forced their way into the town after a bayonet attack. Even then they were not in complete control, since the Neapolitan fleet was anchored in the port of Palermo, and large contingents of the Neapolitan army still occupied the citadel. After ten days of fierce fighting, the Bourbons asked for an armistice, and on June 6 they evacuated Palermo.

From that moment on, the victory of Garibaldi's legendary Expedition of the Thousand was assured. Turin came out in open support of the force, ships from Genoa supplied reinforcements, and Francesco Crispi, Garibaldi's deputy, reorganized the civil administration of Sicily. A final battle took place at Milazzo on July 20, where government forces were still in control. The Bourbons were again defeated.

It remained to be seen whether the brave condottiere would carry on the revolutionary struggle in the south of the Italian mainland. At the request of Napoleon III, Victor Emmanuel wrote an official letter to Garibaldi ordering him not to cross the Straits of Messina to the mainland. Cavour, however, secretly countermanded these orders, and on the night of August 19, Garibaldi crossed the Straits and landed in Calabria. The Bourbon troops

The triumphal entry of Victor Emmanuel into Brescia, where generations of repression led to great rejoicing when Austrian rule was cast off.

Left The famous meeting between Garibaldi and Victor Emmanuel at Teano, outside Naples, on October 26, 1860, at which Garibaldi handed over command of his soldiers to the King.

A photograph of Garibaldi in old age.

A dramatic painting of Garibaldi galloping into battle.

Right A meeting of conspirators. The unification of Italy was hindered by the ambitions and rivalries of European powers.

Marshal McMahon, leader of the French troops in Italy. France's support helped the Kingdom of Naples and the Papal States to withstand for a time the movement for unity.

On October 26, a meeting took place on the outskirts of Naples between King Victor Emmanuel and Garibaldi, who handed over the command of his troops to his monarch and went into voluntary retirement on the island of Caprera, which he had made his home. Now only the fortress of Gaeta remained to be taken. But because of French warships lying off the coast, it was impossible for Victor Emmanuel to blockade the fortress from the seaward side. Once again, the Italian monarch was forced to negotiate with Napoleon III, reproaching him for violating the very principle he himself had laid down at Villafranca—the principle of nonintervention in Italian affairs. The Emperor finally gave way and withdrew his fleet in January, 1861. The fortress quickly surrendered, and on February 12, Francis II, the former King of the Two Sicilies, went aboard a ship that Napoleon had placed at his disposal and made his way to Rome. There he set up residence in the Farnese Palace.

During that same month, the first all-Italian Parliament sat in Turin. On the momentous day of March 14 it was unanimously agreed that Victor Emmanuel was to be proclaimed King of the newly created Kingdom of Italy. The new state was immediately recognized by Britain and, a few weeks later, in April, 1861, by the United States and Switzerland.

It now remained for Venice and Rome, together with the surrounding region of Latium, to be incorporated into the new Italy. For political reasons Rome was clearly going to be the most difficult to conquer, for France, anxious that it should remain the great center of Christendom, persisted in giving the city its protection. Even Mazzini, who had wanted Garibaldi to march on Rome, was persuaded of the impossibility of taking the city at that time and turned his attention to Venice. In 1861, however, the time was not yet ripe for either of them to be conquered, and the Italian nationalists were forced to wait for more favorable circumstances.

Unfortunately, Cavour died prematurely on June 6, scarcely three months after the achievement

stationed there completely lost heart and refused to fight. Garibaldi, most anxious not to lose any more time, hurried on to Naples, accompanied only by a few officers. All along the route he was acclaimed as the great liberator of Italy, and on September 7 he entered Naples in the midst of an enthusiastic reception. The Bourbon King, Francis II, had left the capital the previous day and had made his way to the naval fortress of Gaeta, where he and his remaining supporters took refuge.

Cavour, for his part, was determined that the initiative should remain firmly in the hands of the Piedmontese government. Consequently, he persuaded Victor Emmanuel to act on his own, and Piedmont invaded the Marches and Umbria. The inadequate forces defending these provinces (Catholic volunteers recruited in France, Belgium and Ireland) were no match for the regular Piedmontese troops. In spite of the valor of the "papal zouaves," they suffered a crushing defeat.

of the great task he had tirelessly pursued for twelve years. Before he died, however, he outlined the work that lay ahead for his successors: to make Rome the capital of the new Italy. After Cavour's death, the task was carried on by a group of politicians whose policies and attitudes had been molded by this great statesman. They were just as hard-working and unbiased as he had been, as moderate and realistic in their approach, as utterly devoted to their country. Yet they lacked one essential ingredient: his innate political genius.

Garibaldi, however, had still not relinquished the idea of conquering Rome in a surprise attack similar to that carried out by the Thousand, and from 1862 on, he grew increasingly restless. In August he landed near Catania at the head of twenty-five hundred volunteers recruited in Sicily; he immediately marched into Calabria. Rattazzi, the Italian Prime Minister, would have been quite ready to shut his eyes to what was going on, but Napoleon III made it clear that any attack launched by Garibaldi on papal territory would constitute a declaration of war. Rattazzi had no choice but to give way in the face of Napoleon's threat.

The next efforts to win Rome were diplomatic. The Turin government, led by Marco Minghetti, engaged in lengthy discussions with Paris about the departure of the French garrison from Rome. They finally agreed in 1864 that the French troops should leave within two years in return for a firm commitment on the part of the Italian government that Garibaldi would not embark on any new adventures. As a guarantee of good faith, the capital of Italy was transferred from Turin to Florence. The transfer provoked great disturbances in Turin, and the King himself was seriously displeased. Minghetti was forced to resign and was succeeded by General di La Marmora.

In September, 1867, Garibaldi again resumed his strong propaganda activities throughout the country in an effort to force the hand of the government and to conquer Rome. The Italian government was sent another warning by France, which must have been perfectly aware of the fact that Rattazzi was powerless to prevent the infiltration of revolutionary elements across the open frontiers of Latium or even stop the flight of Garibaldi from Caprera to take over the leadership of the revolutionaries. Finally, Napoleon III decided to take things into his own hands, and in October he ordered his fleet based at Antibes to set sail for Civitavecchia. On October 26 Garibaldi was victorious against the papal forces at the village of Monteretondo, but a few days later, on November 3, he clashed with French troops at Mentana and suffered a defeat.

Italian bitterness over that defeat contributed to the breaking down of the Franco-Italian alliance. In 1870, after war had broken out between France and Germany, King Victor Emmanuel was prepared to send his Italian troops to fight side by side with his French ally of 1859, but his parliament refused to permit him to do so. Instead, when the French garrison had been withdrawn from Rome after the first defeats of the French army, Italian regular troops entered the Holy City. Pius IX was anxious to avoid bloodshed; he rejected, however, the formal agreement between Italy and France, known as the Law of Guarantees, which recognized the complete spiritual autonomy of the Pope and also assured him the status of a reigning monarch over a certain number of buildings in the city of Rome. He considered himself to be a prisoner in the Vatican.

At the end of the nineteenth century, after the colonial setbacks suffered by Italy in East Africa, a new expansionist movement began to develop. After World War I that movement increased enormously under the Fascists. It brought about a reversal in alliances and led to Italy's defeat in 1945 and to the monarchy's fall. MAURICE VAUSSARD

Francis II, the last of the Bourbons of Naples. Their corruption was equaled only by their incompetence. Francis was regarded as a pale imitation of his father, nicknamed Bomba, and as a result was known as Bombalino.

Left Garibaldi's entry into Naples on September 7, 1860, was accompanied by scenes of wild rejoicing, although he was accompanied by only a handful of men.

After the unification of Italy, Garibaldi continued to play an active role in European struggles. This poster, dating from the Franco-Prussian War, 1870, appeals for musicians to join Garibaldi's Army of the Vosges.

RÉPUBLIQUE FRANÇAISE
Liberté, Égalité, Fraternité

ARMÉE DES VOSGES

APPEL AUX MUSICIENS

Les Citoyens sachant jouer du clairon, et voulant concourir à la délivrance de la Patrie, sont invités se présenter au plus tôt, passage des Terreaux, 2° Bureau d'enrôlement des Volontaires de l'Armée de Vosges, sous le commandement en chef du Général **GARIBALDI.**

Vive la République !

LYON, le 23 octobre 1870.

LE CAPITAINE ORGANISATEUR
DE LA LÉGION GARIBALDIENNE,
PASANISI.

LE VICE-PRÉSIDENT
DU COMITÉ CENTRAL ORGANISATEUR
P. GANGUET.

Lyon, imprimerie Rey et Sezanne, rue St-Côme, 2.

Prussia's Germany

The creation of a united Italy—albeit incomplete at first—was watched with great interest in Germany. There, too, there were many who wanted a unified state, and there, too, there was an obvious candidate for its leadership. During the period after the Congress of Vienna, Prussian influence in the rest of Germany had grown steadily, while that of Austria had no less steadily declined. The creation of the *zollverein* (customs union) gave Prussia a dominant role in German affairs, and the risings of 1848 had not affected this. Hanover, the only important north German state to remain outside the *zollverein*, joined in 1853.

The liberals of the "Frankfurt parliament" that had met in 1848 had been enthusiastic supporters of the concept of a united Germany and they had elected Frederick William IV as Emperor of the Germans, an honor that he hastily declined as he wanted to be elected Emperor by the princes rather than the people. Prussia was an autocratic state, and Frederick William was determined that if Germany was to be united, it should be no less a Hohenzollern autocracy than Prussia.

Frederick William IV, King of Prussia.

In spite of Austrian attempts to undermine the *zollverein*—from which she was excluded on the insistence of Prussia—the years after 1848 were a period of rapid economic growth, both in absolute terms and in comparison with the more static economy of the Austrian Empire. The Krupp factory at Essen, which had had no more than seventy-one workers in 1848, had a thousand in 1858 and more than eight thousand by 1868. Although

A cartoon showing the effect on Germany of an imaginary suspension of the *zollverein*.

the growth of Krupp was abnormally rapid, industrial production in the *zollverein* as a whole rose from 815,000 marks in 1850 to 16 million in 1865.

But Prussian hopes of dominating a new German confederation or a unified German state were threatened by internal problems. Frederick William's lunacy and his brother William's regency created an atmosphere of uncertainty. There was also a serious constitutional crisis over the role of the army. A constitution setting up a two-chamber Diet had been promulgated in 1850. The upper chamber was made up of *junkers* (the Prussian landed gentry), while the lower chamber was elected (indirectly) by a system of manhood suffrage that was heavily weighted in favor of large landowners. This had produced a highly conservative Diet, but even so the King had been determined not to allow it any real power over the army, which remained firmly under his royal control. In 1862 William sought to increase the size of the army, but the lower house of the Diet had refused to sanction the necessary budgetary increase.

The ensuing constitutional crisis was only solved when William appointed Otto von Bismarck (1815–98) as Prime Minister. Bismarck adopted the "gap theory" (*Luckentheorie*) to justify the royal claims; since the constitution did not explain what would happen if the King and the Diet disagreed over a budget, the King (who had promulgated the constitution) should find a solution. Inevitably, William's solution was to collect the extra taxes that he wanted and

to increase the size of his army. Prussia was now ready to achieve its domination of the German states and to claim its leadership of the peoples of Germany.

Extremism in America

If unity was a problem in the divided states of Europe, it was little less so in the United States of America. America in the middle years of the nineteenth century was a land still full of hope and promise, but its promise was tragically marred by contradictions in wealth and culture. Literary

Poet Henry Wadsworth Longfellow, author of *Hiawatha*.

leadership was concentrated in a small area of Massachusetts where Henry Wadsworth Longfellow (1801–82), Oliver Wendell Holmes (1809–94), Henry Thoreau (1817–62) and Nathaniel Hawthorne

(1804–64) lived almost under the shadow of the study of Ralph Waldo Emerson (1803–82), making the village of Concord—at that particular moment—an intellectual center almost as eminent as Paris or Oxford and like them, oriented to the Old World rather than the New. But there was a world of difference between the broad visions of the New England intelligentsia and the narrow hatreds and suspicion of the rural masses. The 1854 elections in Massachusetts gave the Know-Nothing Party—a movement composed of "native" Americans who opposed immigrants, Roman Catholics and anyone who championed what they considered to be un-American ideas—an overwhelming victory in the contest for the state senate, the lower house and the governorship.

The Know-Nothings went on to make substantial gains in Delaware, New York State and Louisiana. At the same time extremists ousted moderates from the humanitarian crusades for bettering conditions in the towns and from the crusade to rid the rural South of the scourge of slavery. And in the Southern states themselves, orators like William Yancey (1814–63) of Alabama and politicians like Robert Rhett (1800–76), who expressed his views in his son's newspaper the Charleston *Mercury*, began to beat the drums of secession.

At mid-century the United States was divided into three vast regions: the South, which was still predominantly dependent on a cotton crop; the North, in which factory towns provided the economic

The Unitarian Church at Concord, Mass., an intellectual center almost as eminent as Paris or Oxford.

the North, deepening the rift in American society

base; and a Middle Border region —Michigan, Ohio, Illinois, Iowa, Indiana, Wisconsin and Minnesota—that was almost as populous as the other two traditional areas and provided a vital link with the vanishing frontier, which had already been enclosed by California, lying across the plains and mountains of the frontier's former edge.

Although the issues splitting the nation emerged from the irreconcilable conflict of North and South, it was in the Middle Border region that the greatest changes in the American way of life were taking place. These were the states that held the balance between the older sections. Had the northwestern markets remained tied to the Mississippi and the South rather than to the newly built railroads of the North and West, the great crisis in the American Union might have been resolved in a different way. Chicago, incorporated as a city of four thousand people in 1837, held the key to America's future twenty years later, thanks largely to the establishment in 1853 of a rail link with New York. There at least hope and promise seemed undimmed.

"Hog butcher for the world"

In the early 1850s the largest factory in Chicago was Cyrus Hall McCormick's plant, which manufactured mechanical reapers that were sold to the farmers in the Great Plains. In the ten years before the Civil War it was men such as McCormick—whose family was to become the best known industrial dynasty in Chicago— who helped transform the city into the world's first farming metropolis.

Although Chicago's prosperity was unequaled, it was not alone in finding itself suddenly prosperous. Fifty times as much wheat passed through Milwaukee in 1860 as in 1851, and trade down the Ohio and Mississippi valleys reached such a peak in 1860 that no less than 3,566 riverboat cargoes were unloaded at New Orleans in the last year of peace. The really significant development of those ten years was the growth of railroad mileage in the state of Illinois; it leaped from a mere 110 miles of track in 1850 to 2,867 miles in 1860. Small wonder that in May, 1860, the six-year-old Republican Party held its national convention

in Chicago and chose, on its third ballot, the only presidential candidate capable of carrying Illinois in the ballot—Abraham Lincoln of Springfield.

The Union imperiled

At the end of the prewar period, industry, agriculture and business seemed to be flourishing everywhere except in the older slave states. But in 1857 a cyclical depression (resulting from land speculation and overdevelopment of railroads) threw the economy into momentary confusion. The panic caused real distress in the industrial cities of the East and brought hardship to the sheep farmers of Ohio, but it made little difference to the growing productivity of the wheatlands.

Unfortunately the depression also confirmed the political leaders of the South in the belief that their wealth, based upon cotton and spared by the depression, was "permanent" whereas that of the North was "fugitive and fictitious."

With each year that passed, the divisions that separated North from South grew deeper and deeper. Far more was at stake than even the gross human indignity of slavery. It was the failure of rival societies to understand each other.

America at war

There had already been incidents such as the raid on Harper's Ferry, in October, 1859, by the radical Abolitionist John Brown

(1800–59), but the election to the presidency of the Abolitionist Republican Abraham Lincoln marked the end of any serious hope of peace. After South Carolina's secession and the failure of a peace conference at Washington, in February, 1861, six of the Southern states (the delegates from Texas were delayed) elected Jefferson Davis as the President of their Confederacy.

On a bright spring morning in 1861, the mutual lack of understanding between North and South exploded into the tragic futility of civil war, as the commander of a low, gray Federal fort in the waters of Charleston's harbor defied South Carolina's demand for unconditional surrender. As the lines of war became clearer four more Southern states joined the Confederacy.

The impact of the Civil War on the United States was incalculable, and even in Europe it had an important influence. The war provided an opportunity to experiment with the latest military equipment. The breechloading rifle improved by Christian Sharps was first used at Harper's Ferry, giving a new meaning to the word "sharpshooter." Repeating rifles were introduced; explosive mines and torpedoes were used; railroad transport proved its value in war for the first time; and there were even experiments with the use of aerial warfare—although the balloons were used mainly for signaling and reconnaissance work; communication by telegraph proved a valuable way of passing messages at still longer distances. The

contrast between the American Civil War and the Crimean War a decade earlier shows how rapidly new industrial and technological innovations were having effect.

Perhaps most important and influential of all for the immediate future was the use of armored and heavily armed steamships. Many of the other developments of the Civil War had little real impact until World War I, but at sea the effect was almost instantaneous. Gideon Welles, Lincoln's Navy Secretary, had twenty-four steamships, but every available boat had to be pressed into service in order to blockade the Confederacy. The capture of the shipyard at Norfolk, Virginia, was a serious blow to the Union, as the new frigate *Merrimack* was being equipped there. In March, 1862, the *Merrimack*, renamed *Virginia*, sank the u.s.s. *Cumberland* and was able to close the James River to the Union, but elsewhere the Union's control of inland waterways helped to hold down many Confederate soldiers. Seeing the value of the *Virginia*, the Confederacy ordered two more ironclad steamships, the *Alabama* and the *Florida*, from shipyards in Britain, and these inflicted enormous damage on Union shipping.

But it was on land that the war was really being fought, and it was on land that victory would be won. Two years and eighty days after the first shots were fired on Fort Sumter, the Confederate tide swept over the Pennsylvania market town of Gettysburg, only to recede through wheatfields and peach orchards, after the greatest battle of the Civil War.

The port of New Orleans during the Civil War. The Federal blockade made it almost impossible to export cotton.

A Nation Divided

Spurred by his stunning victory at Chancellorsville, Confederate General Robert E. Lee began to plan an invasion of the populous and heavily industrialized North in early June of 1863. Lee's army of "starving ragamuffins" converged on the Pennsylvania farming community of Gettysburg, and on the last day of June his troops clashed with General George G. Meade's superior Union forces. The battle momentarily appeared to swing in Lee's favor on July 3, when General George Pickett's men broke through the Union lines shortly after two in the afternoon. Pickett's troops were unable to hold the vantage they had gained, however, and twenty minutes later they were forced to withdraw. On July 4, as Lee's bloodied army began its retreat to Virginia, word reached the General that the Southern stronghold of Vicksburg had fallen. In a single day, the Confederacy had been dealt two mortal blows.

It has been said that as Pickett's Virginian Division broke into the Union line on July 3, 1863, the Muse of History for a moment took up her pen to inscribe a new name in the list of nations. In Washington, sixty miles to the south, Abraham Lincoln prayed for victory; the nation, he felt, could not stand "another Fredericksburg or Chancellorsville." What was being decided in the hills above the little Pennsylvanian town of Gettysburg was whether the United States would go forward as a single and major nation. On July 1, 2 and 3, 1863, the scales trembled in an even balance.

The thirteen colonies which declared their independence of Britain in 1776 were scattered down a thousand miles of coast. Their origins and their interests were highly diverse. Only in 1781 was even a loose confederation formed. It was with the greatest difficulty that the states were then persuaded into a closer unity. In 1787 delegates drafted the present Constitution. Over the following seventy years, it became a matter of dispute whether the Union was no more than a contract between states from which any party could, if it wished, withdraw. At first the state loyalties remained intense. It was a President of the United States, John Adams, who, speaking of "my country," meant Massachusetts.

But the North was receiving immigrants without the old local loyalties; and industry and communications developed rapidly. The South, a larger and more rural and scattered area to start with, missed much of this. Economically, too, iron and wheat in the North, contrasted with cotton and tobacco in the South. It was seldom that a trading or banking policy was as beneficial to one as to the other. When in 1831 South Carolina came into collision for the first time with the Union authorities, the issue was not slavery but tariffs. The South Carolina legislature, standing on its overriding "sovereignty," passed a resolution "nullifying" a tariff law. The President, Andrew Jackson,

himself a Southerner, was clearly prepared to enforce the Federal law with troops if necessary, and South Carolina gave way.

But the most important of the issues dividing the country was Negro slavery. From the start the burgeoning new society had been disfigured by this huge and horrible excrescence. At first it seemed likely that it could gradually be restricted, then eliminated. In 1784 an ordinance to forbid slavery in all the territory beyond the Appalachians was defeated in the Congress by only one vote—and this area would have included the future Kentucky, Tennessee, Alabama and Mississippi. The immediate abolition of the slave trade was voted for in 1787 by the moderate states of North and South, like Pennsylvania and Virginia, and opposed by South Carolina and Massachusetts. Under a compromise the trade was finally allowed to go on for twenty years, bringing a huge reinforcement to the slave population.

Meanwhile, just as Southern expansion moved across the rich bottom lands of Alabama and Mississippi, perfect for cotton, Eli Whitney in 1794 invented the cotton gin, and within a decade the new fiber had swept the world. Its harvesting became the great citadel of Negro slavery.

In the first decades of the nineteenth century the movement against slavery still made headway in the non-cotton South. In 1831, a small slave rebellion (Nat Turner's) produced an intense reconsideration in the Virginia legislature. A motion to abolish slavery at that very session was only lost by 73 to 58, while a more moderate bill for gradual emancipation failed by only one vote. But this was almost the last sign of a serious movement against slavery in the South. The beginnings of a powerful Abolitionist movement in the North drew the lines. The Abolitionists must be distinguished from the many moderate Northerners who opposed slavery. The former called for the dissolution of the Union as "an Agreement with Hell and a Covenant

Abraham Lincoln, who was responsible for the abolition of slavery in the United States.

Opposite The Battle of Gettysburg, 1863, where Robert E. Lee's Confederate army was defeated by General Meade's Union force.

General Robert E. Lee and his officers who led the "starving ragamuffins" at the Battle of Gettysburg.

A contemporary drawing showing troops at the Rappahannock before the Battle of Fredericksburg.

southwest, once again raised the question of the political balance between the slave and the free states. By a new Compromise of 1850, designed once again to remove slavery as a major political issue, California was admitted as a free state while for the remainder of the area slavery was to be neither excluded nor imposed.

In 1854, however, the whole basis of previous agreements about the territories was destroyed by the Kansas-Nebraska Act; even in territories north of the Missouri Compromise line slavery was to become legal if approved by a majority of settlers—the so-called "Squatter Sovereignty." This was seen as a Southern political aggression, and it brought many Northerners of moderate views to the reluctant conclusion that they must oppose an insatiable South and support the new Republican Party which now arose with just such a program. It also led to a frightful guerrilla war in Kansas.

In 1857 came the "Dred Scott" decision of the Supreme Court, ruling that Congress had no power to prohibit slavery in the territories, and that, constitutionally, fugitive slaves must indeed be handed back to their Southern owners. This was increasingly abhorrent to Northerners, and several Northern states offered active resistance to the Federal law. This in turn strengthened in the South the feeling that the Union was a fiction already, only obeyed by Northern states when it suited them.

One of the prominent Abolitionist terrorists of Kansas was John Brown. In 1859, with the support of the movement's leaders, he and a small band of followers seized the Arsenal at Harper's Ferry on the Maryland-Virginia border. As Lincoln, repudiating the raid, put it, "It was an attempt by white men to get up a revolt among slaves, in which the slaves refused to participate." Brown was captured and executed for treason—a martyr for the Abolitionists, a portent of terror for the South.

For the election of 1860, Lincoln, by now the

with Death," and they appealed for rivers of blood.

In the South, partly as a result of this agitation, a pro-slavery fanaticism emerged. It no longer became possible to discuss the subject rationally. Abraham Lincoln put it "that the institution of slavery is founded upon both injustice and bad policy, but that the promulgation of abolition doctrines tends rather to increase than abate its evils." As a young man he had seen slave auctions in New Orleans, and detested it. Yet he saw the difficulty of eradicating it at once rather than gradually without "producing a greater evil even to the cause of human liberty itself."

But the slavery question only gradually came to the fore as America's main political theme. In 1820 the Missouri Compromise (by which Missouri was admitted as a slave state, but slavery was otherwise excluded from all the new areas north of 36° 30′) took the issue out of the central area of politics for a generation. But the Mexican War of 1848 and the annexation of vast new territories in the

"Slave Hound of Illinois" to the Abolitionists, won the Republican nomination over more extreme contenders. The Democrats were split in three factions by the slavery issue, and Lincoln won the presidency on a minority vote. But even if the Democrats had combined, Lincoln would still have won with majorities, though not large ones, over almost all the North. Thus the election registered a country already divided along a geographical line.

But Lincoln regarded the preservation of the Union and enforcement of its laws as his overriding duty. When he came to power he offered every conceivable guarantee to the South that no Federal interference with slavery would take place. However, the extremists in South Carolina regarded the mere election of a Republican President as itself grounds for dissolving the Union. On December 20, 1860, they passed an ordinance of secession. Over the next six weeks, this was followed by Mississippi, Florida, Alabama, Georgia, Louisiana and Texas. At the beginning of February these came together to found the Confederate States of America.

The war did not start for some weeks. South Carolina claimed that Federal forces should move from the forts they held in its territory. The crux came when Lincoln, after dispute in the cabinet, decided to send in further supplies to Fort Sumter. On April 14, 1861, the Confederate General Beauregard ordered the bombardment of Fort Sumter, and the war began.

The secession of the other states had been rejected by Virginia, North Carolina, Tennessee and Arkansas, where big Union majorities carried the day. Only when Lincoln now called for troops to put down the Deep South did a revulsion of feeling take place, and the states of the Middle South themselves seceded in turn. Even now four slave states remained on the Union side. And many officers from the seceding states remained with the Union army—the Union division which repulsed

General Grant

Pickett's charge was commanded by the North Carolinian Gibbon. All the same, Fort Sumter finally drew the lines. In North and South alike, fierce patriotisms—one for the Union and one for secession—swept the populations, only to wilt somewhat under the strains of war.

On the face of it, the South had no chance of victory. The North's population was 19 million and the white population of the South only $5\frac{1}{2}$ million. An advanced industrial country was fighting a backward agricultural one; and Southern agriculture was then concentrated on crops irrelevant to survival. In making the struggle after all into such a near thing, "the paramount factor," a Northern historian remarks, "was Robert E. Lee." Opposed to both secession and slavery, he had been approached to take command of the Union Army, but had felt that he could not take arms against Virginia and had "gone with his state." He was to be the only great captain who almost consistently extracted victory, until his resources were at an end, from situations in which he was always in inferior numbers and fighting an enemy equally well-trained and organized and officered, and far better equipped. Even the South's most determined ideological opponents could not forbear a cheer, as when Friedrich Engels wrote to Karl Marx, "they fight quite famously."

The first attempt to deal with the rebels was defeated at Bull Run in 1861. The following year saw Lee's defeat of McClellan in the Seven Days Battle, and of Pope at the Second Manassas, and Jackson's victories over the lesser Union armies in the Valley Campaign. Meanwhile in the West, New Orleans had been captured, and Eastern Tennessee conquered by the North. Powerful Southern counter blows at Shiloh and elsewhere never achieved more than partial and temporary success.

Lee's first invasion of the North was blocked at the Antietam in September. Lincoln took the opportunity to issue the Emancipation Proclamation. All slaves in territory under rebel control (though not in Union areas) were declared free, as from the end of the year, as a war measure.

61

Above A contemporary print showing a typical Southern plantation scene.

Below A photograph showing Federal troops occupying General Robert E. Lee's mansion.

Lincoln had won the old Union men from the start by refusing to abolish slavery and setting the Union first. He now drew on the more radical anti-slavery forces. But above all, the Proclamation, bringing the issue openly to the front, made it extremely difficult for the Confederacy to appeal to the European powers whose support was in the long run as essential to them as it had been to George Washington in the Revolution.

The year ended on the Virginia front with another great victory for Lee at Fredericksburg. In May, 1863, a further Union attempt to march on Richmond, with a greater superiority than ever, ended with Lee's masterpiece at Chancellorsville, where, as the New York papers complained, sixty thousand "starving ragamuffins" defeated 130,000 men of the "finest army on the planet."

On June 2, 1863, Lee set his army in motion for an invasion of the North, with the aim of at best drawing the Union Army out from its impregnable position north of the Rappahannock, and conquering a peace in Washington. At worst, he wished to transfer the fighting from the wasted fields of Virginia. By the end of June he had crushed the Federal forces in the Shenandoah

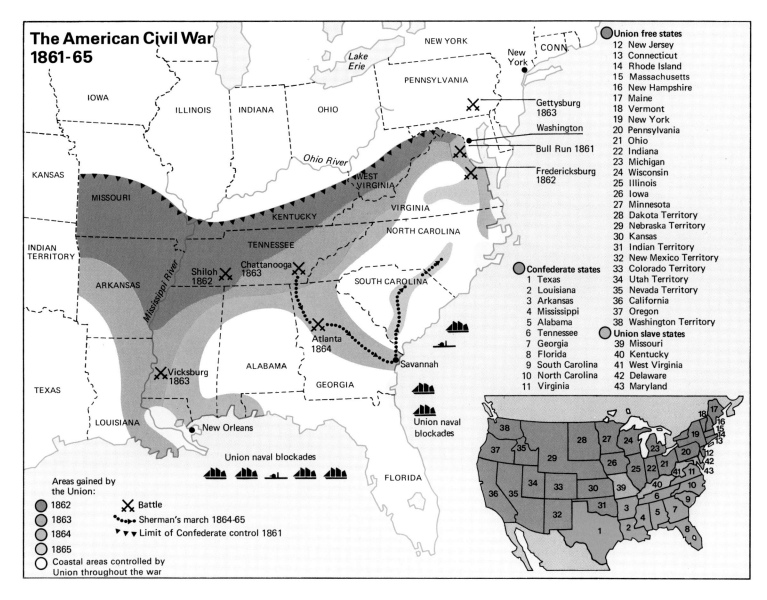

The American Civil War 1861-65

IOWA
ILLINOIS
INDIANA
OHIO
NEW YORK
Lake Erie
New York
CONN
PENNSYLVANIA
KANSAS
MISSOURI
KENTUCKY
WEST VIRGINIA
VIRGINIA
NORTH CAROLINA
Ohio River
Gettysburg 1863
Washington
Bull Run 1861
Fredericksburg 1862
INDIAN TERRITORY
ARKANSAS
TENNESSEE
Shiloh 1862
Chattanooga 1863
Atlanta 1864
SOUTH CAROLINA
Mississippi River
TEXAS
LOUISIANA
Vicksburg 1863
ALABAMA
GEORGIA
New Orleans
Savannah
Union naval blockades
FLORIDA
Union naval blockades

Union free states
12 New Jersey
13 Connecticut
14 Rhode Island
15 Massachusetts
16 New Hampshire
17 Maine
18 Vermont
19 New York
20 Pennsylvania
21 Ohio
22 Indiana
23 Michigan
24 Wisconsin
25 Illinois
26 Iowa
27 Minnesota
28 Dakota Territory
29 Nebraska Territory
30 Kansas
31 Indian Territory
32 New Mexico Territory
33 Colorado Territory
34 Utah Territory
35 Nevada Territory
36 California
37 Oregon
38 Washington Territory

Confederate states
1 Texas
2 Louisiana
3 Arkansas
4 Mississippi
5 Alabama
6 Tennessee
7 Georgia
8 Florida
9 South Carolina
10 North Carolina
11 Virginia

Union slave states
39 Missouri
40 Kentucky
41 West Virginia
42 Delaware
43 Maryland

Areas gained by the Union:
○ 1862
○ 1863
○ 1864
○ 1865
○ Coastal areas controlled by Union throughout the war
✕ Battle
•••• Sherman's march 1864-65
▼▼▼ Limit of Confederate control 1861

Valley at the second Battle of Winchester, and had marched through Maryland far into Pennsylvania. His leading corps, Ewell, was already on the Susquehanna. The Union Army of the Potomac had swung north to keep between him and Washington. The usually faultless Stuart, commanding the Southern cavalry, had been roughly handled at Brandy Station by the Union cavalry commander Pleasonton, and then, to reach his post on Lee's flank, he had ridden all the way round the Union Army, and was now out of touch. So in this alien territory Lee was without his eyes. On June 30 one of his brigades clashed in Gettysburg with the cavalry covering the Union left. Next day two Southern divisions were brought up to develop the situation, and the Northern First Corps arrived before the cavalry were driven in. The battle had begun. During the day the Northern Eleventh Corps came up on the right. But finally Ewell's corps of Lee's army, marching south from the Susquehanna, drove them through Gettysburg on to the hills to the south.

Ewell, under orders to capture the hills if practicable, now failed to advance—the first tactical error of a series. Meade, the new Union commander, came up in the night. Hearing that

the hills made a good defensive position, he had decided to fight there. The battle of the second and third day consisted of a series of Southern attacks from northeast, north and west on his positions; it has been described as being like a fish-hook with its curve to the north at Cemetery Hill, its barb to the east at Culp's Hill, and its longer shank to the west at Cemetery Ridge, running from Cemetery Hill to the hills called the Round Tops at the southern end. The area round Little Round Top is a mass of rocks and gullies, culminating in a small hill a few hundred yards to the west—the Devil's Den. From there the ground dips westward then rises to the Peach Orchard. Lee (76,000 men) had about the same force as Napoleon at Waterloo, Meade (95,000) the equivalent of Wellington and Blücher combined. The Southern infantry had established a marked superiority, but the Northern artillery was greatly superior, in quality as well as quantity.

Lee's plan was to throw Longstreet's corps, less Pickett's division (not yet up) on the Union left. The other corps commanders had orders to demonstrate, converting this into attack as Longstreet's battle got going. Longstreet moved slowly. It was not until 4 P.M. that Hood's division started

63

A photograph of the dead on the battlefield of Gettysburg. This is one of the earliest war photographs; such views showed the grim reality of war.

to fight forward toward Little Round Top, then unoccupied. Warren, Chief Engineer of the Army of the Potomac, had climbed the hill to make a reconnaissance when he saw the crisis—the key to the whole left flank was on the point of being lost, and with it the battle. He hastily detached nearby units on his own initiative and rushed them to the hill, which they were just able to save after bitter fighting. Meanwhile, Longstreet captured the Devil's Den and drove gradually forward in the Peach Orchard. Meade gradually brought up reinforcements until Longstreet was halted by more than half the Union Army. But the other Southern corps failed to take advantage of the weakening of the troops facing them. It was not until 6 P.M. that Johnson's division of Ewell's corps captured part of the Union position on Culp's Hill and only at 8 P.M. did an attack by two brigades actually break the line on Cemetery Hill, having to retreat for lack of the expected support.

The odds against a Southern victory had steadily deteriorated. But it is the third day and the tremendous climax of Pickett's charge which are taken as the high tide of the Confederacy. Lee had again decided on a double blow. Johnson and Longstreet were ordered to strike early and simultaneously. Meade too pressed the fight on Culp's Hill, and by 11 o'clock Johnson had withdrawn to its base. Longstreet's column of nine brigades made its spirited and desperate assault at 2 o'clock. Inadequate support was given on the flanks, but in the teeth of a frightful Northern barrage the column broke into the Union lines on a hundred-yard front. After twenty minutes close fighting the Virginians

withdrew, having lost all their regimental commanders. Meade had no reserves in hand to follow up the shattered units.

With this celebrated incident the battle was over apart from ineffective cavalry actions on either flank.

Gettysburg was no Waterloo. Lee remained on the field the following day, ready for another fight. But he had already decided to withdraw. On July 14, he crossed the Potomac and by August 4, the two armies again faced each other over the Rapidan, and the campaign was over.

As Lee fell back to Virginia the news arrived from the West that Grant had captured Vicksburg, the Southern stronghold on the Mississippi, which he had cut off in a brilliant campaign the previous May, after numerous repulses. The double blow to the Confederacy was, in the long run, deadly. But further efforts were possible. In September the South, for the first time, concentrated slightly superior forces at Chickamauga in northwest Georgia and won a great victory. Grant reversed the verdict at Chattanooga in November. He was then transferred to command against Lee.

1864 saw Sherman in northwest Georgia and Grant in Virginia facing the last great Southern armies, of Joseph Johnston and Lee respectively. Johnston conducted a fighting retreat back to Atlanta, while Lee, in his most remarkable campaign yet, won a series of defensive victories ending in the frightful slaughter of Cold Harbor, and Petersburg, which almost broke the North's will to fight. In August Lincoln considered that he could not win the 1864 election. But the deadlock was

broken by the fall of Atlanta, in September. Several victories in the Shenandoah Valley also heartened the North, as did the capture of Mobile.

In November there was one last scare. A Southern army, under Hood, reentered Tennessee but was defeated there in December. Meanwhile Sherman "marched through Georgia," then the Carolinas. Lee's front remained in being before Richmond, but the whole hinterland was wasting away. In April the break finally came. Lee had to abandon his positions and after a week of desperate fighting, down to 7,000 infantry, he surrendered to Grant at Appomattox Court House. The other Southern armies followed suit in the next two months, and the war was over.

Lincoln, the supreme architect of victory and emancipation, stood for a reconciliation with the South "with malice towards none." His aim was the immediate readmission into the Union of all states accepting, as the South now did, the end of slavery and secession. His successor, Andrew Johnson, took a similar line but, lacking Lincoln's political skill, was soon in conflict with the radical Republicans. A great struggle (in which Johnson was nearly impeached by the Senate) took place over the whole future of the South. It left worse resentments than those of war and defeat.

By the beginning of 1866 all the Southern states had elected new governments, and all except Mississippi had abolished slavery, even before the Thirteenth Amendment became law. But most of them still retained various civic disqualifications for Negroes (as, indeed, did many of the Northern states). The Republican extremists objected to this

on two grounds, one idealistic and one factious. They feared that the South would perpetuate a sort of covert slavery. And they feared that the reentry of the Southern states under white control would mean the end of the Republican grip on Congress. Finally, and more reputably, a Fourteenth Amendment was passed in 1866 granting citizenship and civil rights to everyone. Most of the Southern states failed to carry this out effectively, and in March, 1867, a Reconstruction Act imposed military government on all the ex-Confederate states except Tennessee. Many whites were disfranchised, and most of the South produced Republican governments based on the Negro vote. The Southern states were all readmitted to the Union under these Reconstruction governments by 1870. But it was only possible to maintain these administrations by Federal troops, and the North was not in the long run prepared to use force.

In 1876 the disputed presidential contest was settled on the tacit compromise that the Southern Democrats would acquiesce in the election of the Republican Hayes, while Hayes would withdraw troops from the South. Thereafter, till recent times, the "Solid South" remained Democratic, though it was not until the 1890s that the Negroes were in effect excluded from voting.

Thus the results of the war, in the long run, were that slavery had been abolished, but that the racial problem had not been solved—as it has yet to be. But the Union had been saved, and the foundation, for good or ill, of the huge power of the modern United States had been laid.

ROBERT CONQUEST

The Battle of Hampton Roads in 1862, fought at the mouth of the James River. The Confederate ship *Virginia* sank the Union vessel *Cumberland* but was forced to withdraw, leaving the eastern seaboard in the hands of the Union.

In an ever-shrinking world Britain loses

Federal victory

The American Civil War was the most significant historical event between the collapse of the Napoleonic Empire in 1815 and the assassination of Archduke Franz Ferdinand at Sarajevo just under a century later. It was also one of the longest and bloodiest conflicts involving a major world power. On the afternoon of Palm Sunday, 1865, General Robert E. Lee rode into the village of Appomattox Court House and surrendered to General Ulysses S. Grant. As he did so the Federal soldiers stationed around the surrender site noted that an all-but-forgotten stillness had fallen over the sloping fields and wooded hillocks of Virginia. After four tragic years and the loss of more than six hundred thousand American lives, the war of secession was finally over, and even General Grant (who was by no means a sensitive commander) seemed conscious of the scars of war. "Let all the men who claim to own a horse or mule take their animals home with them to work their farms," he declared that Sunday, modifying the original terms offered to Lee. The Union commander ordered his troops not to cheer at the humiliation of their compatriots, and for a while there seemed to be a hope of reconciliation. That hope was illusory.

AMERICA.

ASSASSINATION
OF
PRESIDENT
L·I·N·C·O·L·N.

ATTEMPTED MURDER OF
MR. SEWARD..

(REUTER'S TELEGRAMS.)
NEW YORK, APRIL 15 (10 A.M.).
At 1.30 this morning Mr. Stanton reported as follows :—
"This evening, at 9.30, President Lincoln, while sitting in a private box at Ford's theatre with Mrs. Lincoln, Mrs. Harris, and Major Rathburn, was shot by an assassin, who suddenly entered the box, and approached behind the President. The assassin then leaped upon the stage, brandishing a large knife, and escaped in the rear of the theatre. A pistol ball entered the back of the President's head, penetrating nearly through. The wound is mortal.
"The President has been insensible ever since the infliction of the wound, and is now dying.
"About the same hour an assassin, whether

Newspaper report of President Lincoln's assassination.

Lincoln was shot at Ford's Theater in Washington on Good Friday, and the sharp agony of battle was succeeded by the nagging sore of reconstruction.

The climax of the Age of Steam

The second half of the nineteenth century saw a continuation of the rapid industrial growth that had characterized the last eighty years, but the pattern of growth changed rapidly. Britain retained the world leadership, but its lead was no longer unchallenged; nor was the supremacy of the four great powers, Britain, France, the United States and Germany. In 1860, the four industrial leaders conducted eighty percent of the world's manufacture, but by the outbreak of World War 1 the figure had fallen to seventy-two percent. The growth rate in Britain was far slower than the world average during that period, and France's was slower still. Among the major powers it was the United States that really set the pace, growing sevenfold in production during the period from the Civil War to 1914. But the European industrial leaders did continue to grow.

The world output of steel grew by seven times in the last two decades of the century, and the production of pig iron more than doubled. The figures for steel production show how rapidly Europe was falling behind the United States, and how, within Europe, Germany was gaining at the expense of her industrial rivals. Between 1870 and 1900 steel production in Britain rose from half a million to five million tons; that of France from one hundred thousand tons to nearly two million tons; that of Germany from three hundred thousand to seven million tons; while American production rose faster still, leaping from one hundred thousand tons to thirteen million tons, almost overtaking the combined production of its three major rivals.

Britain's relative decline was due to many factors. There was no huge and rapidly growing home market that encouraged growth as in the United States; German sales technique was far more dynamic than that of the stolid British, who took their traditional markets for granted and were surprised when they lost them. Germany's victory in the Franco-Prussian War was to

produce financial benefits in addition to the territory of Alsace-Lorraine; indeed, the rapid expansion of Germany's railroad network was largely made possible by the payment of French war indemnities. Both Germany and the United States adopted or permitted protectionist measures that were anathema to the traditional laissez-faire attitudes of most British industrialists and politicians. In Germany the failure in 1873 of court action to prevent the establishment of cartels led to the effective legitimization of price fixing. As a result of this many industrial cartels were set up, and their pricing policies proved an effective means of stifling competition, both internal and external. In the United States Federal and some state authorities took a more vigorous line against cartels and monopolies, and the Sherman Anti-Trust Act of 1890 had some effect, as the eventual breakup of the Standard Oil Trust in 1911 was to show. But the United States adopted a more formally protective policy in order to encourage domestic enterprise, and this, too, found expression in 1890 in McKinley Tariffs. British success in overseas markets was largely due to the cotton trade, and international competition, particularly from the United States, grew rapidly, causing a rapid decline in British cotton exports that was not fully compensated for by growth in other industries. There was also a failure by British industrialists to reap the benefits of British inventions; for example, Germany adopted the Gilchrist-Thomas method of eliminating phosphorus in steel-making—thereby permitting a greatly increased output—while Britain did not.

Although Britain did manage to maintain a reasonable growth rate, it was one that was steadily falling in comparison with both the United States' and Germany's. In addition, because of its dependence on imports, this growth was purchased at the expense of a substantial "visible" balance of trade deficit. At first this was amply covered by "invisible" earnings from finance, insurance and so on. As early as the period from 1870 to 1875 the average annual deficit on "visibles" was running at about £65 million; by the end of the century the overall trade balance was in deficit, and only the dividends and interest

from Britain's huge overseas investments prevented financial disaster.

The weakness of Britain's trade in the later years of the century was the world's gain. Other countries were able to use their trading surpluses for investment, and British investors were responsible for much of the industrial development in South America as well as in the countries of the Empire. But the very success of British investment overseas helped to increase the trading deficit on the current account.

Transportation

Much of the increase in production and commerce throughout the world was made possible by improved transportation facilities, both on land and at sea. In 1840 there was less than five thousand miles of railroad track in the world —two-thirds in North America and the rest in Europe. By 1900 this had risen a thousand-fold, and there were twelve thousand miles in Africa, mostly in the south, twenty-six thousand miles in South America and thirty-seven thousand in Asia. In the United States the completion of the transcontinental Union Pacific and Central Pacific lines in 1869 had an immediate effect on trade and made large-scale settlement of the West possible for the first time. Even more significant was the completion of the great Asian railroads by the Russians; the Trans-Caspian railroad was finished in 1888 and the Trans-Siberian in 1904. These facilitated troop movements and strengthened Russia's hold on Central Asia, presenting a real threat both to other colonial powers and to independent states.

At first the full potential of the railroad for the transportation of goods was not realized, the primary concern of the early railroad builders being passenger movement. This was not the case with the steamship. As soon as technical developments in the 1860s made it feasible, regular services to many parts of the world began, and by 1900 well over half of the shipping tonnage at sea was steam driven. The needs of international trade led to an immense increase in shipbuilding and between 1850 and 1900 the total registered tonnage of the world's merchant marine increased fourfold. This led to the development of large-scale

The Suez Canal, which provided a link between East and West.

Mid-nineteenth-century London dockland view.

port facilities, of which the docks of London were the largest, reflecting both Britain's enormous imports, exports and reexports and the size of its merchant fleet (over half the shipping tonnage of the world in 1900 was British).

The increase in speed resulting from the use of steamships was a major factor in helping to shrink the globe during the nineteenth century. But it was by no means the only factor. The introduction of efficient telegraph systems helped speed communications not only on land but also under the sea. Baltimore and Washington were linked by cable as early as 1844. The first undersea cable came into operation between Calais (France) and Dover (England) in 1850, and the first transatlantic cable was laid between 1857 and 1865. By comparison with the importance of telegraphy, the introduction of the telephone was slow, and by 1900 there were probably no more than one million telephones in use throughout the world.

More important than the telephone as a means of shrinking the globe was the shortening of journeys made possible by the opening of the Suez Canal in 1869. This cut weeks from the journey between Europe and the Orient. The immediate success of the Suez Canal encouraged its engineer, Ferdinand de Lesseps, to attempt to build a canal at Panama. Although per-

mission for this was granted in 1878, the difficulties involved led to long delays and work on the canal —though begun in 1881—was not truly under way until 1904.

Improved refrigeration techniques had a social impact little less important than quicker communications. From 1876, frozen meat could be transported to Europe, where the rapid rise in population over the previous century had put an enormous strain on food supplies. The economic growth of Argentina and Australia particularly was built on the meat trade that developed in the final years of the century.

The rapidly expanding urban population of Europe benefited from these fresh sources of food, but in many cases the farmers were alarmed. A flood of grain from the American Midwest, coupled with the likelihood that railways would soon open up the rich granaries of southern Russia, posed new challenges. Of great concern was the danger to the price of home-grown grain. Farmers in most European countries demanded governmental protection, and industrialists were no less eager to counter foreign competition. Bismarck's Germany erected tariff walls in 1879. France and Austria-Hungary safeguarded their manufacturers in 1881 and agriculture four years later. The Russians and the Spanish (who had never entirely

accepted the principles, let alone the practice, of free trade) increased their tariffs in the late 1870s. Italy turned to protection in 1887, Sweden in 1888 and Switzerland in 1891. The United States responded with tariffs higher than any in Europe. Britain, still the largest exporter of industrial machinery in the world as late as 1880, stuck to the principles of free trade despite a mounting chorus of criticism from farmers and industrialists.

Energy

The rapid expansion of heavy industry, large-scale manufacture and the use of steam for transport put traditional fuel resources under immense pressure. New coal mines were being opened at great speed in Europe and North America, and already the search for mineral fuels was beginning in colonial dependencies. European and American production of coal was still, however, capable of meeting most of the needs of industry. British coal production, for example, rose from eighty-five million tons in 1860 to two hundred and fifteen million in 1900; Germany's from fifteen and a half million to one hundred and five million tons; France's from ten million to thirty million tons. But the natural advantages that America enjoyed over Europe were again apparent in its coal production figures, which rose from seventeen million tons in 1860 to two hundred and fifty million tons at the end of the century.

The relatively high price of coal and its deficiencies, as a source of

light for example, made it necessary to look for alternative fuels. Coal products, particularly gas, helped to make the streets safer by providing efficient lighting and brought a new era to domestic life by making homes light in the evening. But the fuel of the future was oil, and within a few years its drilling, production and sale were to rank with the biggest businesses of all, largely as a result of the activities of John D. Rockefeller and his associates.

Detail of Westminster Bridge as seen from Waterloo Bridge.

Miners underground in the Ruhr coalfield; the enormous coal deposits of the Ruhr Valley helped boost German coal production.

The Birth of Big Business

In August of 1859, a speculator named Edwin Drake struck "black gold" near Titusville, Pennsylvania—and the American oil rush was on. Four years later, John D. Rockefeller and his partners had built their refinery in Cleveland, Ohio. By the end of the decade, Rockefeller and his partners' refinery had become the largest oil-cracking operation in Cleveland. Within twenty years Rockefeller's company controlled over ninety percent of the country's oil pipelines, having established itself as the most important factor in America's petroleum industry. The Standard Oil Company was the first great combination to succeed—an example that would further the trend toward consolidation and monopoly.

John D. Rockefeller, who created the giant Standard Oil Company.

In 1858 an assistant bookkeeper had saved enough from his salary of $25.00 per month to become a partner in a produce commission firm. Four years later John Davison Rockefeller and his partner invested with Samuel Andrews, inventor of an economical process for cleaning crude oil, in a small business that dealt in "oil refining." In 1867 the firm became Rockefeller, Andrews and Flagler. In 1870 Rockefeller, with his brother William, Stephen V. Harkness and other associates, incorporated the firm as the Standard Oil Company with himself as president.

In time the company became so huge that it was decided to form the Standard Oil Trust. For under existing law, corporations chartered in one state were not permitted to own or hold stock property in another. The Standard Oil Trust, formed in 1882, was part of a plan worked out by the company's recently acquired legal counselor, Samuel T.C. Todd, to circumvent these regulations. Under a trusteeship device—by which stockholders of Standard Oil companies agreed to place their stock in the hands of nine trustees, who happened to be Standard Oil chief executives—the Standard Oil Company abandoned control of its corporation to those trustees. That gesture was a mere technicality: the directors of Standard Oil remained in firm control of the huge combine and their ploy signaled the birth of Big Business.

The formation of the trust marked the culmination of a decade of effort by John D. Rockefeller and his associates to bring order and stability to one of the youngest and most chaotic of American industries. From the moment that Edwin Drake's celebrated drilling rig first gushed oil at Titusville, Pennsylvania, in August, 1859, the atmosphere in the producing region had been characterized by hectic exploration, optimistic speculation, soaring land prices, conspicuous waste and rapidly increasing output. Competition was hardly less keen in the refining of crude oil. In 1863, the year Rockefeller

entered the industry, a small refinery could be built in Cleveland for as little as seven thousand dollars—and by the end of the decade Cleveland had at least twenty-six refining firms. Others were located in the oil-producing region around Titusville, in Pittsburgh, and in many of the large consuming centers of the nation. Refineries were also built in New York, Philadelphia and Baltimore to serve the rapidly growing export trade.

Technological developments in the manufacture of coal oil in both Europe and America during the 1850s had helped prepare world markets for petroleum, and the relatively cheap new fuel rapidly displaced coal oil, candles and whale oil as a source of light. Yet the output of crude oil rose even faster than the growing demand—from 2,000 barrels in 1859 to 4,800,000 barrels in 1869 and to nearly 10 million barrels in 1873. As a result of this phenomenal increase, by 1868 both prices and profits were falling.

By the end of the 1860s the firm of Rockefeller, Andrews and Flagler was refining three thousand barrels a day, about 10 percent of Cleveland's output. It was already the largest refinery in the city. But up to that point the firm's growth had been largely internal, derived from ploughed-back profits, bank loans and the investments of a tightly knit, carefully selected group of partners. However, after incorporating the firm as the Standard Oil Company of Ohio in 1870 with a capital of a million dollars, Rockefeller and Flagler began implementing a strategy of growth through combination. As they purchased other refineries in Cleveland (beginning with the plant belonging to their largest competitor), they offered either shares in Standard Oil or cash, at a price based on an appraisal of "use value" rather than a cost of the investment to former owners. By the end of 1872 they had purchased thirty-four firms and had Cleveland's refining capacity firmly within the Standard Oil Company. From there they moved into the oil regions of

Opposite 26 Broadway, headquarters of the Standard Oil Trust in the late nineteenth century.

The Drake oil well at Titusville, Pennsylvania, in 1861. Drake's operation typified the small-scale methods in use before Standard Oil developed more modern techniques.

Pittsburgh, New York and West Virginia, and by the late 1870s they were an interstate group controlling a large share of the refining capacity of the nation. During the years between 1877 and 1881 Rockefeller and Flagler fought a great industrial war with opponents who were as ambitious and determined as themselves, among them the Empire Transportation Company and the Pennsylvania Railroad. Their victory gave Standard Oil control over most of the existing pipelines as well.

To Rockefeller and Flagler the aggressive purchasing of other refineries, undertaken at a time when other refiners were experiencing serious difficulties, was a constructive plan to bring order to a chaotic industry. But to many contemporaries, the plan represented an evil conspiracy. In fact, few can defend the methods by which the combine was created. Standard Oil bargained sharply for rebates and drawbacks from railways on its large oil shipments before pipelines became important. It spied on competitors in order to steal their customers; it cut prices to force competitors to sell out; and it used bribes freely.

To attribute the success of the Standard Oil group simply to a more unscrupulous use of business methods, however, is to miss those factors that explain Rockefeller and Flagler's achievement. First of all, they used bank loans freely to finance their operations. The purchases of the 1870s required considerable amounts of money (since most rivals unwisely took cash rather than shares in the new firm), and Rockefeller and Flagler's willingness to go into debt reflects Standard Oil's faith in the industry's future and contrasts sharply with the fears of many of its competitors. Rockefeller once said that he wore out the knees of his trousers asking for bank loans. The reputation for utter reliability that Rockefeller acquired in Cleveland (*before* he went into the oil industry) gave him

access to these loans and thus the means to act flexibly and boldly.

Another feature of Standard's growth was its persistent and discriminating search for men as well as material assets. The firm eventually absorbed such able and formidable rivals as Ambrose McGregor, H. H. Rogers, Oliver Payne, Charles Pratt and John D. Archbold. One aspect of Rockefeller's genius for organization was his ability to win over other brilliant men to work for him and his careful attention to the choice of both high and middle managers during the company's early years. Once a man was selected, Rockefeller gave him responsibility and trusted him to discharge it. He was always willing to listen to advice and arguments against his own views, and he preferred

Workmen laying a pipeline in the early 1890s.

decisions made on the basis of discussion. In one sense, Standard Oil destroyed individualism in the oil industry and laid the foundations of huge bureaucratic corporate giants. But in its early years it also set a remarkable example of cooperation among highly able and extremely aggressive men who were given full scope for their individual abilities.

A significant development in the 1880s (one which set a pattern for future rivals in the international oil industry) was the increasing tendency toward vertical integration—that is, toward the control of operations covering every phase of oil production. Standard had already purchased a few marketing outlets before the 1880s and had built and acquired pipelines. The firm then moved into the marketing of its own products at home and began acquiring foreign outlets for its growing export trade. This movement into marketing was characteristic of many large firms in America during this decade, for unprecedented urban growth and railway expansion offered great inducements to manufacturers to bypass traditional middlemen.

In some respects Standard was never again to hold so dominant a position in the world's oil industry as it did in the mid-1880s. As new producing regions were opened in Texas, Oklahoma and California at the end of the century, Standard found itself unable to expand fast enough to maintain control, and new firms were created to fill the gap. Standard Oil's worldwide monopoly was further eroded by the discovery of oil in several other parts of the globe during the last two decades of the century. Indonesia, Russia and Burma were beginning production, and in none of these regions could Standard monopolize the new supplies of crude.

By this time Standard Oil had good reason for *not* wanting to appear to be without competitors. Almost from the very beginning of Rockefeller and Flagler's bold initiatives in the 1870s, the firm's activities had been under attack in legislatures and courts. Indeed, much of the popular view of "the monster" arose from publicity attached to legislative hearings in the states in which the company operated, and from civil and criminal proceedings taken against it in the courts by its rivals. As the most highly publicized trust, Standard's reputation suffered not only from the evasiveness of its officers as witnesses, but also from Rockefeller's refusal to undertake public relations activity to answer attacks. Meanwhile Henry Demarest Lloyd's book *Wealth Against Commonwealth* was published in 1894. It anticipated the attacks of other muckrakers—notably Ida Tarbell's *History of the Standard Oil Company*—that became common in the next decade.

As trusts became more powerful, the public

Red Hot, Pennsylvania, characteristic of the boom towns that appeared for brief periods in the 1860s. Red Hot was built in 1869 and has produced no oil since 1871.

An early retailer of oil.

outcry against them became more strident, for such concentrations of wealth conflicted with traditional mores and with the view Americans had of themselves. Further, as common-law prohibitions on restraint of trade proved inadequate to satisfy public opinion or cope with combinations across state boundaries, the clamor for effective legislative restraint grew. As a result, in 1890 the Sherman Anti-Trust Act was put on the federal statute books. This act made it illegal to combine or conspire to restrict interstate or foreign trade.

Few prosecutions were attempted under the Sherman Act until after a huge wave of mergers had been consummated between 1898 and 1904. Once trust-busting had begun, however, Standard Oil was too conspicuous to escape prosecution. The Supreme Court decision of 1911 in the case of Standard Oil constituted a landmark in the continuous search of the American courts for guidelines for dealing with large firms. The court announced the famous "rule of reason," which stated that a combination was contravening the Sherman Act if it harassed competitors unreasonably. Deciding that Standard Oil had done so, the court ordered its dissolution into a number of separate enterprises. This decree could not be made effective overnight, and for a time some community of interest still marked the relations between the constituent firms of the old trust. By 1920, however, Standard Oil of New Jersey, which was still the largest oil company in the world after dissolution, was competing with its former member companies.

Thus Standard Oil had been a factor both in the passing of the antitrust law and in its subsequent elaboration by the courts. This imposing body of complex law undoubtedly played a part in improving business practices, in markedly slowing down the merger movement in manufacturing, and in making oligopoly rather than monopoly the characteristic of large firms in American manufacturing industry. From Thurman Arnold's appointment as Attorney General in the late 1930s to the present, antitrust law has continued to develop vigorously, and antitrust policy has remained a significant watchdog of the private sector. Antitrust law has been more significant than the regulatory commissions, such as the Federal Trade Commission, that were initially organized in response to unregulated growth. Today neither the horizontal mergers of Standard Oil in the 1870s nor the vertical integration of the 1880s would be tolerated. Yet recent sharpening of swords against conglomerates (combines of firms engaged in unrelated activities) indicates that in the 1970s, as in the 1900s, the public's fear of bigness is greater than its appreciation of economic arguments for and against trusts. No firm can have any guarantee against prosecution. In the twentieth century the American public has become persuaded of the economic advantages of size, but it is not convinced that these advantages will necessarily be exploited in the public interest without competition.

As for Standard Oil, in spite of the re-creation of competition within the United States by the courts as well as competition from new oil-producing regions, the firm Rockefeller created prospered. Nevertheless, the dissolution of the combination in 1911 presented the largest remaining firm, Jersey Standard, with a number of problems. Standard of New York had been the marketing agent for exports in Europe and Asia and had owned most of the organization's tanker fleet. The dismembered company was strong in refining but weak in foreign marketing branches and in supplies of crude oil.

Fears that aggressive growth at home might bring antitrust prosecution led Standard Oil of New Jersey to look abroad for expansion. Here it met

Samuel Dodd, an early associate of Rockefeller's.

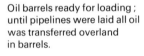

Oil barrels ready for loading; until pipelines were laid all oil was transferred overland in barrels.

rivals worthy of it, notably the Shell Oil Company, which, as a merger of a marketing firm and a rich crude-oil producer, was fully integrated. Other large American firms, fearing a decline in the domestic oil supply, also joined in the scramble for concessions abroad. Over the next half century few parts of the world were untouched by the great international oil firms. Despite the competition, Standard Oil was operating in thirty-four countries by 1966, and four-fifths of its refining capacity was outside the United States. It was the largest of the seven great international oil companies.

The large international oil firms became examples par excellence of the separation of ownership and management. The leading executives of these firms, not the shareholders, made decisions as to how much of the profits were to be retained, how much released in dividends, and how to manage investment of those retained earnings. Decisions by these men affected living standards in the richer parts of the world both directly, through the degree of success in improving and cheapening oil, and indirectly, through the contributions to governments in taxes. Furthermore, as economic growth in developed nations came to depend increasingly upon technological change, the promotion of research to find new products and to improve the means of producing, transporting and marketing oil placed large firms in a key position to help sustain growth. During this process, the great oil firms diversified into new products, mostly related to their central activities. Jersey Standard, for example, has extensive worldwide interests in petrochemicals, synthetic chemicals and fibers, plastics, synthetic rubber, paint and petroleum resins as well as fertilizers, the manufacture of industrial gases and equipment, and chains of motels.

Although there may be little widespread popular suspicion of these large firms in the United States and Western Europe today, they have become a symbol of economic imperialism to much of the Third World. It is not difficult to see parallels with the hostility and suspicion encountered by Standard Oil in late nineteenth-century America. One basis for the suspicion is taxes: modern firms are taxed wherever they operate, but as integrated international firms, they have some control over where they pay taxes and thus over the amounts paid. Another is the relative stability of price and supply of oil over long periods of time, in spite of occasional price wars among the giants and apparently disruptive international incidents such as Iranian nationalization or the closing of the Suez Canal. The great companies have clearly cooperated for certain purposes—for example, in jointly exploiting oil concessions.

Yet in spite of all their evident power (demonstrated recently by a remarkable stability in spite of rapid growth since the late 1950s and the re-emergence of the Soviet Union as a major oil exporter), these huge international business institutions do experience some limitations on their freedom of action. As one example, governments have taken increasing shares of income in the form of taxes and higher royalties. For another, even without the threat of nationalization, these firms now operate within confines of diplomacy and public relations unknown to the founders of Standard Oil. The energy crisis of 1973–74 was in part an attack on the oil companies by the producer countries. The companies have given subsidies to medical welfare, education and highways, and have invested in other types of development in regions where they operate. Further, the growth of oil industries in underdeveloped countries is slowed by a basic drawback: in relation to earnings, it employs so few people. Even a big refinery cannot provide the massive numbers of jobs for rapidly increasing agricultural populations that railway construction, the iron and steel industries and mining did in the nineteenth century. Finally, the American companies are still constrained by the antitrust laws. In 1962, for example, United States courts used these laws to force Jersey Standard and Sonoco to break up a combination of their Far Eastern interests.

Industrial circumstances, of course, have not remained constant since the beginnings of the modern oil industry. The creation of the large firm was an achievement in ordering the environment and pooling resources for cooperative endeavor. But that environment keeps changing. The permanent achievement of Rockefeller and his associates was not the control of an industry but the creation of a massive organization and the means of making it work. To survive, bureaucratic firms have had to remain somewhat flexible and aggressive. In the late 1950s the appearance of new supplies led to falling prices. But this trend was sharply reversed after the Arab-Israeli war of 1973, and prices increased sharply.　　CHARLOTTE ERICKSON

Wall Street, New York, in the late 1800s, looking toward Trinity Church and Broadway.

Henry Flagler, who encouraged Rockefeller to take control of the oil pipelines.

Bismarck consolidates Prussia's gains

Spanish America

While American industry was being transformed by the creation of large-scale business enterprises, the most protracted war of the era was being fought in South America. Its casualties were to dwarf those of the campaigns of German Field-Marshal Helmuth von Moltke (1800–91) in Europe and of the conflict between the Union and the Confederacy in the United States.

Helmuth von Moltke, who made the Prussian army into an almost invincible war machine.

In 1865, General Francisco Solano López, the dictator of Paraguay, carried his country into a struggle with Brazil, Argentina and Uruguay that lasted until López himself was eventually killed, five years later. This bitter war cost the Paraguayans more than three-quarters of a million lives in battle and in its aftermath, and the Republic of Paraguay, which had been as efficient as any in Latin America, became impoverished and unstable. After 1870 it was permitted to exist only through the rivalry of its neighbors and the goodwill of arbitrators in distant Washington, D.C.

The Paraguayan tragedy passed almost unnoticed in the Western world, and caused little stir outside South America. It was otherwise with Mexico, where the folly of Napoleon III disastrously involved the French army in an expedition that had originally been intended to support the claims of Western bondholders against Benito Juárez (whose near-bankrupt government had announced the suspension of payments on all foreign debts). With the United States racked by civil war and unable to enforce the Monroe Doctrine, Napoleon III and his ministers gambled on building

Benito Juárez, who suspended payment on foreign debts in Mexico.

an empire in Mexico to replace the territory of Louisiana, which had been sold to the United States at the beginning of the century. Napoleon wanted to create a state that would be independent in status, but would be closely linked with France for purposes of commerce and investment.

In June of 1864 Maximilian of Hapsburg, brother of the Austrian Emperor Francis Joseph, was crowned Emperor of Mexico and established an orderly and liberal administration. His power, however, rested on no more substantial basis than the twenty-five thousand French bayonets that kept the supporters of Juárez isolated in the mountains and cowed in the towns. There were occasional skirmishes, although more casualties were caused by disease and the climate than by guerrilla attacks. Once the Civil War ended north of the Rio Grande, the United States government was free to adopt a menacing attitude toward the European adventurers, and Napoleon III was forced to withdraw his soldiers. The last units left on March 12, 1867, and Maximilian's charade of empire barely survived their departure. Within nine weeks he had

The execution of the Emperor Maximilian of Mexico, whose power rested solely on French arms.

been captured by Juárez, and within fourteen he was dead—shot by a firing squad on the hillside above Querétaro. Nothing remained of the Mexican Empire except clusters of graves among the cacti, a widowed and demented empress living in exile in Belgium and an oil painting by Manet—who had been so moved by the death of Maximilian that he had tried to capture the poignancy of the moment on canvas.

War and peace: the paradox of the 1860s

Paradoxically, at no other time was man so aware of the hideous realities of war or so incapable of restraining his appetite for bloodshed as in the 1860s. These were the years of the Geneva Convention for the protection of the wounded

Leo Tolstoy, one of Russia's great novelists.

and captured and of the foundation of the Red Cross movement (1864). They were also the years in which Leo Tolstoy, working on his estate in rural Russia, had destroyed the glamour of battle in the searing pages of his great novel *War and Peace*.

Yet in that whole decade there were only three months free from reports of military campaigns, and even this brief interlude witnessed a punitive expedition by British troops against the Maoris in New Zealand. In September of 1862 the newly appointed chief minister of Prussia, Otto von Bismarck, declared: "The great questions of the day will not be decided by speeches and majority votes—that was the great mistake of 1848 and 1849—but by iron and blood." His words startled even his fellow-Prussians, and yet they were not so much a threatening boast as a simple statement of fact, which was valid for Europe and beyond.

The Iron Chancellor

The shadow of Bismarck hung heavily over the 1860s and even more heavily over the 1870s. In a rare moment of self-criticism in his later years Bismarck reproached himself: "Without me three great wars would not have happened and eighty thousand men would not have perished." At the time, however, such considerations left him unmoved. Convinced of the inevitability of German unity—but absolutely determined that it should come about under the direction of Prussian landowners rather than of middle-class liberals —Bismarck took advantage of each successive emergency to fulfill his political and military objectives.

Bismarck's supremely opportunistic instinct prompted him to lead Prussia (in alliance with Austria) into a war with Denmark in 1864 that brought Prussia the partly German-speaking province of Schleswig-Holstein. That war also enabled him to use the future disposal of this territory as the excuse for a further war against Austria-Hungary and some of the other German states in the summer of 1866. The Danish campaign had been brief, lasting only ten weeks; the Austrian was shorter still and was over within seven weeks.

The invincible Prussian army was a new and unique military machine that had been perfected by von Moltke, who had become chief of the general staff in 1857. Its success sprang from four main causes: the work of staff officers who had been trained to see war as an exact science; the use of railroads for the rapid transportation of troops; a revolution in firearms that enabled the Prussian breech-loading rifles to fire six times as fast as the older weapons of their opponents; and the ability to mobilize the whole country in a mass army.

The victory of Prussia over Austria in the Battle of Sadowa—fought on the Bohemian Plain on July 3, 1866—stunned Europe. The balance of power swung decisively in Bismarck's favor; the North German Confederation came into being, uniting all the German states north of the Main River under Prussian leadership; and indirectly forced the defeated Austrian Emperor to agree to the creation of the Dual Monarchy of Austria-Hungary. Nor were the ultimate effects of Bismarck's triumphs limited to Central Europe. With ominous foresight one of Napoleon III's marshals declared: "It is France that is defeated at Sadowa."

Napoleon III

Indeed France had much reason to fear the rise of Prussia. The unfortunate Mexican episode had dealt a crippling blow to the already waning prestige of Napoleon III. In the ten years that had followed the Crimean War, "the sphinx of the Tuileries" seemed the natural arbiter of the world's problems. A French garrison protected the Pope in Rome from the dangers of a united Italy; a French force had been sent to police Lebanon and Syria when disorder shook the Levant in 1860; and a French expedition had marched beside the British to Peking, where Chinese discourtesy to Western diplomats was punished by the burning of the Emperor's Summer Palace.

Napoleon III's influence did not depend entirely on military dispositions. The Rumanians, as a Latin people, could count on his support for freedom from the Sultan; the Tsar's Polish subjects had his sympathy and, occasionally, his encouragement; and Prince Nicholas of Montenegro, whose reign was to last from 1860 to 1916, owed his survival to French diplomatic intervention when Turkish troops marched on the tiny mountain principality a few months after his accession. A portrait of Napoleon III was still hanging in a place of honor in the royal palace at Cetinje when the Austrians finally drove Nicholas into exile.

Elsewhere, however, gratitude had a less enduring quality. Sadowa and Querétaro helped to dissolve the aura of French primacy, and the Emperor became conscious that he had overtaxed his resources. In December of 1866 he withdrew his garrison from Rome in order to strengthen his army watching that of Prussia across the Rhine. His cleric-advisers, terrified by the Garibaldian specter of Italian nationalism, forced Napoleon to send them back again ten months later; after seventeen years Pius IX could not conceive of government without French military support. Napoleon's grip on events seemed to slacken both at home and abroad, and as pressure mounted from the radical opposition, autocracy gave way to representative government. In the first months of 1870 a liberal empire (headed by a prime minister who was responsible to a parliament rather than the emperor) was proclaimed. Napoleon himself might declare that he had always believed in "liberty with order," but there were many in Paris who felt that it was a little late to be discovering first principles and that the reluctant donor of these concessions was an old and tired man.

Splendor of the Second Empire

Nevertheless the last years of the Empire glittered with superficial achievements. Baron Haussmann's wide boulevards—and the landscaping of the Bois de Boulogne—gave Paris a grace that other capitals sought in vain to emulate. The Exhibition of 1867 surpassed both its predecessor and London's Crystal Palace in splendor. And while the Mexican adventure was reaching its tragic anticlimax, Napoleon was host to an unprecedented galaxy of foreign potentates: the Tsar of Russia; the Sultan of Turkey; the kings of Belgium, Denmark, Greece, Prussia, Sweden and Spain; the Prince of Wales; and even Bismarck.

Earnest visitors to the gaslit capital found much that was frivolous and even vulgar that summer. Entertainments included the Folies Bergère, the masked balls, the lilt of Jacques Offenbach's music and the scandal of the cancan. But the exhibition caught the spirit of the Second Empire. It was an assertion of industrial progress, a parade of military panache and proof that France remained a center of the arts. Its fifteen million visitors seemed most interested in locomotives, interior furnishings and a lightweight metal called "aluminum"—and the greatest thrill was certainly going up in one of the many balloons from which all Paris could be seen.

But a gallery of art did exhibit works by Corot and Ingres, and the private pavilions of Manet and Courbet set up on the outer fringe of the grounds displayed the new Impressionism to a public that resolutely declined to understand it. The Emperor, who had long been conscious of the social problems of industrialism, insisted that there should be sections of the exhibition concerned with housing and the conditions of factory life. He had lost none of his talent for window dressing.

The Eiffel Tower, a Paris landmark for 1889.

Paris retained its gaiety throughout three seasons after the exhibition closed. On May 25, 1870, an elegant audience enthusiastically applauded the first night of a new ballet at the Opera. The work was entitled *Coppelia*, and the triumph of the evening belonged to Giuseppina Bozzacchi, a seventeen-year-old Italian. She was hailed as a great ballerina in the making—but her career was doomed, for *Coppelia* was the last grand premiere of the Second Empire. Within two months the diplomats had blundered into war with Prussia; within four, France was a republic and Paris was encircled by an invading army; within six, the Parisians were eating dogs, cats and rats and the young Signorina Bozzacchi was dead, a victim of "siege fever."

The decade was ending, as it had begun, in carnage and destruction. The devastation that had blighted the American South and turned Paraguay into a desert threatened Paris. The royal château of Saint-Cloud, like the Summer Palace at Peking, was left a charred ruin. And in the aftermath of war, flames consumed the Tuileries.

Papal troops in formation reading "Long live Pius." Pius was utterly opposed to the new Italian nationalism.

A Proclamation at Versailles 1871

In 1789, the year that the Bastille fell, Germany did not exist. Middle Europe was a patchwork of 350 sovereign states, dominated—but not controlled—by Prussia. Internecine squabbling was frequent at that time and national self-awareness was nonexistent. Ironically, it was Napoleon Bonaparte, Prussia's greatest foe, who first sparked a feeling of patriotism in the German people by annexing half of Prussia in 1807. Six years later—following Napoleon's humiliating and catastrophic Russian campaign—Prussia formed an alliance with the Tsar. By midcentury, it had become a power to reckon with—and by 1870, Prussia's Chancellor, Otto von Bismarck, felt sufficiently confident of his nation's military prowess to provoke France into a declaration of war. Prussia's victory was swift, and on January 18, 1871, William I of Prussia was proclaimed Emperor of Germany at Versailles. The German Empire had been born.

On January 18, 1871, Prussian troops in full-dress uniform formed ranks outside Louis XIV's palace at Versailles. At the time, the Franco-Prussian War was only some six months old, but Prussian forces had already routed the French troops at Sedan, captured the Emperor Napoleon III and 100,000 of his troops, besieged Paris and established their general headquarters at Versailles. And now the German states were to be formally unified; Germany was about to be proclaimed an empire under the Prussian King William I; and the Hohenzollerns, once petty local princes, were on the point of becoming the most powerful rulers in Europe.

January 18 had been chosen for the ceremony because it was the anniversary of the crowning of the first Prussian King, Frederick I, at Königsberg in 1701. The choice of setting was also symbolic: in the Hall of Mirrors at Versailles the brilliant court of Louis XIV had attended the Sun King's ceremonies. Now delegations from all the German regiments in the field were mustered in the enormous room, and they presented their battle-torn flags in a forest of color. In the middle of the gallery, between two tall center bays, an altar had been set up, and opposite it a raised dais had been built.

Precisely at midday a roll of drums was heard from outside, an abrupt military command echoed down the gallery—which had suddenly fallen silent—and the King of Prussia made his entrance followed by other German rulers, princes and generals. He mounted the small dais and took his seat. On his right was the heir to the throne, the Crown Prince, and on his left was Chancellor Otto von Bismarck, wearing the uniform of Colonel of the Horse Guards. A detachment of infantry played a fanfare on muted trumpets, and the official court preacher delivered a long sermon. At the end of his harangue a choir of soldiers sang the Te Deum.

In a brief speech William I thanked the representatives of the German states who had offered him the title of Emperor and declared it his duty to accept it. Bismarck then read the Emperor's proclamation:

Accordingly, we and our successors will bear henceforth the title of Emperor in all affairs concerning the German Reich. We hope that with God's blessing we shall be able to lead our country, under the banner of its former splendor, toward a happier future. We shall assume the imperial dignity in a spirit of national fidelity, to preserve the rights of our Reich, to ensure peace, to defend our independence in prosperity, and to defend liberty.

At this point the Grand Duke of Baden, a man of enormous stature, cried loudly: "Long live His Majesty the German Emperor William I!" The whole assembly broke into frenzied cheers and some officers drew their swords and brandished them in the air. The German Empire had been born.

Strictly speaking, the ceremony had not been a coronation but simply a proclamation. But that was enough. "It was a historic day and a day of rejoicing," the Chancellor's secretary noted in his diary. "The ceremony was impressive, and was held amid a great military display. Everybody who was present said that it was an unforgettable sight." In point of fact, the event had transformed the fate of Germany, had changed the map of Europe, and it would ultimately affect the destinies of the whole world.

The achievement of German unity satisfied a relatively recent aspiration. The Holy Roman Germanic Empire, which had reached the apogee of its power in the Middle Ages, would later be referred to as a forerunner of the German Empire, but the two empires were actually vastly different. The First Reich, as the Holy Roman Empire came to be called, had been a loose, haphazard group of principalities that made no pretension to be the embodiment of any racial or national sentiment. It comprised such disparate territories as the Kingdom of Italy, the Kingdom of Arles, Holland and the Duchy of Burgundy. One Emperor, Frederick II

William I of Prussia, who was proclaimed Emperor of Germany at Versailles.

Opposite An English cartoon of Bismarck, who was regarded by many as Europe's most capable statesman. In the "Ems dispatch" he deliberately provided a *casus belli* for the French.

A French newspaper attack on the unpreparedness of the French army. The Battle of Sedan allowed the German army to enter Paris almost unopposed.

The proclamation of William I of Prussia as Emperor in the Hall of Mirrors at Versailles.

German nation." In fact, such signs were hardly discernible before 1807. But in that year Napoleon I reduced Prussia's territory by more than half by the Treaty of Tilsit. This brutal treatment embittered the Germans and brought about a national self-awareness; hatred for France became the banner of German nationalism. A year later the first patriotic association, the *Tugendbund*, was founded. Its outspoken members urged all Germans to unite in resistance to foreign oppression, but in less than two years the *Tugendbund* was dissolved at the insistence of the French Emperor. German patriots were given another opportunity to vent their passions against the French in 1813, following Napoleon's disastrous and ill-advised Russian campaign. The whole of Germany rose against the French Emperor in the early months of 1813 and replaced the alliance with France by a treaty with the Tsar.

It was the German revolt that sealed Napoleon's fate. In October of 1813, the great conqueror suffered a decisive defeat at Leipzig—thanks in large part to the efforts of his former German allies. By April, 1815, a Frankfurt financier was able to write: "The memory of the humiliating domination that Germany suffered for ten years has developed a national spirit that has dispersed small local jealousies." The idea of a German nation had been launched; the man who was indirectly responsible was Napoleon.

In 1815 the government at Berlin initiated a German Confederation, a military alliance that included Austria as well as the German states. For the next several decades Austria and Prussia vied

of Hohenstaufen, who was the grandson of Frederick Barbarossa, spoke Italian, French and Arabic—but no German.

In 1789, the year the Bastille fell, what is now called Germany was a patchwork of 350 sovereign states. Bismarck noted in his *Thoughts and Recollections*: "In Germany up to the outbreak of the French Revolution there was no sign of the emergence of a

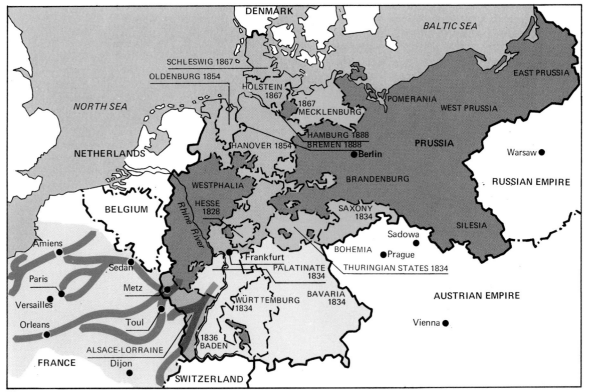

Unification of Germany 1865-71 and the Franco-Prussian War 1870-71

■ Prussia in 1865

■ Prussian acquisitions 1866-67

■ North German Confederation 1866-70

■ German Empire 1871
── Boundary

── Route of Prussian army in Franco-Prussian War 1870-71

□ French territory occupied by Prussia during Franco-Prussian War

■ Territory annexed by Germany after Franco-Prussian War

Dates show when states joined the Customs Union or *Zollverein*

for a position of dominance in the Confederation. Not until one or the other established hegemony would unification move forward. The issue finally was decided in the Austro-Prussian War of 1866: Prussia triumphed at the Battle of Sadowa, and the war came to a swift and abrupt end.

Before the 1866 war, Prussia's growing ambitions had aroused lively reactions from the other German kingdoms, who feared that their independence was threatened. They could foresee the day when they might find themselves completely absorbed by their bigger neighbor. At the outbreak of war Bavaria had openly taken Austria's side. But Prussia's victory at Sadowa not only eliminated the Austrian competition, it also unleashed enormous patriotic enthusiasm throughout Germany. From then on Prussia acted as a rallying point for the German territories.

On June 25, 1867, Prussia founded the North German Confederation. At the time, the Confederation comprised only Saxony and the small principalities that were too insignificant and weak to offer any obstacle to Prussian predominance. The other German states made a great point of holding themselves aloof. The southern states—Bavaria, Württemberg, Baden and Hesse-Darmstadt—showed themselves more and more reticent in the face of what they called the "will for leadership of Berlin." The most antagonistic without doubt was the King of Württemberg, Charles IV, brother-in-law of the Tsar of Russia. He made no secret of his feelings and of his will to resist anything that could be interpreted as disguised annexation. When he received Prince Frederick Charles of Prussia in 1868, he treated him with such coolness that it was tantamount to an

insult. Charles even thought of linking the other southern kingdoms into an independent league that would be opposed to the northern confederation, although this meant that Germany would be cut in two.

This diplomatically perilous situation was to be temporarily resolved when Bavaria, Württemberg, Baden and Hesse all affirmed their resolution to

The Prussian Bully being turned out of Luxembourg, a Punch *cartoon of 1867.*

79

preserve their freedom. At the same time, in separate treaties, each concluded a defensive military alliance with Berlin. It was agreed that if one of the signatories were to be attacked by a third power, the others would come to its assistance immediately. France almost immediately tested those new alliances—and in the process provoked the final achievement of German unity—by making the disputed succession to the Spanish throne an international issue. At the beginning of July, 1870, the Spanish throne was vacant. Leopold of Hohenzollern-Sigmaringen, a petty German prince and a distant cousin of King William I, declared his willingness to accept the Spanish throne, and he did so with William's full permission. When the news became public, the French were furious. They asserted vigorously that the arrival of a Prussian on the throne of Spain constituted "an encircling movement against France." Buoyed by their recollection of Napoleon's exploits, they proclaimed their complete unwillingness to suffer "this intolerable provocation."

William I was astounded and extremely troubled by the violence of these reactions. At seventy-three, he was anxious for peace, and he agreed to bring pressure on his cousin to persuade him to withdraw

his candidacy, which the young prince promptly did. For France the diplomatic victory was a sizable one, and the incident was considered closed. Unfortunately, when news of the concession reached Paris it inflamed the high feelings that had been aroused. France's demands escalated, and it now insisted on what it called "guarantees for the future." The French Ambassador presented these new demands to William at Ems, where the King was peacefully taking the waters. William answered that the renunciation of the throne was sufficient in itself. The meeting between the French Ambassador and the King took place in an atmosphere of extreme courtesy, but in Berlin Chancellor Bismarck, urged on by the military faction, deplored the evidence in his sovereign of what he considered "an excess of goodwill." He released the account that he had received of the meeting (now known as the "Ems dispatch"), but first he edited it in order to make it as offensive as possible to the French. The German text, already couched in unpleasant terms, was mistranslated by the French, and consequently the truth became doubly distorted.

No one in Paris was interested in checking the accuracy of the dispatch, which had no official sanction whatsoever. The people of Paris were enraged, and Emperor Napoleon III, aging and in failing health, was not sufficiently strong to resist such an outbreak of popular anger. In what was undeniably an unprovoked act of aggression, France declared war on Prussia on July 16, 1870.

France's move gave the other side of the Rhine the chance to implement the defensive alliances concluded in 1867. King Louis II of Bavaria, who was extremely anti-Prussian, hesitated for some hours, but under pressure from his compatriots he finally agreed to support the spirited resistance that had swept over the rest of the country. In fact the southern states were unanimous in declaring their "solidarity with Prussia, who was a victim of French megalomania." In two days the German bloc cohered. Bismarck was to admit later:

I considered a war with France entirely necessary for our national development. I never doubted that the establishment of the German Empire must be preceded by a victory over France. The nation could only achieve unity through a common cause for anger.

France's declaration of war was to prove cause enough. On September 3, 1870, the very day after the Prussian triumph at Sedan, Bismarck set about the task of giving his dream of a unified empire concrete form. He summoned Rudolph von Del-

Opposite above Paris cooked in its own juice—by Germany and the Devil—a French cartoon of 1871.

Opposite below A railroad bridge near Dijon being patrolled by German soldiers during the Franco-Prussian War.

The Prussian Bully takes his share of the Plunder, a *Punch* cartoon of 1864. The Franco-Prussian War helped Prussia consolidate her gains in Germany.

A cartoonist's view of the aging Napoleon III. Like the Prussian King, he had no wish to fight, but popular feeling in France made war inevitable.

Louis II of Bavaria. The mad King of Bavaria, more interested in Wagner's music and in building grandiose castles, proved no match for the pan-German ambitions of the wily Bismarck.

brück, who had been his closest collaborator in Berlin, to Versailles and charged him with drawing up a proposed constitution. The text was ready by the end of September. It predicted the formation of a German Empire, subject to the control of Prussia, into which the states would become integrated. The text was to be submitted to the interested parties.

At this point a rather strange thing happened: William I of Prussia, who was foremost among the "interested parties" and most likely to benefit from Delbrück's proposed constitution, proved extremely hesitant about the entire matter. The King was adverse to the title of Emperor, which he considered strongly reminiscent of the Holy Roman Empire, and it took considerable time to persuade him that the title was the only acceptable one. He finally resigned himself to it with what his son tells us was a "feeling that he was being given a cross to bear that would weigh heavily on his shoulders and on the Royal House of Prussia."

Although this first obstacle had been overcome, there still remained the difficulty of obtaining the agreement of the states who were being invited to surrender any real degree of sovereignty. The negotiations were delicate, but Bismarck was to display all the qualities of a great statesman. He

directed his first efforts to winning over Bavaria, whose acceptance he thought would bring the others in its train. The negotiations were protracted. As Bismarck was later to explain:

The King of Bavaria, Louis II, expressed his agreement with the cause of German unity but nevertheless his primary concern was to maintain the federal principle which safeguarded the privileges of his country. I well remember the idea that he put forward during the discussions at Versailles and that from a political point of view was quite unrealistic. He demanded that the Presidency of the Confederation should alternate between the Royal House of Prussia and that of Bavaria. I was perplexed as to how I could give so impractical a plan some reality.

Fortunately for Bismarck, Louis II, intelligent as he was, was an artist rather than a statesman, and his sensibilities were more highly developed than his resolution. Among other eccentricities, he was possessed with a mania for building palaces of all kinds. The Chancellor accordingly encouraged these expensive tastes by giving him, under the pretext that it was a "contribution to the arts," a personal subsidy of 100,000 *thalers* a year. Louis rapidly came to the conclusion that he could not long stand out against the movement that was infecting all the German peoples. What he now sought was

the maximum personal advantage. Bismarck was prepared to make concessions as long as they did not compromise the essential matter. He agreed that Bavaria was to be accorded favorable treatment: it was to maintain its own diplomatic representation abroad and it was to continue to issue its own postage stamps. Furthermore, Bavaria's coinage would still bear the head of its ruling prince, and its army corps would maintain their separate designations. It was even stipulated that if the House of Hohenzollern became extinct, the royal crown would pass to the House of Wittelsbach at Munich. Satisfied with all these concessions, Louis II ratified the constitution.

On November 23, Bismarck entered the room where his secretaries were working. "Gentlemen," he said in a shaking voice, "the Bavarian treaty has been signed. German unity is a fait accompli and our King has become the German Emperor!" He ordered champagne to be brought and then, sitting down in the middle of his colleagues, he gave his version of events:

It is possible that I might have gained more from Munich. Our newspapers in Berlin will not be satisfied. Whoever later on writes a straightforward historical account will blame me for being too accommodating. He will say: "The fool could have demanded more and the

German guns bombard Paris.

other party would have had to concede it." But it is my contention that the other party should be satisfied. The agreement that we have signed is not perfect, but it is all the more firm for that. Treaties mean nothing when those who enter into them have only signed under duress.

In truth the minor rulers had no illusions about their ability to resist the Emperor; they knew what was in store for them. Bismarck himself, in safeguarding the individualities of old Germany, did not seem in fact to have wished to do more than to contrive the means for change. The ministries in Berlin quickly developed their overwhelming ascendancy, as the natural tendency toward centralization came irresistibly into play. The constant absorption of the smaller and weaker states by the more powerful and dynamic ones became ever more rapid; a system that had once been flexible became ever more rigid. Soon there was only one rule: "The state rather than the province." The law of the German Empire—rather than local law—predominated. In a short space of time the federal German Empire became a monolithic Empire. And this was not the only distortion. From its very beginning, the Empire carried the seeds of far more formidable things to come.

The Empire was conceived at a time of war and had its infancy in a time of victory. It began by inheriting the responsibility for Alsace and Lorraine, which had been annexed against the wishes of their inhabitants. As soon as elections were held in 1874, the populations of these provinces elected as their representatives to the Federal Parliament fifteen deputies devoted to protest. The two provinces whose destinies had been disposed of by force were never to accept the imposition; and the annexation was to engender a lasting hatred among the French, who were intent upon revenge. There followed an armaments race that lasted for half a century and bore heavily on the fate of Europe.

As far as Germany itself was concerned, the ceremony of January 18, 1871—in an invaded country and in a historical setting whose very choice was a mark of insolence, among all the trappings of war and the rattling of sabers—was to stamp upon the new German Empire a military character that was to permeate and dominate it. All this was to lead inevitably to the catastrophe of World War I and its natural consequence, World War II. German unity was a perfectly natural aspiration, but the manner in which it came about had deplorable consequences, and both Germany and France were responsible for the results.

GEORGES ROUX

Léon Gambetta, who led the resistance to the Germans after the defeat at Sedan.

German learning

The magnitude of the Prussian victory in 1871 ensured Bismarck's supremacy among the world's diplomats for the next two decades. All major international problems—apart from disputes between Britain and the United States—were referred to the German Chancellor for advice and guidance, if not always for solution. And when the statesmen of Europe met in 1878 to settle the affairs of Turkey and her Balkan neighbors, it seemed natural that they should gather in the German capital for their formal deliberations. Similarly it was in Berlin that a fourteen-nation conference met from November of 1884 to February of 1885 to determine boundaries for the newly acquired spheres of colonial settlement in Central Africa. Both France and Italy sought Bismarck's support when they vied for the acquisition of Tunis in the early 1880s—and it is a testimony to Bismarck's powers of dissimulation that each government subsequently thought that it and it alone had received his assurance of sympathetic patronage for its endeavors and ambitions.

Yet the Age of Bismarck witnessed more than the triumph of German statecraft. It also saw the influence of specifically German culture and learning reach its zenith. During this period Teutonic "higher criticism" subjected biblical passages to ponderous analysis; Ernst Haeckel (1834–1919) asserted man's mastery of the universe; and Wilhelm Wundt (1832–1920) anatomized man's physiological psychology. In an equally specialized but different field, Nikolaus Otto (1832–91) and Gottlieb Daimler (1834–1900) perfected the first internal combustion engines—Otto in 1876 using a four-cycle gas engine and Daimler, a decade later, using liquid gasoline. In that same year, 1886, Heinrich Hertz (1857–94) proved the existence of electromagnetic waves, a discovery that was used some nine years later by the Italian inventor Guglielmo Marconi (1874–1937) for transmitting the first radio messages.

Nor was the German achievement limited to the physical sciences. Those were the years in which the cult of Wagnerian opera

Gottlieb Daimler, the German technologist who developed the first liquid gasoline-powered internal combustion engine.

—the very apotheosis of Romanticism—spread beyond the confines of the composer's fatherland. Historians throughout Europe followed Leopold von Ranke (1795–1886) in his search for a new objectivity, and Heinrich Schliemann (1822–90) promoted the study of archaeology with the thoroughness of a Prussian and the enthusiasm of a born romantic. Even socialist thought, which had been predominantly French in inspiration earlier in the century, looked to the Germans Wilhelm Liebknecht (1826–1900) and August Bebel (1840–1913) for leadership. It was only in the field of fiction with Emile Zola (1840–1902), Alphonse Daudet (1840–97) and Guy de Maupassant (1850–93) and in the visual arts that France retained her traditional supremacy; nothing in European painting could match the imaginative craftsmanship of the Impressionists, whose genius dominated the Parisian salons of the 1870s.

Germany under Bismarck

Bismarck took little personal interest in the culture of his age. He remained loyal to the stolid Lutheranism of the Junkers, the class of Prussian landowner that he typified and represented. During the nineteen years in which he was Germany's Chancellor, he championed the established order, and during his tenure the political

balance of Europe acquired a permanence not unlike the equilibrium that Metternich had sought to sustain half a century earlier.

The Chancellor believed that the wars of 1864, 1866 and 1870 had won for Germany all the territory that could be absorbed without a fundamental change in its social structure. The Reich of 1871 was large enough to satisfy the patriotic ardor of the German people and was yet sufficiently limited in size to be administered by the Prussian civil service and the Junkers. Bismarck knew that the concept of a greater Germany was an illusion of the middle classes —a dream whose realization would involve the political elimination of the Junkers. He therefore resisted all pan-Germanic movements, whether they had the backing of industrial magnates or of members of the General Staff. He would never have approved the expansive policy of Hitler's Third Reich.

Yet Bismarck could not entirely ignore new ideas. He bowed reluctantly to the general demand for colonies, and authorized settlements in Tanganyika, the Cameroons and Southwest Africa in the 1880s. The Chancellor's gesture was a temporary one, designed to mollify his critics; Bismarck recognized that such undeveloped territories could be no more than expensive and dangerous toys for the German people for years to come. By the 1880s he was prepared to experiment with social welfare schemes for industrial workers, although he remained narrowly conservative at heart. And while he was particularly opposed to all forms of "internationalism" (whether Roman Catholic or socialist in origin), he was no less suspicious

of the bellicose nationalism of the younger generation. So long as William I remained Kaiser, Bismarck rested secure in the knowledge that his sovereign shared his viewpoint. The accession of the twenty-nine-year-old William II in 1888 changed the situation, and Bismarck's failure to understand the spirit of the new Germany he had created led to his dismissal two years later.

Bismarck's foreign policy

German foreign policy after 1871 reflected Bismarck's general desire for stability. He became a pillar of peace because he feared that any European war—even one that did not involve Germany directly— would enable the victor to impose a new settlement on the great powers and thereby destroy his achievement. He knew that the greatest danger for Germany was a war of revenge initiated by France, but he assumed that the French would not risk a campaign without allies and he believed that he could counter any such threat by keeping France isolated diplomatically.

The key to Bismarck's foreign policy lay not so much in his negative attitude toward France as in his dealings with his mighty neighbor to the east. Good relations with Russia were essential, for the Russians were natural geographic allies of the French in any struggle against Germany. Except for a brief period in 1879, therefore, there was throughout the age of Bismarck a close understanding between the governments of Berlin and St. Petersburg.

The Chancellor also favored

A German cartoon attacking the role of missionaries, both Roman Catholic and Protestant, in Africa.

cooperation with Austria-Hungary, partly to forestall any Paris-Vienna cooperation and partly to hold in check the dangerous friction between the Austrians and Russians in southeast Europe. The League of the Three Emperors, a loose understanding between Germany, Russia and Austria-Hungary, enabled the East European autocracies to work together from 1873 to 1875, but it could not survive the strain of the Eastern Crisis of 1875–78. The League was renewed more formally in 1881 and lasted until 1887 (when Balkan tensions once again aggravated relations between the Austrians and the Russians). Bismarck maintained close relations with the Russians during his last three years

The emperors of Germany and Austria and the Tsar of Russia meeting in 1884.

in office, however, and a secret Russo-German pact known as the Reinsurance Treaty was signed. This kept the wires to St. Petersburg open from 1887 to 1890.

Collaboration with Russia was only one aspect of Bismarck's diplomacy. He built up a system of secret defensive alliances at the same time to ensure support for Germany if it were attacked by Russia or France at some future time. An Austro-German alliance formed in 1879 was transformed into a triple alliance in 1882 by the admission of Italy, and that combination of Eastern and Central European powers lasted—at least theoretically—until the coming of World War I. The weakness of Bismarck's system of alliances was that it required a chancellor of his caliber to make it function, and none of his successors could reach his heights of statesmanship.

Turkey

The problem of racial minorities was one that caused difficulty in Asia, Europe and America, al-

though the form it took differed from country to country. It was a problem that was posed in a more and more acute form as the century continued, owing to the rapid extension of the European empires. But the well-established empires found similar difficulties. In the Ottoman Empire, for example, nationalist ideas, which had already been felt so strongly and with such a major effect in Greece and the Balkans, were beginning to have an impact elsewhere. An additional problem that faced the Sultan's government was that of religious minorities. In the Middle East, Druzes and Maronite Christians were no less eager for national independence than the Arabs as a whole. That these religious minorities could rely on the support of the Western powers (particularly of Russia and France, both of which saw themselves as the protectors of Christians) merely added to the difficulties of the Sublime Porte. The bankruptcy of the Ottoman government in 1874 further increased the many difficulties of the Sultan's officials.

Austria-Hungary

In the Austrian Empire the situation was even worse. The loss of Lombardy and Venetia in the 1860s had shown how strong were the centrifugal pressures at work. The 1850s and 1860s saw almost continual conflict between the imperial government and the various national assemblies, which increasingly formed focal points for nationalist ideas. The situation was exacerbated by inequitable electoral arrangements; in the Czech assembly, for example, the deputies

The Hradshin Castle, Prague, in the mid-nineteenth century; nationalist movements among Czechs and others helped weaken the Austrian Empire.

for the German districts of the city of Prague represented 2,800 inhabitants each, while for the Czech areas they represented 32,000.

Linguistic differences were a source of anger to the minorities; German was the common language of the whole Empire and German-speakers could not understand why Hungarians and others should not give up their languages just as they were supposed to have given up their loyalty to their individual region for the sake of a greater Austria. Nor could German liberals see the benefit of giving way to nationalist ideas, for many of the nationalist leaders were great nobles who were seeking to enhance their own power, while the imperial government was at least prepared to make gestures in the direction of liberal reforms. A federalist solution had little attraction—the example of the American Civil War was enough to put most nineteenth-century liberals off the idea of federalism. So the imperial government was able to rely on widespread support against making concessions to nationalism. As a result the Poles in Galicia and Cracow, the Czechs and Slovaks of Bohemia and Moravia, and the Slavs in the south were forced to wait for national self-determination.

Only the Magyars of Hungary gained any real measure of autonomy. As the most powerful of the minority groups, they were able to persuade the Emperor Francis Joseph that by giving Hungary a limited measure of self-determination, he would find it easier to retain Austrian control over the rest of his possessions. The Hungarians were not committed to the

The Hungarian nationalist leader, Count Julius Andrassy.

principle of *national* self-determination, only to that of Hungarian self-determination. One of the Hungarian leaders, Count Julius Andrassy, said of the Slavs, "They are not fit to govern—they must be ruled," a sentiment with which Francis Joseph did not disagree. In 1867 the Emperor was crowned as King of Hungary, and his empire became a dual-monarchy, Austria-Hungary. As a result the other minorities were all left with an additional feeling of grievance.

America

Elsewhere, too, the problem of minorities remained an intractable one. Sometimes, as in Ireland, it was connected with land-ownership. It was often, however, a problem of scattered and persecuted groups, as were the Jews in many European states. Not even America avoided the problem of minorities. Negroes, whether born free or newly emancipated, were usually discriminated against. They were often excluded from education, land-ownership and the vote, as well as being forced to use separate facilities. That was a problem that America chose to ignore until the twentieth century. But the problem of the Indians could not be ignored. With each step farther west, America came into contact with more Indians. Sometimes amicable agreements were made by smooth-talking government officials—often with the added incentive of whiskey —but the Americans usually broke the treaties they had made, and Indian trouble remained a minor but recurrent threat, which occasionally, as in 1876, caught the headlines.

Custer's Last Stand 1876

Toward the end of the nineteenth century the United States expanded westward—across the Plains and into Indian territory. Slowly the Indians lost ground. In 1867, the Sioux and Cheyenne signed a treaty giving up most of their land for a guaranteed territory including their beloved—and sacred—Black Hills. When lust for gold caused the treaty to be broken the tribes rose in outrage. The force sent to quell them included a flamboyant cavalry officer with a history of insubordination—George Armstrong Custer. In a frantic search for glory he disregarded his orders and led his troops into one of the most celebrated massacres in history.

By the 1870s, the life of the Plains Indians—dependent as it was on the horse, the buffalo and the freedom to roam great tracts of land—was seriously threatened. The great overland trails and the spreading network of railroads cut across the prairies bringing, after the respite afforded by the Civil War, new waves of emigrants. Each was anxious to claim and settle land by right of individual ownership—a notion as alien to the nomadic Indians' thinking as it was hostile to their way of life. In 1871 began the uncontrolled slaughter of millions of buffalo by professional hide-hunters, an activity encouraged by officials who foresaw in the extermination of buffalo the extermination of the Indian. The Indians rose up to resist the white man but failure was inevitable. For them war was an affair of the moment, against the enemies of the moment; as they were numerically too few, tribally fragmented, and short of firearms and ammunition, they could not sustain a campaign. When they yielded, they had to cede their hunting grounds in exchange for increasingly barren reservations.

In the western half of South Dakota and the adjacent parts of Wyoming and Montana, the northern Plains Indians had retained much of their land by force of arms. In 1866 the government had tried to negotiate with the Sioux for a right of way along the Bozeman Trail, a route in western Wyoming leading to the gold fields of Montana. The Indians refused, but the army went ahead and built three forts along the trail. Throughout the winter Red Cloud's Oglala Sioux, with allies from other Sioux and Cheyenne tribes, made war on the forts. On December 21, 1866, they lured eighty-one soldiers led by Captain William Fetterman into an ambush and killed every man. In 1867 the army abandoned the forts, and the Sioux and Cheyennes signed a treaty that gave them the Powder River country and the surrounding area of Wyoming as a hunting ground, as well as establishing a reservation

and agencies in western South Dakota. This reservation included the Black Hills, the *Paha Sapa* of the Sioux—the most sacred place on earth. In return Red Cloud promised never to make war again.

Red Cloud kept his word, and urged his people to do likewise. Yet from the start there was trouble over the treaty. Many Indians maintained that what they had been promised and what had been ratified in Washington were two quite different things, and they raided settlers who encroached on what they claimed as their territory. In 1873, railroad surveyors, plotting the course of the Northern Pacific on the north bank of the Yellowstone River, were attacked and called in the army for protection. Then, in the summer of 1874, in response to rumors of gold, and in violation of the treaty, the government sent an expedition of miners and soldiers into the Black Hills. The soldiers were the Seventh Cavalry and their commander was Colonel George Armstrong Custer. As a dashing cavalry officer with a flair for publicity, Custer had been the youngest Brevet General on the Union side in the Civil War, but little of his early promise showed in his career as an Indian fighter. As was his custom, and defying specific orders, Custer included a group of newspapermen in his expedition to the Black Hills.

When the miners found gold there the news spread like wildfire. The trickle of prospectors quickly became a flood. Rather than try to stem the tide, the government sent a commission to negotiate with the Indians for the sale or lease of the Black Hills. More than 20,000 Indians—Sioux, Cheyenne and Arapaho—came together to hear, and to reject, the commissioners' proposals. Some came wearing war paint. Crazy Horse, who had fought under Red Cloud and who was, now that Red Cloud had become an agency Indian, the chief of the free-roaming Oglala Sioux, did not attend. Instead he sent a spokesman, Little Big Man, who said that he

General George Armstrong Custer, whose disregard for orders led to the massacre of Little Big Horn.

Opposite Little Big Man, spokesman for the Oglala Sioux, who flatly rejected government proposals to lease the sacred Black Hills.

Above *Custer's Demand*, by Schreyvogel

Right Custer, photographed on his graduation from military academy.

would kill the first Indian who advocated selling the Black Hills. Similarly Sitting Bull, the great medicine chief of the Hunkpapa Sioux, sent a message that he would not sell the white man so much as a pinch of dust. When the commissioners reported their failure to Washington they added a recommendation that Congress should now enforce the appropriation of the Black Hills. Meanwhile the Indians resumed their attacks on the prospectors.

On December 3, 1875, the government published an order directing all Sioux and Cheyennes to report to their agencies by January 31; all who remained outside would be considered outlaws. But it was impossible for this order to be obeyed. Nor could its authors have imagined otherwise; in effect they were announcing their intention to kill the Indians. Lack of communication meant that many Indians would not even hear of the order before the deadline, while snow, blizzards and extreme cold made it impossible for those who did hear to move their families and ponies. In any case the agencies did not have the resources to support an influx of Indians; by March many of the Indians who had already reported had to leave the reservation to hunt for food.

When news of the government order reached Sitting Bull and Crazy Horse they both sent word they would go when the weather made it possible to travel. The army gave them no chance to prove their promises; its plan to sweep the Indians out of the Black Hills was already in motion.

The army planned a three-pronged invasion of the Indian heartland. In the early summer the roving bands of Sioux and Cheyennes would gather in the Powder River country for the Teton Council, a great annual convocation, both a religious and a social event. To this rendezvous Brigadier-General George Crook would bring up one column from the

southeast; a cavalry force under Colonel John
Gibbon was to set out eastward from Fort Ellis,
Montana; and the third force—commanded by
General Alfred Terry and including most of Custer's
Seventh Cavalry—was to march west from Fort
Abraham Lincoln in North Dakota. Crook's
column, making a preliminary foray toward the
Yellowstone River in March, was responsible for the
first bloodshed. In a predawn blizzard the advance
guard of cavalry under Colonel J.J. Reynolds
came upon an Indian village. Reynolds did not
know, and did not wait to find out, that the village
was composed of Cheyennes and Oglala Sioux who
had wintered legally on the reservation and had
only recently left to forage for food. The cavalry's
first charge into the sleeping village was easy enough.
But once the braves rallied they offered Reynolds'
men a stiffer fight and the cavalry withdrew. The
Indians, in tatters and without food, marched for
three days seeking the village of Crazy Horse and his
Oglalas.

If Crazy Horse had had doubts before, he now was
determined to fight. When the weather improved,
he broke camp and moved north to join Sitting Bull
and his Hunkpapas at the mouth of Tongue River.
From there they again moved back toward Rosebud
Creek. Bands of other Indians joined them along the
way—Minneconjous, Cheyennes, Brules, Sans Arcs,
Blackfoot Sioux. Some were reservation Indians who
had left to exercise their rights as hunters. But many
young braves were burning for a fight, despite the
advice of the older chiefs. Sitting Bull fasted and
tortured himself for three days until he fell into a
trance; at the end he cried out that he had seen
soldiers falling like grasshoppers and Indians riding
over them.

With his column of fifteen companies of cavalry
and five of mule-mounted infantry, Crook too had

headed for the Rosebud. On June 16 he made camp
along its banks, and early the next day, knowing that
hostile Indians were nearby—he had been so in-
informed by Sitting Bull and Crazy Horse—he
rode out with some 1,200 men to look for them.
Crook had been enraged by Reynolds' escapade,
which he regarded as a disgrace to his command. He
had acquired quite a reputation for his campaigns
against the Apaches in Arizona. But for all his
experience, he was quite unprepared for the attack
Crazy Horse unleashed on him that day, when,
suddenly, there stood before him a massed force of
Indians, equal, if not superior, to his group in number. Crazy Horse was a tactician. Since Red Cloud's
war he had studied the Bluecoats and their methods
of fighting. He had sought guidance too in the visions
through which he believed he gained access to the
real world.

Crazy Horse's charge caught Crook with his
cavalry deployed to the left of his infantry. Barely in
time, the infantry formed a defensive circle on high
ground. The cavalry itself, heavily engaged by
mounted Sioux, could not get back to them, and the
circle broke and broke again, into three and then
into four groups. But the individual groups remained
intact and the Indians drew back. For a time they
remained on a ridge, just out of shot, taunting the
soldiers. After some two hours, and for no apparent
reason, the Sioux dispersed. Crook, severely shaken,
moved his expedition back to a camp on Goose
Creek, just inside the Wyoming border. He
remained there, making no effort to warn Gibbon or
Terry in the north—an extraordinary lapse in so
experienced a soldier.

Meanwhile Terry had been making his way up
the Yellowstone in a flat-bottomed riverboat, the
Far West, with his column keeping pace with him
along the bank. On June 7, at the mouth of the

89

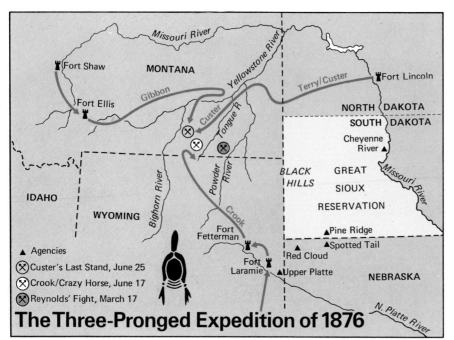

The Three-Pronged Expedition of 1876

▲ Agencies
⊗ Custer's Last Stand, June 25
⊗ Crook/Crazy Horse, June 17
⊗ Reynolds' Fight, March 17

Powder River, he linked up with Gibbon. A conference was held aboard the *Far West* and on June 22 Custer rode out with six hundred men. As he left Gibbon called out to him, "Now, Custer, don't be greedy. You wait for us." Custer replied, "I won't." Whatever he meant by that, he carried with him a written instruction from Terry not to engage in any major battle; if he located a hostile encampment he was to wait until Terry and Gibbon's combined force came within striking distance. The overall plan of movement was vague, but the general intention was that Custer should make his way south up the Rosebud and then swing west to join Gibbon and Terry on the Big Horn. However, being politically as well as militarily ambitious, he evidently decided that the publicity that would follow a dramatic personal coup could only be to his credit.

The pace Custer set proved his determination. On June 23 the regiment marched thirty-five miles, and on the next day, between 5:00 A.M. and 8:00 P.M., forty-five. That day some of Custer's forty-four Indian scouts reported signs of a massive Indian movement heading westward toward the Little Big Horn River. The cavalry swung into action, covering an additional ten miles that night. When they finally pitched camp around 2:00 A.M. they were, unknown to Custer, within ten miles of where Crazy Horse had beaten back Crook's column one week before. By now men and horses were suffering from thirst and exhaustion because the water they found along the way was too brackish to drink.

Shortly after dawn a Sergeant Curtis, backtracking to look for a mule pack that had been lost during the night, found the pack being dismembered by a party of Sioux. On his way back to camp he saw other Indians observing the regiment from high ground. Custer therefore assumed that the main force of Indians knew all about his encampment. A

little later, some of his Indian scouts sighted a huge herd of ponies on a ridge just west of the Little Big Horn, some twenty miles off. The tepees of the village were obscured by trees, but the number of ponies indicated that the village was large. Ignoring the scouts' nervousness, Custer told his officers he proposed to attack as soon as possible before the tribes had a chance to run away. By noon, the regiment had advanced to the divide from which it could see into the Little Big Horn Valley. Custer halted and split up his column, an unusual move, as he did not know the strength of the enemy.

Three companies of forty men each under Major Frederick Benteen were ordered west to scout the South Fork and beyond, prior to turning north toward the known enemy encampment. The pack train and a one-troop escort commanded by Captain Thomas MacDougall were to follow a similar line. Three companies under Major Marcus Reno were sent in pursuit of Indians who had been spotted galloping along the flat ground on the far bank of the river toward the southern end of the village. Custer himself swung the remaining five companies to Reno's right. Reno, having failed to catch up with the Indians, charged onward to the outskirts of the village, where, incredibly, he took the Indians completely by surprise.

The Hunkpapa Sioux, who occupied this southern upstream end of the village were prepared for another battle. Sitting Bull had told them his prophecy had not been fulfilled at Rosebud Creek. But they expected the battle to be of their own choosing; it had not occurred to them that they could be attacked in broad daylight when they and their Cheyenne allies were mustered together in such strength. The braves who had reconnoitered Custer's camp early that morning had not even bothered to report their findings to the village. News of the cavalry's approach was brought by hunting parties later in the day, but the chiefs remained unconcerned—until suddenly there was gunshot all around. Women and children as well as men fell to the ground. Led by the Hunkpapa war chief Gall, the Indians quickly rallied. The women and children were taken to safety downstream and Reno found himself facing an overwhelming force of mounted Sioux braves, with more closing in on his left flank. A small grove on the riverbank offered a possible site for a stand; if the Sioux circled round it and did not come too close, and if ammunition lasted, it could be held. But the cover was not really adequate, there was no sign of the promised support, and the men had begun to panic. Suddenly Reno rode to the high ground back across the river, followed by those soldiers who could mount up in time. Some were shot down crossing the river, but when Reno halted at the top of the bluffs he found that the Indians had stopped their pursuit. He had lost forty men and three officers.

Custer had sent two observers part of the way with Reno. They waited just long enough to see Reno's charge upon the undefended fringes of the village, and then galloped back to report to Custer that Indian resistance was weak. This news may have sharpened Custer's fears that the Indians were about to run away. Sending messages to tell Benteen and MacDougall to bring up the reserve ammunition and join him, he moved northward with his five companies. It seems that Custer, appreciating the steepness of the bluffs along his side of the river opposite the Indian camp, intended to find a point where he could attack the lower end of the encampment from downstream. This was what the Indians anticipated.

A ride of some twelve miles, taking perhaps ninety minutes, brought Custer to a point level with the lower end of the Indian camp. His column was strung out over more than three-quarters of a mile and, though still on the east bank of the river, it had crossed onto the western side of the ridge. Now the

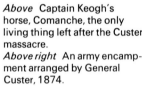

Above Captain Keogh's horse, Comanche, the only living thing left after the Custer massacre.
Above right An army encampment arranged by General Custer, 1874.

Indians had them trapped. The vanguard was halted by frontal fire from a band of mounted Cheyennes. More mounted braves came up from the river behind the rear column. Looking for a way out, most of the soldiers began to make their way down toward the river, thereby becoming a hopelessly over-extended line, partially dismounted and incapable of organized fire. Near the river, concealed by the terrain, the main force of Sioux and Cheyennes were waiting. Watching from across the river, thirteen-year-old Black Elk saw only a cloud of dust, from which horses emerged with empty saddles. Both sides were fighting in a fog of smoke and dust caused by the encircling braves. Many of the Indians had dismounted and were closing in from rock to rock.

According to Red Horse, some soldiers, when they saw they would be overwhelmed, threw away their guns and begged for mercy. But the Indians took no prisoners that day. However, around Custer the soldiers stayed together, set their horses free and fought to the last man. Several Indians later claimed credit for killing Custer, and the legend persists that he was the last man to die. With Custer approximately 225 cavalrymen died, plus a handful of civilians, including his brother, three other relatives and a newspaper correspondent. The sole survivors were some Indian scouts who, having a shrewd idea of what their commander was riding into, had held back. One of these, a seventeen-year-old Crow named Curly, eventually brought news of the disaster to General Terry. The number of Indian braves involved was approximately four thousand.

On receiving Custer's orders to close up, Benteen had no clear idea of where to go. The sound of heavy firing in the distance gave him a line to follow, which presently brought him to the point on the bluffs to which Reno had just scrambled with the remnants of his men. Benteen's forward company, under Captain Thomas Weir, pressed on and arrived at the high point of the ridge. There he saw, some two miles off, the last moments of the Custer battle—no soldiers standing, and a horde of Indians quartering the ground searching out and killing the wounded. By now Indians were also heading for the bluffs, and there was barely time for Weir, Benteen and MacDougall to join forces and consolidate Reno's position before they came under heavy siege.

It was a brave defense, kept up throughout the following day. Then in the later afternoon of June 26, the Indians withdrew, setting fire to the grass in the valley as they went, and disappearing into the Big Horn Mountains with their encampment. The chiefs had received reports of the Terry-Gibbon column advancing from the north; they were short of ammunition and they had to find food. As they headed into the mountains, the tribes dispersed along different trails.

The next morning a reconnaissance by Lieutenant James Bradley of Terry's column revealed the nature of the calamity. The Indians had stripped the bodies of the soldiers and burned their uniforms. Though

some of the corpses had been ritualistically muti-
lated, that of Custer was untouched. Some Indians
claimed later that this was because of their respect
for him as a warrior; others said simply that they
had not recognized him.

Crook and Terry finally rendezvoused in August,
and for the rest of the summer they pursued the
scattered tribes. A solitary and limited success
came at Slim Buttes on September 9, when Crook's
forward detachment under Captain Anson Mills
destroyed the village of the Sioux chief American
Horse, who died of wounds received in the fighting.
A counterattack on Crook by Crazy Horse and six
hundred warriors was repulsed. Except that Custer
paid the full price for his impetuousness, the
campaign was typical of the army against the
Indians. Casual or gloryhunting commanders, lack
of communication, superficial reconnaissance—all
had precedents. Cynics at the time said that the
cost to the United States for each Indian killed by its
armed forces was a million dollars. Even if Sand
Creek (1864), Washita (1868), and later Wounded
Knee (1890), boosted the army's balance sheet
with a high bodycount of women and children, it
was not until the winter that the Sioux and Cheyennes paid for their victory at the battle at Little Big
Horn. Custer was a national martyr and the
nation demanded vengeance.

In the summer the average cavalry remount was
no match for a lightly laden, well-fed Indian pony.
Come winter, when both the ponies and their
riders were half-starved and feeble, the relative
mobility of soldier and brave was reversed. As the
weather hardened, so did Crook and, working in
tandem with Colonel Nelson Miles, he harassed the
Indians to the breaking point. He set new standards
of preparation and reconnaissance and he brought
in field guns which the Indians dreaded. Meanwhile a new government commission bludgeoned
the agency Indians into ceding all their hunting
grounds and moving to barren, hated reservations
along the Missouri River. In May, 1877, Crazy
Horse surrendered. Sitting Bull and the remnants
of his braves were fugitives in Canada. The war for
the Black Hills was over.   PATRICK ANNESLEY

An Indian view of the massacre
of Little Big Horn.

In the great age of European imperialism

The Meiji restoration

The nineteenth century was the great age of European imperialism. Only one non-European state—apart from the white colonies and the United States—was appreciably stronger at the end of the century than at the beginning. The success of Japan in avoiding the fate of most of Asia and Africa was largely due to the resurgence of imperial power and the collapse of the Tokugawa shogunate which had exercised all real power in Japan for centuries. The shogunate never recovered from the blow to its prestige by the enforced ending of its policy of isolation, dealt by the Americans in 1854, nor from the British bombardment of Kagoshima in 1863. Anti-Tokugawa plots became increasingly common and they found a focus in the *sonno* (honor the emperor) movement.

In 1868 there was a rising in support of the sixteen-year-old Meiji Emperor. Although the Tokugawa cause still found many supporters, the Shogun himself quickly re-

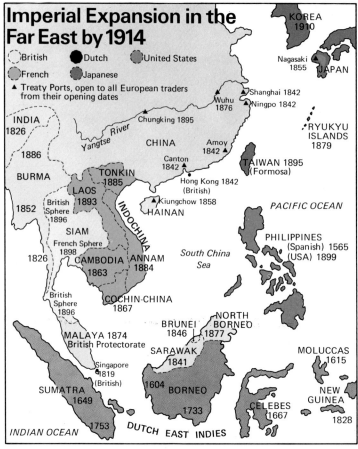

Imperial Expansion in the Far East by 1914

British · Dutch · United States · French · Japanese

▲ Treaty Ports, open to all European traders from their opening dates

KOREA 1910
Nagasaki 1855
JAPAN
Shanghai 1842
Wuhu 1876
Ningpo 1842
Chungking 1895
RYUKYU ISLANDS 1879
INDIA 1826
Yangtse River
CHINA
Amoy 1842 ▲
1886
Canton 1842 ▲
TAIWAN 1895 (Formosa)
BURMA
TONKIN 1885
Hong Kong 1842 (British)
LAOS 1893
1852
British Sphere 1896
Kiungchow 1858
HAINAN
PACIFIC OCEAN
SIAM
French Sphere 1898
1826
CAMBODIA 1863
ANNAM 1884
South China Sea
PHILIPPINES (Spanish) 1565 (USA) 1899
British Sphere 1896
COCHIN-CHINA 1867
MALAYA 1874 British Protectorate
BRUNEI 1846
NORTH BORNEO 1877
MOLUCCAS 1615
SARAWAK 1841
Singapore 1819 (British)
1604 BORNEO
NEW GUINEA 1828
SUMATRA 1649
1733
CELEBES 1667
INDIAN OCEAN
1753
DUTCH EAST INDIES

acy. Railroads and telegraphs were built. No less important was the government's commitment to industrialization. In addition to ordinary industrial and commercial development, naval shipyards and several arms factories were built. Within a few years the whole apparatus of a modern Western state had been set up, and Japan was ready to take its place as an equal with the powers of Europe and the United States.

Japan's determination not to be overwhelmed by the West was demonstrated by the territorial greed that it quickly showed. Japan had been threatened by both Russian and Chinese expansionism before the Meiji restoration, and its enthusiastic espousal of armaments was largely due to this. The policy of isolation from external contacts, although at first beneficial, had latterly proved unfortunate. Korea was a source of contention with China, since it was Japan's nearest mainland neighbor and was also virtually a Chinese colony. After several years of effort the Meiji government succeeded in making a commercial treaty with Korea. The consequence of this was a further deterioration in Japan's relations with China,

particularly as the Japanese made no effort to disguise their determination to extend their influence in Korea and ultimately to conquer it. Finally, in 1894, war broke out between China and Japan over Korea. The Sino-Japanese War showed the extent to which Japan had succeeded in modernizing itself during the previous forty years, and Korea became a vassal state. Although for a few years, with the help of Russian troops, Korea succeeded in regaining its independence, the Sino-Japanese War had signaled Japan's arrival as a colonial power. Elsewhere in Asia, however, European power was reaching its peak.

India after the mutiny

The suppression of the Indian Mutiny and the handing over of the British East India Company's empire to the government began a great period of consolidation. The Indian civil service, recruited by examination in England, rapidly became the most prestigious branch of British public service. Far more attention was paid to the wishes of the native Indians, particularly the princes, than before; the

government of India, under a viceroy whose court was no less splendid than that of Queen Victoria herself, began to concentrate on systematic investment and development: an extensive railroad system, the finest in Asia, was built, irrigation methods were improved and irrigated areas vastly increased. In 1876 the Queen was proclaimed Empress of India, the inheritor of the glories of the defunct Mogul Empire. There was, however, opposition to the British administration after the 1870s, and in 1885 an Indian National Congress met and pressed for improved conditions. The Congress soon became a major political force.

The large British army in India was used chiefly in neighboring areas, particularly Afghanistan and Burma. In the former country there was a constant threat from the ever-expanding Russian Empire. Although the independence of Afghanistan was eventually assured, Britain continued to have trouble along the border, the notorious Northwest Frontier. Relations with Burma had been difficult throughout the early part of the century,

Nagasaki harbor, Japan, in the 1860s.

signed, and his supporters too abandoned the struggle after a year. The Meiji restoration—as it is known—did not bring power into the hands of the Emperor at once, but rather gave it to an alliance of nobility, samurai and merchants. Americans and Europeans were kept at arm's length, but what they had to offer was eagerly learned.

Feudalism, which had tended to reduce the effectiveness of the central government, was swept away. The cult of the emperor was replaced by a new emphasis on Shintoism as the official religion of the state. Universal primary education was introduced in 1871, making Japan one of the first modern states to eradicate illiter-

British colonial officials in India.

and the period had been marked by occasional wars, which eventually deprived Burma of the whole of its coastline. In 1885, alarmed by the growth of French power in Indochina, the British invaded and annexed Burma, making it part of the Indian Empire.

Indochina

The role that the British played in India was played in Indochina by the French; but the late arrival of the French and the rapidly changing standards of French colonial administration left a very different heritage. Although there had previously been trading and mis-

apan takes its place as a colonial power

sionary contacts, French interest in the Annamese Empire only really began in the 1850s. Saigon was captured by a French expeditionary force in 1859, and French influence in the area grew rapidly, as Cambodia and other regions that feared Annamese expansionism placed themselves under French protection. French expansionism was, however, no less of a threat than that of Annam; the French saw that trade with inland China would be possible along the Mekong River, and this encouraged further colonial expansion. By 1904 the whole of Indochina was effectively in French hands, although each country had a different relationship with France.

Explorers and missionaries in Africa

Although Africa had from time to time excited the greedy interest of the European states, it remained the "dark continent" until the middle of the nineteenth century, and most of inland Africa remained unconquered until the end of the century. There was, however, increasing interest in exploration and missionary work, particularly from the 1870s. There were many reasons for this: colonies were being acquired in coastal regions, for both trade and the

Henry M. Stanley, intrepid explorer of darkest Africa.

mining of precious metals, and occasionally to offset threats (usually imaginary) from other European powers. Many of those who went to Africa felt that they had a divine mission, bringing the benefits of Christianity and civilization to the natives, even in those areas that had not yet been conquered by European states.

The nineteenth century was the great age of the missionary, and Africa was the inspiration that sent thousands of doctors and clergymen to discomfort—and often an early death. Organizations such as the London Missionary Society and the Church Missionary Society flourished. Missionaries often acted as the vanguard for later colonial conquest. The Scottish David Livingstone (1813–73), for example, explored much of the Upper Zambesi River, and was the first white man to see the Victoria Falls. A few more professional explorers, such as the British Richard Burton (1821–90) and John Speke (1827–64), who discovered the source of the Nile River, were to be found, but they were outnumbered by the missionaries. Discovery was, however, dangerous, as it benefited slave traders no less than government officials and missionaries. Indeed the value of the nineteenth-century missions has often been questioned, but judged by the standards of their time they had a beneficial influence on Africa.

European expansion in Africa

In North Africa, in 1830, the French invaded Algeria, a task that took eighteen years to complete. The slow progress in the conquest of Algeria was due to lack of French interest, as the government, whose main ambition was to control the western end of the Mediterranean, had little incentive to press home the conquests inland.

In West Africa the decline of the slave trade had been signaled by the founding of Liberia as an independent state for free American Negroes in 1820. Elsewhere along the west coast the European powers were becoming increasingly interested in the region's economic potential. The Gold and Ivory Coasts attracted European traders and miners. A rush for West Africa did not at once ensue, as the Europeans found that a major

problem to conquest and colonization was the fierce independence of the native tribes. For example, on the Gold Coast the British found the native Ashanti kingdom a far more serious obstacle to expansion than the rival Dutch and Danish settlements.

On Africa's east coast there was a major attempt at colonization and conquest between 1820 and 1860, but it was made by Moslems rather than Europeans. Both Egypt, which had thrown off Turkish rule, and the Sultanate of Oman in southern Arabia, in search of slaves to sell, sought to extend their control of the East African coast. In origin the close links between Arabia and East Africa date back to biblical times, but never were they closer than in the mid-nineteenth century. The growing importance of its East African possessions led the representative of the Sultan of Oman to establish his seat of government on the island of Zanzibar in 1840. He introduced clove trees, which rapidly made the island the world's largest producer of cloves. The possession of rifles encouraged the Arabs to extend their empire inland. Although slave trading became increasingly difficult as the century continued, due to British pressure, the clove trade helped to ensure Zanzibar's prosperity even after its partition from Oman in 1850.

Farther north, Egyptian interest in the Upper Nile threatened the independence of Ethiopia. However, the opening of the Suez Canal brought Egypt itself under increasing European control; consequently the threat to Ethiopia diminished. European dominance, however, spread most rapidly in southern Africa.

Southern Africa

The British had begun to show an interest in southern Africa in the late eighteenth century, and in 1814 the government bought the Cape Colony, which had been captured in 1806, from the Dutch. Although the purpose of this was to make the Cape route from Great Britain to the Far East absolutely secure, it had a major effect on the later development of southern Africa. The Dutch colonial farmers, settled for generations around the Cape, had become almost totally divorced from their relations in Holland,

The Zulu chief Chaka.

both culturally and linguistically. These "Afrikaners" had little love for firm government of any kind, but their dislike of the British was increased by the determination of the colonial administration to root out slavery, one of the pillars of Afrikaner society. The Calvinist Afrikaners believed that the natives were the biblical "sons of Ham," whom God had made into slaves. In order to escape the emancipating power of Britain, the Afrikaners moved northward, where they came into conflict with powerful settled African tribes who showed no enthusiasm for the fate that the white man's God had decreed for them—a cause of most of southern Africa's subsequent difficulties. The Zulu chief Chaka, who died in 1828, had welded together many of the tribes of Natal into a highly effective barrier. It was inevitable that the Afrikaners, forced to trek even further by the extension of British power in southern Africa, should clash with the Zulus. This was largely due to the "Great Trek" of 1835–37, which led to the foundation of an Afrikaner state in Natal in 1838 after a brief but bloody war with the Zulus. The foundation of other Afrikaner states, the Orange Free State in 1853 and the South African Republic in 1856, soon followed. Britain was not able to avoid involvement either in the affairs of the Afrikaner republics or in those of the native tribes and confederations, of which the Zulu was the most important. War with the Zulus was inevitable. In 1879 it broke out.

The Zulu War

1879

Africa's southern extremity was colonized by Boers and British, who found there few organized tribes—except the Zulu. Under their great leader Chaka, the Zulus had formed a large, united, warlike nation determined to rule its own destiny. The British invasion of Zululand was met by Cetewayo, a nephew and successor to Chaka. By skillfully deploying his forces, Cetewayo was able to inflict a calamitous defeat upon the British. However, reinforced and resupplied, they returned the following year and the Zulus were defeated. From then on Africa quickly fell under the colonial yoke.

To the early explorers, South Africa was little more than a watering place on an inhospitable coast—a halfway house on the long run to the Indies. Many, beginning with the Portuguese sailor Bartholomew Dias in 1488, paused there, but few stayed. Those who did remain found the indigenous population consisted of tribes who ruled themselves, preyed on their neighbors and had no conception of political cohesion. Because of these factors, the colonization of Africa by Europeans progressed slowly but inexorably. For more than a hundred years there was "trouble," particularly along the Great Fish River in what was known as British Kaffraria, where the fighting was savage and bloody. It would not be until the emergence of Chaka that any easily identifiable milestone appeared beside the road toward African "civilization."

Chaka was born about 1787. He grew to be a man of six foot three inches—immensely powerful and an expert in the use of the assegai, the spear used for killing by the Zulus. He originated the battle drills and tactics that established the Zulus as the dominant Bantu tribe in southern Africa. The Zulus, over a period of eighteen years, killed nearly two million people, virtually depopulating vast areas of land.

In 1816 Chaka began shaping the Zulus into a nation dedicated to war and conquest. In 1828, having lived by the assegai, he then died by it, being assassinated by his successor. Later, in 1873, Chaka's nephew Cetewayo became the king of the most powerful nation in black Africa.

For more than a hundred years the Bantu tribes, the Boers and the British had been struggling against one another—the white men either subjugating the blacks or driving them north and east, away from the ever-expanding Cape Colony. The Boers had no love for the British, who had taken Cape Town from the Dutch in 1806. Since then the Boers had been seeking a life free of British rule. It was this quest that brought the Boers and in their wake the British into conflict with the disunited Bantu tribes.

When the Boers encountered the Zulus the story was, however, very different. Chaka's legacy to his people was the Zulu army, which was well-organized, well-commanded and had high morale. Cetewayo had a force of forty thousand men with which to resist the white man. This army was regarded as a permanent threat by the British settlers in neighboring Natal who feared what would happen to them if the Zulus decided to extend their frontiers. They demanded and received imperial troops to protect them; but mere protection was not enough. The Zulus stood in the way of expansion and the advancement of "civilization." They had to be crushed.

It is doubtful that Cetewayo planned to invade Natal. He was an intelligent man who took the trouble to learn something of the power and resources of the British Empire, and his policy was to avoid any involvement with the white administration across his frontier. He built his royal kraal, or village, at Ulundi, on high ground above the valley of the White Umfolozi River and did his best to rule his country in peace. But in the person of Sir Henry Bartle Edward Frere, appointed High Commissioner of Native Affairs for South Africa in April, 1877, the Zulus had an adversary who was prepared to take any opportunity to annex their country, by force if necessary.

The chance came from a minor border incident in July, 1878. A Zulu crossed over into Natal with a small party to recapture two of his father's wives who had been unfaithful and were hiding in the villages of some of the Natal border guards. One woman was dragged back into Zulu territory across the Buffalo River, and clubbed to death. The other was taken back across the ford at Rorke's Drift and shot. The incidents, greatly magnified, were made the basis for an ultimatum that Cetewayo must disband his army within thirty days.

The Zulu leader Cetewayo, whose defeat ensured the rapid spread of British colonial power in southern Africa.

Opposite The Battle of Isandhlwana, the major British defeat in the Zulu War.

97

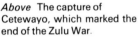

Above The capture of Cetewayo, which marked the end of the Zulu War.

Above right The Battle of Ulundi, which effectively ended the war.

Opposite Zulu warriors being reviewed by a chief.

The British military commander, Lord Chelmsford, had been assembling troops, transport and supplies since the previous August. He had a force of nearly seventeen thousand men under his command in South Africa. He also had two million rounds of ammunition and a wagon train of oxen, mules and horses capable of conveying his logistical support to Cetewayo's capital of Ulundi, some sixty miles from the border. Posting his line-of-communication units he then divided his army into three columns of approximately equal strength. The left-hand column, commanded by Brigadier-General Evelyn Wood, was to invade across the Blood River, near the scene of the decisive defeat of a Zulu impi (armed force) of twelve thousand warriors by a Boer commando under Andries Pretorius in December, 1838. The right-hand column, led by Colonel Charles Pearson, was to cross the Tugela River by the Lower Drift. Chelmsford and his staff were to move with the center column, which was under the command of Colonel Richard Glyn. The center column was to ford the Buffalo River at Rorke's Drift, and all three columns were to converge on Ulundi.

Several weeks before setting out, Chelmsford had a conversation with Paul Kruger, a Boer leader with considerable experience of fighting the Zulus. Kruger emphasized the importance of using scout parties to locate the highly mobile enemy, and of fighting in the concentrated formation of either a square or wagons in a circle or laager. He also spoke of the need to laager the wagons in a defensive formation every night. Chelmsford agreed. Using information supplied by a border agent, he had already provided all his company commanders with

a map of Zululand and a handbook giving the complete Zulu "Order of Battle" with the details of every regiment and its commander. The British knew practically everything about the Zulu army, except where it was.

In fog and drizzling rain Chelmsford's column began to cross the Buffalo River before dawn on January 11, 1879. Lieutenant Gonville Bromhead was left with a company to garrison the small mission station at Rorke's Drift and guard the river crossing. By January 20, the center column had covered only ten miles to a camp pitched on open ground below the Nqutu Plateau, almost in the shadow of a large hill known as Isandhlwana. Despite Kruger's warning, they did not make a circle of the wagons to fortify the camp against attack. The Zulus, reported by Chelmsford's native spies as having left Ulundi to attack the invaders, had not as yet been located.

Very early in the morning of January 22, Chelmsford received a message from one of his scouting outposts that contact had been made with a force of more than two thousand Zulus twelve miles to the west in the direction of Ulundi. Aware that this could not be the main force, Chelmsford believed the much larger group must be nearby and that his detachment was in danger. Leaving behind five companies, one section of two guns and some colonial volunteers and Natal Kaffirs to protect the camp, he moved out with the other half of his force at 3:30 A.M. He intended to meet the main Zulu army in the open. He and his staff rode on ahead to find the outpost, reaching it at 6:00 A.M. Apart from a few Zulus seen moving through the bush, the open slope ahead which during the night

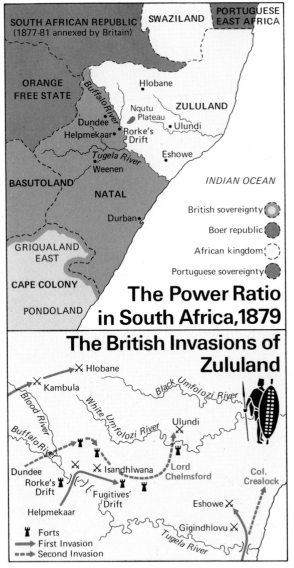

The Power Ratio in South Africa, 1879

The British Invasions of Zululand

the valley they took their battle positions and set out for the camp.

Pulleine watched them coming at him—a dark river more than a mile wide. His only hope was to draw his force of eighteen hundred men into the traditional square, front rank kneeling and rear rank standing, and rely on their firepower and discipline. The great tide of yelling, stabbing Zulus swept over them.

When Chelmsford rode back toward Isandhlwana in the afternoon and saw what had happened, he realized that the force under his command had suffered a terrible defeat. The units he had taken out that morning bivouacked not far from the slopes where three thousand five hundred bodies, white and black, lay stiff and cold in the starlight. Later, when his men, still under threat of attack, lay uneasy in the darkness, they heard the sound of prolonged firing. A red glow in the western sky told the anxious commander that the mission station at Rorke's Drift was on fire and he knew where the Zulus had gone.

Yet, fortunately for the tiny garrison, it was not the main Zulu force which came down to the Drift. Only three regiments, a total of four thousand five hundred warriors, pursued the fugitives who were all trying to get back across the Buffalo River.

In the afternoon two lieutenants of the Natal Kaffirs, fleeing from Isandhlwana, had brought news of the disaster and of the extreme danger now threatening the small garrison. A Lieutenant Chard, realizing that there was no time to evacuate the sick, began to put the place in a state of defense, using existing walls, wagons and bags of grain. While this work was going on the chaplain, Rev. George Smith, and a soldier named Wall climbed the hill behind the mission station to watch for the enemy.

Soon other refugees from Isandhlwana crossed the Drift, refusing to stay and reinforce the garrison,

had been dotted with Zulu campfires was now bare. The main group still had not been found.

Meanwhile, Lieutenant Colonel Pulleine, who was in command of the force left in the base camp, heard of enemy movement four miles away on the Nqutu Plateau, and sent troops to investigate. They saw one or two Zulus driving cattle up a slope in front of them. The troopers gave chase and the herdsmen ran over the crest of the hill and disappeared. The cattle stopped. One of the troopers only just managed to pull up his horse in time to prevent it falling over the edge of a ravine that had been hidden by the crest.

Glancing down, the trooper froze with fear. Packed close together, motionless and squatting in silence, twenty thousand Zulu warriors stretched like a black carpet as far as the eye could see. Thousands of feathered headdresses lifted. As the Zulus began climbing out of the ravine, the trooper galloped back to his companions.

The Zulus had not intended to fight that day, January 22, because it was the day of a new moon and therefore inauspicious; but now there was no alternative. As the warriors came boiling up out of

Opposite above Lieutenant Chard, V.C., wearing his Victoria Cross; with other officers he successfully defended Rorke's Drift.

Right The funeral of the Prince Imperial, Louis Napoleon. The death of the Prince led to the government's decision to replace Lord Chelmsford as the British commander.

Lord Chelmsford and his staff looking for Ulundi from a hilltop. The mountainous conditions made it hard for the British to pin down a Zulu force.

thus causing a panic among the native troops guarding the ford. All of them, including their colonial officers, fled, leaving Chard with a hundred and forty men, including the sick, to hold three hundred yards of wall. Some time after 4:30 P.M. Smith saw the Zulu regiments led by their commanders mounted on white horses coming toward them on the Natal bank of the river. He and Wall rushed down the slope to give warning.

The soldiers were still feverishly building the defenses with bags of grain and boxes of rations when the enemy came in sight. They just had time to get their rifles and ammunition pouches and take up their positions when the host was upon them.

The initial charge of the Zulus was across open ground. Their casualties were heavy, but they pressed on. Many armed with rifles took cover on the high ground behind the misson and fired at the backs of the defenders; despite fierce hand-to-hand combat, most of the British casualties were caused by gunshot wounds. It was not until 4:00 A.M. that the Zulu attacks subsided.

When dawn came and Chard was able to take stock he found eighty of his men still standing; fifteen had been killed and two were dying. Nearly all were wounded. Beyond the wall lay hundreds of enemy corpses. The Zulus had retreated.

The invasion of Zululand now came to an abrupt halt and Chelmsford retreated into Natal. Colonel Pearson with the right-hand column had beaten off a Zulu attack but was subsequently besieged and had to be rescued by a relief expedition. Only Brigadier Evelyn Wood and his column on the left, which had defeated the Zulus at Kambula, was still comparatively mobile and fit for battle.

"We have certainly," said Chelmsford, "been seriously underestimating the power of the Zulu army."

Yet the Zulu army had paid dearly for its victory at Isandhlwana. Cetewayo described the battle as "an assegai thrust into the belly of the nation." In truth, the Zulus never recovered from the cost of Chelmsford's initial defeat. They had never expected such resistance from the British troops and their own experience with firearms had not in any way prepared them for the devastating effect of the British volleys.

Yet, by having brought the invasion to a standstill, the Zulus were in the strongest position they had ever attained. This caused a panic in Natal where there were no British reserves to defend the long frontier with Zululand. There was no force in Natal able to offer effective resistance if Cetewayo decided to invade, and no British reinforcements could be expected for at least two months. Natal and Cape Colony lay open. The Zulu nation, mobilized and victorious, had the white settlers at its mercy; but Cetewayo had achieved his ambition by driving the invaders out of his country.

A few months later, reinforced by ten thousand

troops, Chelmsford once again took to the field and set off for Ulundi. He took with him the Prince Imperial, Louis Napoleon, only son of Napoleon III and the Empress Eugénie. He was a popular young man who caused considerable anxiety to his commanders by his daring and enthusiasm when out on patrol. On June 1, 1879, soon after the force had crossed into Zululand again, he went out to reconnoiter and sketch the ground to be covered the following day, and was killed in a Zulu ambush.

News of the Prince's death received far more publicity than either the disaster at Isandhlwana or the defense at Rorke's Drift, and was regarded by many as evidence of the importance of relieving Chelmsford of his command. The cabinet did replace him with Sir Garnet Wolseley, and the campaign in Chelmsford's mind became a race to defeat the Zulus before Wolseley could reach Africa and take over the command.

Chelmsford was careful not to repeat the errors of the previous January. He had recovered much of his confidence at the successful Battle of Umisi on April 2, when he had led the expedition to relieve Pearson at Eshowe, and he now moved steadily on Ulundi with a force capable of destroying any attacking Zulus. The final battle was fought on July 4—before Wolseley had arrived—on the plain in front of Ulundi; the British, forming a huge square of infantry around the cavalry, were supported by guns and field pieces. The Zulus had mustered twenty thousand men, all that remained of the warriors of this warrior nation, most of them inexperienced and eager to fight.

The regiments charged and were cut down in swathes. For the last time in their history the Zulus fought with desperate valor to defend their villages and their cattle, their country and their king. Cetewayo escaped from the ruins of Ulundi, which was burned to the ground, but he was tracked down and captured a month later, and sent to England in 1882.

Later he returned to Zululand and was reinstated, but his people never recovered from the war. Eighteen years later they were annexed to Natal and in 1906 made a last, desperate attempt to regain their freedom. Their rebellion was easily crushed, and they exist now only as one tribe among many in the Republic of South Africa. If Cetewayo had inherited Chaka's ambition, his lust for power and urge to conquest, the story of the European colonization of Africa might have been entirely different. The rise and fall of the Zulus may have stained the pages of South African history with much blood, but it is their unity, their organization and their self-sacrificing determination to hold back the tide of European domination for a time that has earned them their place in world history.

JOCK HASWELL

Rorke's house at the Drift.

In a rearguard action, Pius IX assert

Nineteenth-century religious life

Religious speculation was still the greatest intellectual exercise during the third quarter of the nineteenth century. This was true not only of Victorian England but of Europe in general. Even Giuseppe Mazzini (1805–72), the fiery Italian patriot who was regarded by the Roman Catholic Church as a "red revolutionary," claimed to be acting in the name of "God and his people," and his personal manifesto, *The Duties of Man* (1860), listed service to God alongside service to the family and the nation as the obligations of a good citizen. Similarly, Auguste Comte, the Frenchman who founded Positivism, stated that it was impossible to transform philosophy into the worship of humanity without incorporating a mystical element and compiling a Positivist catechism to ensure an ordered scheme of life. The strength of religious feeling and its domination of intel-

Cartoon of *Kulturkampf*.

lectual life was shown by the sharply hostile reaction to Darwinism.

In England the Oxford Movement hatched a progeny of "ritualists" who did much to add both religion and color to the drab lives of unchurched slum dwellers. There was also a successful revival of monasticism in the Church of England. In general, however, the religious initiative remained with

smaller nonconformist bodies, such as the Salvation Army, which was founded by the evangelist William Booth (1829–1912) in 1878.

The Roman Catholic Church showed little willingness to compromise with the new intellectual movements. From 1854 to 1870 Pope Pius IX endeavored to counter what he regarded as irreligious tendencies by resolute pronouncements on doctrine. In 1854 the Pope proclaimed the dogma of the Immaculate Conception of the Virgin Mary. Although he had been politically liberal in the early part of his pontificate, Pius' horror at the events of 1848 led him to adopt views that even the Austrian government regarded as reactionary. The insecurity of his rule over the Papal States made him distrust liberalism still more, and in 1864 his *Syllabus of Errors* condemned the fashionable ideas of science and the political liberalism that the French cleric Félicité Robert de Lamennais (1782–1854) had urged the Church to accept. This new ultramontanism posed questions of conscience for sincere believers in many lands and the air was heavy with ponderous theological debate.

Nor did the debate grow less heated as the years passed. In 1870 Pius held a general council of the Roman Catholic Church at the Vatican, while French troops continued to hold the advocates of a united Italy at bay. Pius' alarm at the widespread and speedy success of the *Risorgimento*, which threatened his temporal power, led him to glorify the spiritual side of the papal office. Against the advice of most distinguished theologians, but with Pius' enthusiastic support, the council adopted a definition declaring the pope to be infallible when he pronounced *ex cathedra* on matters of faith or morals. This led to a small schism as many Roman Catholics, particularly in Germany and Switzerland, felt unable to accept the definition, and the Old Catholic Church was founded.

Secular governments, too, were concerned about the social implications of the dogma of papal infallibility. Between 1873 and 1879 a fundamental conflict of beliefs, or *Kulturkampf*, arose in Germany. During that struggle the authorities sought—unsuccessfully—to subordinate the Roman Catholic Church to the State, by

insisting on inspection of Church schools, and attempting to forbid priests to introduce politically controversial topics into their sermons.

Relations between the Roman Catholic Church and the State were also strained at this time in Austria, Spain, Italy and Belgium. However, the most protracted dispute over Church rights in education arose in France in the 1880s and, apart from a brief interlude in the early 1890s, continued till the eve of World War I. The radical statesman Jules Ferry (1832–93) was responsible

French Prime Minister Jules Ferry.

for the momentous law of March, 1882, which established free, nonclerical and compulsory primary education in France, but which insisted on the teaching of essentially Christian ethics without the propagation of a specifically religious faith. (This was based on legislation passed in England in 1870, when, because of nonconformist opposition, the government was forced to abandon the idea of a denominational religious teaching in state schools.) Later, radical politicians attacked the alleged support given by Roman Catholic bishops to anti-republican movements of the right, and in 1905 the French government even went so far as to abrogate the Concordat that had regulated Church-State relations since Napoleon's time.

In Italy the immediate aftermath of the Vatican Council was disastrous. On the day after the declaration of papal infallibility, the Franco-Prussian War broke out and Napoleon III withdrew his garrison from Rome again. This enabled the Italians to complete their conquest of the Papal States. Only the Vatican and a few small

View of the Salvation Army's work

estates were left under papal sovereignty. Pius, furious, withdrew into the Vatican. But the loss of political power caused a new awareness of social problems, and his successor Leo XIII recognized trade unionism in his 1891 encyclical *Rerum Novarum*.

The Balkan Question

"The whole of the Balkans are not worth the bones of a single Pomeranian grenadier," Bismarck once remarked in disgust, and the sentiment was one with which most of his compatriots would have agreed. But Balkan questions plagued the European chanceries in the 1870s and 1880s, just as they were to do—with tragic consequence for Germany and the world—from 1911 to 1914. Misrule by the Sultan's servants in the Balkans provoked risings in the Turkish provinces of Bosnia-Herzegovina and Bulgaria in 1875–76, just as it had done in Greece earlier in the century; in practice many communities were used to a very large measure of freedom and resented any attempt by the Sublime Porte to restrict it. These revolts were suppressed by Turkish irregulars with a bestiality that was widely reported by British and American newspaper correspondents. Inevitably, the Russians, who—despite the Treaty of Paris—saw themselves as the champions and protectors of all Slavs and Orthodox Christians, seized on the reports as evidence that the Turks were unfit to administer these territories.

Public opinion in Britain was divided over the news of the Balkan atrocities. The two political parties turned somersaults in their attempt to satisfy the electorate; the normally *laissez-faire* Liberals adopted an energetically interventionist policy, while the Conservatives—usually the upholders of interventionist policies—favored mild support for the Ottoman Empire against the Russians. Led by William Ewart Gladstone, the greatest political figure in nineteenth-century England, the Liberal opposition campaigned vigorously for concerted action that would force the Turks to make concessions to the Balkan nationalities; the Conservative government of Benjamin Disraeli, fearing that any limitation of the Sultan's sovereignty would only favor Russia, disputed the reports

The Balkans after the Treaty of Berlin 1878

RUSSIA

to Russia

AUSTRIA-HUNGARY

BOSNIA and HERZEGOVINA (administered by Austria)

TRANSYLVANIA

Belgrade

RUMANIA

SERBIA

Bucharest

Nis

to Rumania

ADRIATIC SEA

Sofia

BULGARIA

BLACK SEA

EASTERN ROUMELIA

MONTENEGRO

San Stefano

MACEDONIA

Adrianople

TURKEY-IN-EUROPE

Salonika

Constantinople

IONIAN SEA

AEGEAN SEA

OTTOMAN EMPIRE

GREECE (independent from Turkey 1830)

Athens

○ Independent States

Cyprus to Britain ▶

as press exaggerations. There was some justification for the Conservative position. Like the Russians, most of the inhabitants of Bulgaria and Bosnia-Herzegovina were Slavs and members of the Orthodox Church, and public sentiment in the Russian Empire was strongly pro-Slav. It came as no surprise, therefore, when Alexander II declared war on Turkey in April, 1877, and sent a powerful army southward through the Balkan mountains to liberate Bulgaria and expel the Turks from Europe.

Although the Russians were held up for several months at Plevna by Turkish resistance, whose fierceness surprised the Russians, the first Russian units reached the Sea of Marmara by early 1878. The Sultan sued for peace and in March signed the Treaty of San Stefano. That agreement startled and horrified the European powers for, besides giving the Russians considerable territory in the Caucasus, it created a Bulgarian principality that included almost all of Macedonia and a long stretch of the Aegean coast. It was assumed that this Greater Bulgaria would become a Russian satellite, and the treaty was viewed by the Western powers as a means by which the Tsar could extend his power into the western Balkans and to the shores of the Mediterranean Sea.

Opinion rapidly hardened against the Treaty of San Stefano both in Vienna, where the new Bulgaria had trespassed on Austria's Balkan interests, and in London, where there had long been an exaggerated fear of Russian influence in the eastern Mediterranean. The Tsar reluctantly accepted an offer from Bismarck to act as an "honest broker" in settling the Eastern Question and the Congress of Berlin was summoned in July, 1878.

Russian troops on the march through the Balkans.

Treaty of Berlin

The resultant Treaty of Berlin destroyed the work of the Pan-Slavs. The Russians kept their gains in the Balkans, but Greater Bulgaria became little more than the dream of a few Pan-Slav nationalists in Sofia. A small autonomous Bulgarian principality was set up, but the southern part of Bulgaria remained subject to Turkish rule under a Christian governor; most of Macedonia was restored to Turkey; the Austrians were authorized to occupy Bosnia-Herzegovina and the British to annex the island of Cyprus, although both these territories remained nominally part of the Turkish Empire. Essentially, the Berlin settlement determined the fate of the Balkans for the next thirty years (even though this division of Bulgaria was ended in 1885 by a further revolt); but the artificiality of the imposed solution satisfied almost nobody.

The Treaty of Berlin provided neither a good nor just settlement, but in the short run it was remarkably effective. Only in Russia did its terms arouse widespread resentment. Pan-Slavism had been the first sentiment to stir the Russian masses since 1812, when they had rallied in defense of their country to defeat the Napoleonic invasion. The Russian press and the Russian Church—a curious combination of the new and the old—had fanned Russian indignation until war with Turkey assumed the proportions of a crusade. Even before the 1877 invasion, volunteers had set out from Moscow and St. Petersburg to aid their brother Slavs in the Balkan lands, and a Russian translation of Gladstone's pamphlet denouncing the Bulgarian massacres had sold ten thousand copies in a few weeks. Small wonder that the Treaty of Berlin was seen as an anticlimax.

Inevitably these events had repercussions on Russia's internal politics. While the Pan-Slav agitation was at its height, most of the Russian intelligentsia resigned themselves to the absence of constitutional liberties. After the Treaty of Berlin, however, demands were made for representative institutions. Alexander II was not given an opportunity to respond to the demands, for the politics of murder triumphed over those of reason.

Assassination of Alexander II

Even before the 1825 Decembrist Revolt—an abortive military coup that Nicholas I, Tsar of All the Russias, had ruthlessly suppressed—underground terrorist groups were plotting to overthrow the Romanov dynasty. By the middle years of the nineteenth century, plots to assassinate his son Alexander II were as frequent—and as notorious—as the blizzards that swept the Russian steppes. In an effort to placate his enemies, Alexander inaugurated a program of Great Reforms—culminating in the 1861 decree that emancipated Russia's serfs—but his foes could not be appeased. In 1879 a Nihilist organization known as People's Will secretly condemned the Tsar to death. Their initial attempts to execute that sentence were thwarted, but on March 13, 1881, the anarchists achieved their goal: Tsar Alexander was mortally wounded by a bomb blast that shook every European throne.

Nicholas Rysakov, Tsar Alexander's assassin, from a drawing made during his trial.

Opposite Tsar Alexander II who was assassinated by members of the terrorist organization People's Will. By contemporary Russian standards Alexander was a liberal ruler.

In the early afternoon of Sunday, March 13, 1881, the Emperor Alexander II of Russia set off for his Winter Palace in St. Petersburg after a routine visit to the Mikhaylovsky Cavalry Parade Ground. He sat alone in his carriage. A liveried coachman rode on the box, mounted Cossacks wearing fur caps and scarlet coats escorted him, and sleighs conveying the St. Petersburg Chief of Police and other officers followed behind. It was a dull day and the gaudy imperial cortege contrasted sharply with the dirty snow underfoot.

As the Tsar himself had every reason to suspect, revolutionary conspirators had been keeping him under surveillance for several months in an effort to establish the pattern of his movements within the capital—a necessary preliminary to killing him with high explosives. These plotters, sometimes known as Nihilists, belonged to the underground terrorist political organization People's Will. They had secretly condemned Alexander to death in the late summer of 1879, and since that time they had made several determined attempts on his life: Nihilist saboteurs had blown up a train in which the Tsar was thought to be traveling north from the Crimea, and they had engineered a huge explosion inside the Winter Palace that killed many unintended victims but left the Tsar himself unscathed.

On March 13, 1881, those abortive attempts were finally crowned by success. As the Emperor's carriage swept westward down Engineer Street toward the Catherine Quay, Sophia Perovsky, the terrorist and qualified schoolmistress who directed the assault in the field, posted herself on the far side of the canal at a point where she could observe the Tsar's approach. When his carriage came into view she signaled with her handkerchief, alerting the four young men under her command who lurked on the Quay, each holding a cumbersome hand grenade disguised in an improvised wrapping.

After reaching the end of Engineer Street, the imperial carriage turned north along the Quay. It had covered about a hundred yards when the first Nihilist, Nicholas Rysakov, threw his bomb, which exploded with a great crash near the back axle. The vehicle held together, and Alexander would have been well advised to drive on at full speed without pausing to investigate, but he insisted on dismounting and walking back to where his assailant, already under arrest, stood amid a group of police and onlookers. Some words were exchanged and the Tsar turned back toward his carriage. At that moment a second member of the murder squad, Ignaty Grinevitsky, suddenly struck, throwing his grenade directly at the Emperor from close range.

Alexander was hurled back against the canal railing, mortally wounded. His blood gushing over the snow and his clothing in tatters, the monarch called weakly to be taken to his palace to die. He perished there soon afterward, and at 3:55 P.M. the palace flag was lowered in mourning. The Tsar's assailant also died, a victim of his own bomb.

Within a few days the police had arrested many of those involved in the conspiracy, and on April 15, 1881, five condemned terrorists of People's Will (including Sophia Perovsky and Rysakov) were hanged on an enormous scaffold that was erected for the occasion on the Semyonovsky Parade Ground. The execution, which was performed most inexpertly by a drunken, red-shirted hangman to the sound of drum rolls, was attended by foreign diplomats, Russian military units and a huge crowd of sightseers.

The Tsar's assassination climaxed a decade of increasing revolutionary violence. At the beginning of the 1870s, the Russian revolutionary movement was expanding, but political conspirators still numbered in the hundreds, and they remained relatively peacefully inclined. Most of these dissidents hoped to effect a change of regime through the peasantry. That downtrodden and ill-used social

и блистательные подвиги русскихъ войскъ въ борьбѣ за свободу славянъ 1877 года.

The Winter Palace,
St. Petersburg, to which
Alexander was returning when
he was assassinated.

Sophia Perovsky, the
schoolmistress and terrorist
who gave the signal when
the Tsar's carriage was
approaching.

A drawing from the *Illustrated
London News* showing
Rysakov's bomb exploding.

group seemed ripe for mutiny—and it was potentially well-poised to overturn the Tsar, if only because peasants comprised four-fifths of the Russian population. But how were these "dark people" to be shown the light and plunged into revolutionary action? Hundreds of young revolutionaries went out into the rural areas of Russia in the summers of 1873 and 1874 and attempted to teach the *muzhik* to revolt—but with poor results. Most Russian peasants were loyal to the throne.

Frustrated in their attempts to agitate rural Russia, the revolutionaries switched their attention to the towns during the late 1870s. They formed more tightly knit conspiratorial associations at the same time, but their frustrations continued to grow. Many of them were arrested and thrown into prison without a trial. Their periods of incarceration provided the rebels with plenty of opportunities to hatch revolutionary plots, and in 1879 a number of them banded together to form People's Will, a group specifically organized for the purpose of political terror by assassination. The slaughter of the Emperor in 1881 was only the climax to a series of assassinations that had taken the lives of several prominent victims.

Alexander's assassination echoed around the world, and the *New York Herald* was not the only periodical to regret the death of such a "far-seeing and beneficent prince." Although many deplored the tragedy, many others applauded the assassination as a severe blow to the monarchic principle. (The *New York Herald* also printed a paean in honor of Sophia Perovsky, for example.) Marx and Engels saw the event as one that would eventually lead to the establishment of a Russian commune.

Inside Russia the assassination did not provoke a general uprising, nor did it frighten the new Tsar into enacting far-reaching liberal reforms. After a brief spasm of excitement, the population at large relapsed into political indifference, and soon thereafter the new Tsar, Alexander III, revealed himself to be a far more reactionary ruler than his father had ever been. He rejected certain modest political concessions that had been accepted in principle by Alexander II just before his death, and he submitted to the influence of such diehard reactionaries as Konstantin Pobedonostsev and Count D.A. Tolstoy. Alexander III's regime enacted a series of counterreforms that whittled away—but by no means undid—the progressive measures that the assassinated Alexander II had introduced in the early, liberal years of his reign.

Meanwhile, a reorganized political police force was engaged in crushing the broken remnants of People's Will. Some of the conspirators were sent to Siberia and some were incarcerated in fortress dungeons, while others sought refuge in foreign exile. The few active revolutionaries who remained in the Russian Empire virtually abandoned tsaricide as a political tactic, although the year 1887 did bring the hatching of a plot to kill Alexander III— on the anniversary of his father's death and by a similar method. The conspiracy was foiled by the police and led to the execution of Alexander Ulyanov, Lenin's brother. Lenin himself was a mere schoolboy at the time, and the prospects for a Russian revolution seemed distant indeed in the middle of Alexander III's reign.

Although the assassination on the Catherine Quay proved disastrous to the assassins' immediate cause, it did shake the confidence of Russia's autocrats to a greater extent than any other event of the century, including a previous attempt to unseat a tsar. That occurrence, known as the Decembrist Revolt of 1825, had instead led to a temporary strengthening of the monarchic principle. It was, nevertheless, the first revolutionary outbreak in Russian history.

For some years before 1825, political conspirators—most of whom were army officers—had been plotting to overthrow the Russian autocracy and to replace it with a constitutional monarchy or republic. After the death of Alexander I in November, 1825, Nicholas I's claim to the throne was widely disputed, and in the ensuing confusion the disaffected officer-revolutionaries—the Decembrists— struck the blow that they had been secretly discussing for so long. They persuaded the rank and file of certain units to mutiny and then led the mutinous soldiers—several thousand strong—to the Senate Square in St. Petersburg, hoping that their presence would spark a general rising among the troops. Throughout most of the freezing day the soldiers paraded in the square. They undertook no military operations, but they also refused to heed numerous appeals to disperse. In the end, the new Tsar was forced to bring up artillery units and drive the rebels off with gunfire, causing many casualties.

The "first Russian revolution" was over. It was followed by a rigorous investigation and trial that appeared to have effectively destroyed the infant revolutionary movement and that provided the new Emperor—a notorious martinet—with an opportunity to assert his authority at the very outset of his reign. He then set up a special security organization, the Third Section and the Corps of Gendarmes, to combat subversion in his Empire. Strict censorship and control of education helped to hold the country in an iron grip during his regime (which is sometimes regarded as a prototype of the twentieth-century police state). Like Catherine the Great, Paul I and Alexander I before him, Nicholas I was

obsessed with the idea that an upheaval comparable to the French Revolution of 1789 might take place in Russia. A series of minor revolutions did indeed occur in Central and Western Europe during Nicholas' reign, and they prompted the Tsar to impose even stricter regimentation inside his Empire.

The death of Nicholas I in 1855, and the accession of his son Alexander II, brought about an immediate rise in morale in most sections of Russian society. Hopes of a change for the better were encouraged when, in the year following his accession, the new Tsar solemnly announced that he intended to emancipate the serfs of his Empire, claiming that it was better to accomplish that reform "from above" than to allow it to come "from below." Fear of peasant revolution may have inspired that great reform, but Alexander also sponsored important new legislation affecting many other branches of the administration. For a time the notoriously backward Russian Empire seemed likely to enter the second half of the nineteenth century as a nation aspiring to a degree of political, social and economic development comparable to that attained in the more advanced countries of the world.

At the very time that the Great Reforms were being enacted, however, general disillusionment was setting in. The year of emancipation—1861— was also a year of widespread peasant rioting. The first important student demonstrations broke out in St. Petersburg the same autumn. Nihilists distributed secretly printed pamphlets calling for the massacre of the Tsar, while terrible fires—of unknown origin but attributed by some to revolutionary arsonists—devastated parts of St. Petersburg. To cap these disasters a revolutionary ex-student, Dmitry Karakozov—who was, in effect, the first practicing Russian political terrorist—made an unsuccessful attempt to assassinate the Tsar by shooting at him in the Summer Garden in St. Petersburg on April 16, 1866. In the following year a Pole fired at Alexander during a visit to Paris.

Fearing unknown assassins, Alexander gave

The hanging of the terrorists convicted of the assassination of Alexander II.

V. K. Pleve, the Minister for the Interior, who tried to exterminate the terrorists. He himself was assassinated in 1904.

The coronation of Tsar Alexander II in 1856. The splendor of the Russian court and high society contrasted with the miserable conditions of the populace.

The barricades of the unsuccessful 1905 Revolution. After Alexander's assassination the revolutionary movement grew gradually in size and reached its peak in 1917.

virtual control of the Empire's internal management to Peter Shuvalov, his chief of political police from 1866 to 1874. During the last decade and a half of his reign, the Emperor's reforming impetus was very much in abeyance and accordingly those were years of comparatively severe political reaction. Even so, Alexander II remains the most effective sponsor of humane reform among Russia's supreme rulers—Tsars and Soviet dictators alike— and it was a harsh dispensation of fate that decreed that he, rather than Nicholas I, should be struck down by revolutionary violence. (Some four years after Alexander's death a similar fate overtook Abraham Lincoln, who shares with the Russian Emperor the achievement of having abolished slavery in an extensive section of the globe.)

After a long setback following the assassination of Alexander II, the Russian revolutionary movement gradually gathered new strength in secret. From the 1880s onward, Russian subversives living in temporary or permanent exile abroad played an especially important role in plotting the overthrow of the imperial system. But until the turn of the century, Russian revolutionary development, both at home and abroad, proceeded very largely on the plane of words. The age was one in which revolutionaries concentrated more on hammering out doctrine than on initiating action. Expatriate Russians published many pamphlets and periodicals on presses located outside Russia and smuggled such material into the Empire in quantity. During that period those same expatriates remained comparatively inactive in fomenting strikes and street demonstrations; no leading Russian statesmen were assassinated during the years 1881–1901.

If fringe groups such as the anarchists are excluded, Russian revolutionaries can be said to have fallen into two opposed camps by the turn of the century. One of these groups was the Narodniks (Populists), so termed because they continued to champion the *narod*, or common people (in effect, the peasantry). That group ultimately took the name Socialist Revolutionaries and founded, at the beginning of the twentieth century, the Socialist

Revolutionary Party, a largely clandestine body. At the same time they secretly established a small and virtually independent fighting organization, which was to revive the tactic of political terror by assassination on a scale unprecedented in Russia.

That terror campaign began in a small way in 1901, when a former student murdered the Minister of Education. The next year saw the assassination of D. S. Sipyagin, who was Minister for the Interior and therefore included overall responsibility for the police among his many duties. His successor was V. K. Pleve, who tried to contain growing revolutionary violence by severe repressive measures. Despite such tactics—or because of them—Pleve himself fell victim to an assassin: on July 27, 1904, his carriage was blown to pieces by a bomb.

The following year saw the outbreak of the unsuccessful Russian Revolution of 1905, sometimes termed the dress rehearsal for 1917. Widespread military and naval mutinies, manifold peasant riots, large-scale strikes and popular demonstrations— all lacking any effective central organization—were features of that disturbed year. Other significant episodes of 1905 were a sizable uprising in Moscow and a short-lived operation in St. Petersburg of a Soviet of Workers' Deputies which attempted to usurp some of the functions of government. Its members were arrested wholesale on December 15, 1905.

Meanwhile political assassination—chiefly of minor police officials, but including a governor-general of Moscow, a town captain of St. Petersburg and several provincial governors—increased to the point where victims numbered in the hundreds. Reprisals by police and troops, combined with numerous summary death sentences awarded by military courts and field courts-martial, caused thousands of fatalities among the population. Those operations completely eclipsed the political terror and counterterror of Alexander II's last years. And though no successful attempt was made on the life of Nicholas II, who had succeeded to the Russian throne, several plots to kill him were devised. The police, using a network of informers

posing as revolutionaries, managed to thwart those plots, and by 1907 the imperial government had so effectively asserted its authority that revolution once more appeared to be on the retreat.

The other large semiclandestine revolutionary group of the late imperial period, the Russian Marxist movement, attracted less public attention than the more flamboyant Socialist Revolutionaries. That lack of notoriety was partly due to the Marxists' rejection of assassination as a means of accomplishing revolution—not as a matter of principle, but because they considered it ineffective. In 1898 the Marxists founded the Russian Social Democratic Workers' Party at Minsk; five years later, at the Second Congress in London, the Party split into two violently opposed factions—the Bolsheviks and the Mensheviks. Lenin, who was the leader of the Bolsheviks, did not seem particularly dangerous to the Russian political police of the period. On the contrary, his habit of quarreling viciously with rival Social Democrats (while recruiting a small and apparently harmless cadre of followers who were blindly loyal to him) seemed a positive advantage to the authorities for it split, and so weakened, an important section of the revolutionary movement.

Although Lenin would not have sponsored Alexander II's assassination (which he regarded as a mistaken political tactic), he was wholeheartedly committed to the use of violence wherever he saw a prospect of political gain. Indeed, the assassination of Tsar Alexander II gains new significance when examined in the context of Lenin's successful revolutionary coup of November, 1917. Unfortunately for Russia, political changes such as have often occurred in other countries through peaceful evolutionary means have frequently been brought about there by violence. The slaughter of the reforming Tsar was just such a tragic landmark in history—and it dealt a serious blow to the increasingly discredited monarchic principle throughout Europe. It shook every throne in Europe by removing an autocrat who, for all his reforms, had some claim to be regarded as the world's premier despot.

RONALD HINGLEY

Tsar Alexander III, whose reign was more repressive than that of his father, Alexander II.

Russian Expansion in the Nineteenth Century

Areas gained or contested by Russia
Dates show when acquired by Russia
Areas of Russo-British rivalry

FINLAND 1809

St. Petersburg

SIBERIA

Sakhalin 1875

Terek Cossacks 1781-1825

Moscow

DAGHESTAN 1805

TURKESTAN 1864-65

Khiva 1873

Bokhara 1868

AMUR PROVINCES 1858-60

POLAND

GEORGIA 1801

Erivan 1828

Kars 1878

Crimean War 1854-56

MINGRELIA 1802

Thwarted ambitions in Balkans and Mediterranean

MANCHURIA
Occupied 1900-1905

Kirgiz 1801-55

PERSIA

Constantinople

AFGHANISTAN

ARMENIA

JAPAN

Eastern expansion halted by Russo-Japanese War 1904–1905

Parliamentary developments

"Parliaments are the great lie of our time." With that caustic generalization Konstantin Pobedonostsev, the chief minister of Tsar Alexander III, inadvertently epitomized the difference between Russia and the other nations of Europe in the late nineteenth century. While the Russian Empire tightened the bonds of autocracy through a series of laws in the 1880s, representative governments flourished in other parts of Europe on a far broader basis than had seemed possible thirty years before. Universal manhood suffrage was established in France and Germany in 1871; in Switzerland in 1874; in Spain in 1890; and in Belgium in 1893. It was introduced—with certain minor exceptions—in Britain in 1884 and in Holland in 1890. The franchise in Italy, although broadened in 1882, remained limited by property and educational qualifications until the eve of World War I. Lip service was paid to the concept of democratic control in the Balkan states, but political realities fell far short of constitutional provisions. There alone, perhaps, Pobedonostsev's remark had some justification.

The Emperor Mutsuhito of Japan, who was responsible for establishing the beginnings of representative government in Japan in 1889.

In Britain the last third of the nineteenth century saw the classic parliamentary duel between the Liberalism of Gladstone and the Conservative policy of empire and social reform grafted onto the old Tory Party by Disraeli. It was also an era of great parliamentarians on the Continent. The German Center

Party, led by Ludwig Windthorst (1812–91), and the National Liberals, led by Count Rudolph von Bennigsen (1824–1902), ensured that the *Reichstag* in Berlin was no mere echoing vault for Bismarck's thunder. The eloquence of such master-craftsmen as Léon Gambetta (1838–82), Jules Ferry (1832–93) and Georges Clemenceau (1841–1929) made the Chamber of Deputies in Paris the real center of French political life and the bastion against the neo-Bonapartism of the right. And the Parliament in Budapest—although by no means representative of all Hungary's nationalities—achieved a dignity comparable to the institutions of Westminster under Kalmán Tisza (1830–1902).

Nor were these developments limited to Europe. The Congress of the United States was more powerful than the presidency in the last decades of the nineteenth century, and in 1889 the Japanese Emperor approved a constitution that established a chamber of peers and a diet elected on a limited franchise. On the other hand, Sultan Abdul Hamid II rescinded political concessions forced on Turkey by the great powers during the Eastern Crises of 1875 and 1878 and continued to rule Turkey despotically until 1908. In Latin America power remained in the hands of self-perpetuating oligarchies that reduced parliamentary life to a completely empty formula.

On liberty and liberal reform

The most venerated theorist of Western liberalism was John Stuart Mill (1806–73), whose great plea for minority rights, *On Liberty*, was published in 1859, the same year as Darwin's *The Origin of Species*. Though Mill was primarily concerned with British institutions, he was much influenced by French traditions and spent several months of every year in France. He enjoyed a respect on the Continent of Europe that was rare among English political writers, and his work was even translated into Serbo-Croat by the exiled Peter Karageorgevich (1844–1921), who was to ascend the Serbian throne in 1903. In Britain, Mill educated both the political parties: it was Disraeli, a Conservative, who pushed through the second Parliamentary Reform Act of 1867 (which gave the vote

John Stuart Mill, the most venerated theorist of Western liberalism and author of *On Liberty*, the classic plea for minority rights.

to more than a million town laborers) but it was Gladstone, a Liberal, who passed the third Reform Act of 1884 (which extended the franchise to two million agricultural workers). Yet there was a significant limit to Mill's influence even in his own native land. During the debates on the 1867 Act, Mill proposed that any woman who paid taxes ought, by right, to enjoy the vote. His motion was overwhelmingly defeated in the House of Commons and his championship of female suffrage was scorned by *Punch* and satirized by Gilbert and Sullivan, whose comic operas were then at the height of their popularity. The first country to give women the right to vote was New Zealand, which did so in 1893.

The 1870s and 1880s were decades of domestic reform in Britain. Under Gladstone's leadership the Liberals laid the foundations of a

Upper-class children at play; Juvenile Ball in the Mansion House, London, in 1875.

national system of education, checked the scourge of alcoholism by controlling the sale of liquor, recognized the principle of privacy in casting votes in an election,

Mealtime at an orphanage, 1870; social contrasts were pronounced.

established a more equitable system of entry into the higher ranks of the Civil Service and the army and centralized the administration of justice. Disraeli and the Conservatives were responsible for the

View of a women's club; women were beginning to demand the vote.

iberties—"the great lie of our time"

earliest attempts to deal with slum clearance on a national scale and for giving governmental backing to local authorities' attempts to improve sanitation and hygiene (and thereby to stamp out cholera and limit the advance of other diseases). The Disraeli government of 1874–80 was also the first administration to allow trade unionists to undertake peaceful picketing during a strike. And it was the Conservatives, under Lord Salisbury, who extended the principle of democratic control to smaller communities by the Local Government Act of 1888.

The Irish Question

Throughout this period British politics were dominated by the Irish Question and, in particular, by Parliament's failure to understand the Irish tenancy system or to perceive that the life of an Irish tenant farmer was more akin to that of an Eastern European serf than to that of an English farmer.

Charles Stewart Parnell, leader of the Irish Party, whose brilliant tactics forced Gladstone to support Home Rule for Ireland.

Gladstone's Irish Land Act improved the status of tenants, but it came too late to check violence and outrage. The brilliant political tactics of Charles Stewart Parnell (1846–91) and his Irish Party in the House of Commons kept the Irish Question in the forefront of the public mind for nearly a decade—until finally in 1886 Gladstone himself became convinced that only home rule for Ireland would provide the answer. Nearly a hundred of Gladstone's supporters at Westminster revolted at Gladstone's proposal to set up an Irish parliament at Dublin, and the Liberal Party was sundered (just as Peel's Tories had been forty years before over repeal of the Corn Laws). It was not until after World War I that a compromise

solution partitioned the country, giving self-government to southern Ireland, and even that settlement retained Westminster's sovereignty over the Parliament of the north of Ireland.

Marxism

The failure of the 1848 revolutions to impose a more liberal structure of government on the states of Europe might have destroyed ideas of reform, whether liberal or socialist. However, socialist ideas, although their adherents were without political power or influence, grew rapidly in popularity after 1848. Urban and industrial

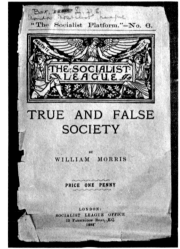

Title-page of William Morris' *True and False Society*.

development were the key to the growth of socialism as they had been to its birth.

One of the most serious problems of socialism in its early years was the lack of a consistent intellectual framework and vision of society. This difficulty was ended with the publication in 1867, 1885, and 1894 of *Das Kapital* by Karl Marx (1818–83), the last two volumes of which were completed by Marx' collaborator Friedrich Engels (1820–95). The aim of *Das Kapital* was to provide an intellectual basis for Marx' views "as a process of natural history." Marx put forward an evolutionary view of human history, which made his debt to Darwin very apparent. Engels was later to claim that, "Just as Darwin discovered the law of development of organic nature, so Marx discovered the law of development of human history." In its view of human society, Marx' book was little less revolutionary than

Darwin's had been. Both excelled in the destruction of accepted ideas. But the real intellectual debt that Marx owed was to the German philosopher Georg Wilhelm Friedrich Hegel (1770–1831) rather than to Darwin. Marxist dialectics sprang from those of Hegel, and the synthetic nature of Marx' thought formed a major part of its appeal.

At the root of Marx' thought was the idea of a class struggle, which was bound to become fiercer as the logic of capitalist economics—the concentration of ever-greater wealth into the hands of an ever-diminishing proportion of the population—grew more apparent to the wealthless proletariat. The proletariat would rise against its masters and create a revolutionary state, which would introduce economic policies that would allow the worker—instead of the entrepreneur—to enjoy the full fruits of his labor. As a result the class struggle would end and the state itself would become unnecessary.

By Marx' emphasis on the importance of the revolution, socialism was given a new dynamism. At the same time the size and scope of *Das Kapital* meant that it could no more be ignored than could *The Origin of Species*.

The growth of socialism

Despite Marx' emphasis on violent revolution, the second half of the nineteenth century saw the arrival of socialism as an effective political movement. The romantic and utopian socialism of the French thinkers, Claude de Saint-Simon (1760–1825) and Charles Fourier (1772–1837), at the outset of the century gave way not merely to the pressure of Marxist ideology, but also to the need for effective political and economic organization. The first socialist organizations had been more like political clubs than political parties, and they would have been incapable of capturing the allegiance of the rapidly expanding electorate of most of the Western countries, even if they had tried.

In France, the labor movement had been forced underground by Napoleon III, but as a result of the Franco-Prussian War of 1870 it was able to emerge from hiding. The humiliation of France led to a revulsion of feeling against Napoleon III, despite the valuable

benefits that his government had brought. Bismarck's insistence that a new French National Assembly be elected on the basis of universal manhood suffrage produced a highly conservative body.

Influenced by the National Guard, whose pay had been canceled by the National Assembly, Paris revolted in 1871, both in defiance of the conservative Assembly and as a socialist gesture. The government sent an army to suppress the rising, but the troops refused to attack their fellow countrymen. A commune was set up, but its failure to appreciate its military weakness led to its dissolution. The commune was suppressed with great brutality—it is calculated that over twenty thousand supporters of the commune were massacred by government troops—leaving the French workers' movement stunned. Yet from the ensuing fragmentation there emerged five Socialist parties in France with national influence. However, their disagreements meant that they posed little danger to the governments of the Republic.

The evolution of socialism in Italy was similar to the French pattern in its violent origins, but in Germany it was very different. The first effective socialist party was founded in 1863 by Ferdinand Lassalle (1825–64), but its aims were very limited. Far more important was the Social Democratic Working Men's Party, founded in 1869 by disillusioned Liberals. In 1877 the party won half a million votes, and by 1890 it was able to win almost one and a half million votes.

The electoral successes of Socialist parties—modest though they appear by later standards—was due in part to the rapid growth of the cooperative movement, but in larger measure to the development of factory-floor organization. Trade unions were illegal in Britain until 1871 and in France until 1884, but this did not prevent them from achieving a rising membership, and legalization provided an extra spur to recruitment. In the United States the Knights of Labor, founded in 1869, proved to be too general to be effective and gave way to smaller unions linked to the American Federation of Labor, founded in 1886. Violence played a large part in the early years of American trade unionism as the Haymarket Affair was to show.

The Haymarket Affair

In the labor troubles that followed the Great Upheaval, as the depression of 1884–85 was called, a meeting was held in Chicago's Haymarket Square to protest the death of a striker, killed in a fracas with strikebreakers and police. The meeting was peaceful enough—even dull—until police officers decided to disperse the crowd. A bomb was thrown and one policeman lay dead. In the ensuing hysteria, eight men were brought to trial and were railroaded to conviction. Four were executed, one committed suicide, two had their sentences commuted to life imprisonment, and one received fifteen years in prison. The Haymarket incident not only created America's first labor martyrs; it also diverted labor's energies away from unproductive agitation and into more political—and ultimately successful—channels.

Chicago Historical Society

August Spies. A meeting he was addressing outside the McCormick Works was broken up by the police, precipitating the Haymarket affair.

Opposite Report of the Haymarket affair in the *Chicago Daily News.*

The violence in Haymarket Square in Chicago on May 4, 1886, occurred as the United States was emerging from the depression of the early 1880s. During that time there had been an unusual amount of protest, agitation and organization among the political parties of the left and among the industrial working class. Known as the Great Upheaval of 1884–85, this activity came at a time when the country's economy was being transformed. Industry's techniques of mass production began to dominate. In addition, the trend toward monopoly, perceived and feared by the workers, brought ruthless price competition and fluctuation, as large industrial units struggled for control of raw materials and markets. Consequently profit margins declined and wage reductions hit the semiskilled and unskilled workers especially hard.

The Great Upheaval was characterized by an increase in labor organization rather than in political action, the chief agent of which was the Order of the Knights of Labor. After a series of successful strikes the membership of the Knights soared from 100,000 to 700,000 in six months. The significance of this increase was that the Knights had become the means by which angry and desperate unskilled workers now made their uncompromising demands—all this despite a conservative and timid leadership that rejected strike action and advocated cooperation and arbitration. Divided into district assemblies of workers within a particular industry or occupation without distinction as to trade or skill, the Knights' rank and file spoke of war between capital and labor. The industrialists panicked and responded with strikebreakers, private and local police, militia forces and blacklists, causing concern among the more traditional trade unions.

Although the trade unions admitted unskilled laborers to membership, they were essentially craft-based and dominated by skilled workers. However, with the spectacular growth and activity of the

Knights, the trade unions realized that their influence within the labor movement was waning. To draw attention to itself, arouse its membership and regain prestige, the Federation of Organized Trades and Labor Unions (FOOTALU), headed by Samuel Gompers and Adolph Strasser, presented at its 1884 annual meeting a demand for an eight-hour day. The FOOTALU wanted the eight-hour day to be introduced by legislation rather than by industrial action; if that were not achieved before May 1, 1886, a general strike would be called for that day.

The eight-hour-day tactic of the trade unions received little sympathy from the leaders of the Knights who saw this proposition merely as a flurry of activity on the part of a rival organization in a period of decline. But, while the Knights' leadership was wary of a campaign which was quite likely to fail, the rank and file saw its potential as a device for focusing their anger at the employers. Also aware of the campaign's possibilities were the anarchists, particularly those in Chicago who had become a powerful force in the city's trade unions and who looked to the radical trade unions as agents for overthrowing the existing capitalist order. The Chicago anarchists had been helping to foster the Central Labor Union, a progressive and successful alternative to the established and conservative city trades assembly. August Spies, Albert Parsons and others organized parades, meetings and demonstrations directed at mobilizing workers around the demand for an eight-hour day.

By early 1886, their efforts were proving so effective that it was thought if the campaign succeeded anywhere, it would be in Chicago, and on May 1. The city's business leaders were prepared. Labor strife had been fierce and frequent in the 1880s; at the time the eight-hour campaign was coming to a climax the McCormick Harvester Works was on strike, contributing to the prevailing air of watchfulness and unease. Moreover,

THE CHICAGO DAILY NEWS.

EVENING ISSUE—VOL. X.—NO. 106.　　WEDNESDAY EVENING, MAY 5, 1886—SIX PAGES.　　EVENING ISSUE—

WITH SUPPLEMENT

This issue of the Evening News consists of SIX PAGES, and purchasers are entitled to, and should demand, the complete issue.

EXTRA
9:15 O'CLOCK A. M.

LOCKED UP.

Anarchist Leaders Arrested by the Police Early This Morning.

August Spies, His Brother, and Editor Schwab Captured by the Police.

They Have the Temerity to Come Down Town and Consult with Each Other.

Taken to the Central Police Station and Placed Securely Behind the Bars.

The Anarchistic Editor Is Thoroughly Frightened When He Is Searched.

No One Is Allowed to Talk to Him Except the Officials.

August Spies is under arrest. He was captured by the police a trifle this morning. The anarchist and "secondary editor of the Arbeiter Zeitung—who was the first one to address the meeting at Desplaines and Randolph streets, who occupied the space from which, it is charged, the dynamite bomb was thrown which did such bloody work last night, who was one of the speakers at the meeting on the prairie near McCormick's Monday afternoon, whose inflamed the mob until it was ready to burn down the great factory—had the temerity to appear in the editorial rooms of his paper this morning.

EXTRA
11:00 O'CLOCK A. M.

MEN KILLED.

Bloody Conflicts Between Rioters and Officers of the Law at Bay View.

Unable to Stop the Advance of a Crowd the Militia Fire—Five Persons Slaughtered.

Many Others Are Severely Wounded—The Mob Quickly Scattered.

Another Gang Attempt to Destroy Best's Brewery—More Shooting Occurs.

MILWAUKEE, WIS., May 5, 9 a. m.—Reports from Bay View say the militia fired on the mob this morning. The rioters are known to have been killed.

A mob is marching toward the Allis works, which started up under military protection this morning. The light-horse squadron is on the way to the Allis works.

Wrecking Stores.

Ten Thousand Rioters Attack Rosenfeld's Drug Store and Completely Gut It.

Then Their Vengeance Is Turned Against a Saloon—It Is Also Demolished.

Charged With Murder.

Substantial Help.

EXTRA
11:30 O'CLOCK A. M.

FIELDEN SHOT.

The Man Who Incited the Mob Last Night Locked Up This Morning.

He Was Wounded in the Melee by a Gunshot and Now Walks Lame in His Cell.

Sam Fielden, the rabid anarchist and companion of August Spies, is under arrest. He it was who spoke the last words to the mob last night which led to the slaughter. He was found this morning and safely caged at the central station.

THE EVIDENCE.

Copies of Last Night's Incendiary Circular Found at August Spies's Office.

The Forms from Which They Were Printed Still Standing in the Composing-Room.

ATTENTION, WORKINGMEN!

DYING POLICE OFFICERS.

Scenes of Misery Witnessed at the County Hospital This Morning.

MINOR MATTERS IN BRIEF.

EXTRA
1:00 O'CLOCK P. M.

ARMS SEIZED.

The Police Raid a Canal Street Establishment and Confiscate Some Firearms.

Selling to Socialists Charged by the Officers, But Denied by the Owner of the Place.

Lieut. Hubbard, with twenty men of the central detail, made a raid about noon to-day on the work-shop of C. H. Rinell, on the fourth floor of the building at 53 south Canal street.

FINDING MUSKETS.

A Raid Made on the Headquarters of the Anarchists.

ARMING FOR WAR.

Guns and Ammunition Being Distributed from the Central Police Station by the Chief.

EXTRA
THREE O'CLOCK P. M.

PROCLAMATION.

Mayor Harrison Orders the Dispersal of Any Large Bodies of People.

He Alludes to the Condition of Affairs Now Existing and the Scenes of Last Night.

Every One Advised to Remain at Home—A Document that All Should Read.

The following was issued by the mayor to-day:

THE MAYOR'S OFFICE.

Many Business Men Call to Give the Executive Advice.

THE HON. O. B. FICKLIN.

Death at Charleston, Ill., of the Noted Fifty Illinois and Lawyer.

New Corporations Licensed.

THE ST. PAUL HOUSE.

Work Proceeding on Consul-To-Day—Witnesses Remain Passive.

SWITCHMEN REFUSE.

EXTRA
FIVE O'CLOCK P. M.

The Bomb Thrower

Seen by a Young Man to Light the Fuse and Hurl the Missile.

Detectives Are Now on the Track of the Dastardly Villain.

It Is Hoped that His Capture Will Be Effected in a Short Time.

Buried Alive.

Twenty-Three Men Caught in a Falling Building at Minneapolis This Afternoon.

ST. PAUL, MINN., May 5, 4 p. m.—Rumor just reached here that the Bracket block at Minneapolis, corner 1st avenue south and Third street, has fallen in, burying twenty-three men.

FREIGHT-HANDLERS.

The Wabash Road Imports Some Germans from Decatur, Who Refuse to Work.

EXTRA
SIX O'CLOCK P. M.

THE INQUEST.

Officer Degan's Tragic Death Being Officially Investigated This Afternoon.

August Spies and Editor Schwab Brought Before the Jury Under Guard of Detectives.

An Abstract of the Testimony Given by a Brother of the Deceased and Other Witnesses.

An inquest was commenced this afternoon on the body of Officer Degan who was killed in the riot last night. It was held at one of the offices in the city hall, great privacy being observed.

AMMUNITION FOUND

The Arbeiter Zeitung Building Still Continues to Yield Up Destructive Missiles.

They Are Stowed Away Under an Old Sink Ready for Use.

CONTESTING A WILL.

Strange Allegations Set Up by a Disinherited Nephew.

A bomb exploding among the police as they approach the rostrum.

the city police had frequently been used to protect plants and to attack strikers. By 1886 its officers saw themselves as the right arm of the meat packers, the railroads and the McCormick Company.

Ironically May 1, a Saturday, passed relatively quietly and there were no incidents. Fifty thousand workers struck for the eight-hour day and tens of thousands paraded through the center of the city. The anxiety which had been further aggravated by a fearful press and civic leadership dissipated. The police, however, did not relax their guard. On May 3, one of the anarchist leaders, Spies, was addressing a meeting of strikers outside the McCormick Works when the strikebreakers began to leave the factory. A fight ensued and several hundred police appeared; in the turmoil one worker died and several were wounded. Incensed, Spies ran to the office of his newspaper and called for a mass meeting next evening in the Haymarket.

Only a few thousand gathered that night to protest the police violence of the previous day and to hear Spies, Parsons and Samuel Fielden, leaders of the eight-hour movement, speak. The speakers found it difficult to arouse their audience and it was a disappointing affair. At 10:30 P.M., as rain began to fall, Fielden decided to bring the meeting to a close. Mayor Carter Harrison, who had been present as an observer, had left, but on his way home had notified Captain Bonfield that his detachment of two hundred police could assume that there would be no trouble as the meeting was about to break up. However, as Fielden was concluding, Bonfield and his men appeared at the rostrum and ordered him to end the meeting. Before Fielden could do more

than tell him, "We are peaceable," there was a blinding flash and then pandemonium as guns blazed from both the police and the audience. A bomb, hurled into the police ranks, had exploded and in the ensuing panic those with guns had fired. One policeman was killed and seventy injured. Officially it was reported that one worker had died and, undoubtedly a gross underestimate, twelve had been injured.

Reaction in the city was as widespread as it was extreme. The major Chicago newspapers were unanimous in their demand that the socialists and anarchists be hunted down and executed before there was revolution or anarchy in the city. Newspapers and spokesmen throughout the entire country agreed. The Chicago police searched for suspects and arrested and interrogated anybody linked in any way with radical parties or the labor movement. So intense was the panic and paranoia that the city council even voted to eliminate the color red—labor's color—from all Chicago street signs. So incensed was public opinion that many who were disposed to criticize the police were forced to keep their silence. Many labor and left-wing party leaders, aware of their guilt by association, either remained silent or joined in the general denunciation. They confined their criticism to the deed itself, which they did not condone, rather than to those assumed to be responsible.

From the two hundred suspects arrested, thirty-one were indicted and eight stood trial for the murder of Police Officer Degan. Three of the eight had addressed the Haymarket meeting and a fourth had been present for part of it—August Spies,

Albert Parsons, Samuel Fielden and Michael Schwab. All were well known to the police for their public speeches, their newspaper writing, their involvement with the Central Labor Union (c.l.u.) and in the eight-hour-day campaign.

Spies was the most able and influential but Parsons was the most interesting. Although it was assumed that anarchists were foreign-born and of inferior origins, Parsons had impeccable credentials; his ancestors had arrived on the *Mayflower* and fought in the Revolution. He himself was from Alabama and had fought for the Confederacy; after his arrival in Chicago he had become a Socialist and, on the Socialist Labor ticket, had twice run for alderman. In the 1880s he rejected electoral politics and edited the anarchist paper, *Alarm*. Samuel Fielden was an English-born teamster associated with Parsons in his newspaper and organizational work among the English-speaking workers, while Michael Schwab engaged in similar functions with Spies among the German-speaking workers. The four others charged were not anarchist leaders but in varying degrees were associated with them though none was present at the Haymarket. George Engel addressed a meeting on the evening of May 3 at which violence and disruption were discussed, but in general terms only and not related to the next day's Haymarket meeting. The prosecution, however, presented this as the occasion when the conspiracy was planned. Louis Lingg was an anarchist who actually made bombs and had left some of them in Neff's Hall, a saloon near the Haymarket, on the afternoon of May 4, and it was argued that the bomb thrown was one of Lingg's. Finally, there were Adolph Fischer and Oscar Neebe, both only vaguely associated with the anarchists, and neither was present at the meeting.

From the start of the trial, it was apparent that matters were biased against the defendants. In the empaneling of jurors, Judge Joseph Gary made it clear that even friendship with one of the wounded policemen or a hatred of anarchists was insufficient reason to disqualify anyone. Regardless of the judge's attitude, the prosecution's case was tenuous and only supportable in the context of Illinois' somewhat vague conspiracy statute. The prosecution asserted that by their speeches in the past as well as on May 4 the accused had generated a climate of disturbance and were therefore accessories before the fact. Based on this circumstantial evidence, a conspiracy theory was proposed. Yet the man who actually threw the bomb could not be identified, and therefore his relation, if any, with the accused could not be proved. The defense, however, continually asked why the bomb could not have been thrown by an agent-provocateur and why the police suddenly had appeared when the peaceful meeting was about to disperse.

All of these reasonable doubts were as nothing compared to the innuendo that made up the prosecution's case. And so the verdict of guilty, with death by hanging as the sentence, was returned. Neebe alone escaped death and was given fifteen

years in prison. Appeal was made to the Illinois Supreme Court but on both the law and the evidence the lower court decision was upheld. Appeal then was made to the United States Supreme Court on the grounds that the rights of the defendants guaranteed under the Fourteenth Amendment had been denied them during the trial, but the Court rejected this argument and disclaimed jurisdiction. The courts had in effect tried the men for their

The police attacking the protest meeting in the Haymarket.

The Haymarket, Chicago.

Adolph Fischer. Not present at the Haymarket and only vaguely associated with the anarchists, he too was hanged

Right George Engel. He was hanged although he did not attend the Haymarket meeting and was not closely linked with anarchist politics.

An advertisement for the meeting to protest against the police attack on the McCormick strikers.

Attention Workingmen!

═══ GREAT ═══

MASS-MEETING

TO-NIGHT, at 7.30 o'clock,

═══ AT THE ═══

HAYMARKET, Randolph St., Bet. Desplaines and Halsted.

Good Speakers will be present to denounce the latest atrocious act of the police, the shooting of our fellow-workmen yesterday afternoon.

Workingmen Arm Yourselves and Appear in Full Force!

THE EXECUTIVE COMMITTEE.

Achtung, Arbeiter!

Große

Maffen-Berfammlung

Heute Abend, 8 Uhr, auf dem

Heumarkt, Randolph-Straße, zwischen
Desplaines- u. Halſted-Str.

☞ Gute Redner werden den neueſten Schurkenſtreich der Polizei,
indem ſie geſtern Nachmittag unſere Brüder erſchoß, geißeln.

☞ Arbeiter, bewaffnet Euch und erſcheint maſſenhaft!

Das Executiv-Comite.

opinions rather than their deeds, and there was no recourse left unless the Illinois governor would exercise clemency.

Perhaps the most dramatic moments of the whole affair occurred at this stage as the Amnesty Association, formed a year earlier to aid prisoners, sent in a petition. Civic leaders including Lyman Gage, later President William McKinley's Secretary of the Treasury, personally beseeched Governor Oglesby for mercy. Leaders of labor, particularly Samuel Gompers, now intervened to try to save the innocent men. Oglesby did not want to take an inflexible position on the matter, although he was forced to do so by Chicago's business leaders. A way out was provided when Fielden and Schwab wrote to Oglesby saying they would accept a reprieve, whereupon the governor commuted their sentences to life.

On November 11, 1887, Spies, Parsons, Fischer and Engel were hanged. (The day before the execution, Louis Lingg committed suicide.) The city breathed a sigh of relief, the *Inter Ocean* announced that "Armed anarchy is dead in this city, and dead by force of law and reason." The national magazine *Harper's Weekly* concurred: "Their crime was so wanton and their pleas for it so wild that any other verdict would have been startling." Nonetheless, the Haymarket affair remained a central issue in Illinois politics for another seven years, as pressure mounted from middle-class reformers, workers and others to have the surviving anarchists pardoned. And in 1893, as one of his first acts in office, the newly elected reform governor John Peter Altgeld not only released the surviving three, but he also strongly criticized the conduct of the trial, suggesting that the prisoners had been "railroaded."

The Haymarket incident was used as proof that trade unions were imbued with violence and dominated by newly arrived immigrants, unfamiliar with American customs and inspired by fanatical foreign ideas. Therefore, labor activity was suspicious, subversive, violent and foreign. Anti-foreign organizations multiplied just after Haymarket, and at the same time a number of state laws were passed increasing restrictions on foreigners and facilitating their deportation. Among working men themselves, there was suspicion of the foreign born.

Samuel Gompers judged that the riot was responsible for "killing" any hope for a shorter work day, as many employers stood firm or else retracted the concessions forced from them before the bomb was thrown. And finally, the trial of the Haymarket defendants demonstrated that the courts were opposed to labor unions and strikes. The courts were prejudiced and they had the means, such as the charge of conspiracy or later the injunction, to curb or destroy organizations that seemed to threaten the new industrial system.

If capital had used the riot to denigrate labor organizations and politics, it also produced something else as well—the Haymarket martyrs. American labor's first heroes were Spies, Parsons and their comrades. By their eloquent statements just before receiving sentence and by their insistence on their innocence, they had made a deep impression on a number of younger radicals—Emma Goldman, "Big Bill" Haywood, the future leader of the Industrial Workers of the World (I.W.W.), and the rising Socialist and railway union leader, Eugene Debs. The anarchists' funeral at Waldheim cemetery in Chicago was a moving event attended by a quarter of a million people; the anarchists' graves became a

Far left Albert Parsons. An activist of impeccable American background, he edited the anarchist paper *Alarm*.

Left *Liberty is not Anarchy*, a cartoon from *Harper's Weekly*. The men being crushed in the hand of Justice are the seven who were convicted and subsequently executed for their association with the affray in the Haymarket.

shrine and the day of their execution, November 11, became an official day of remembrance in the American labor movement for the next fifty years.

And after May 1, 1890, the day when workers in America and Europe demonstrated for the eight-hour day, May 1 was annually celebrated internationally by Socialists. Haymarket was really the first episode in United States labor history that had repercussions abroad and meetings were held in support of it in France and in Britain. Anarchists throughout Europe praised the Chicago martyrs and extolled their example as inspiration for others.

There were two further respects in which Haymarket had a salutary effect. First, after rejecting electoral politics in the late 1870s and early 1880s in favor of union action or individualistic "propaganda by deed," the labor movement once again turned to politics. The years 1887–88 saw the emergence of United Labor parties in many cities, including Chicago, New York and Milwaukee. In these local elections, coalitions of Socialists, Knights, trade unionists and middle-class reformers drew together elements on the left that before Haymarket had been disparate and autonomous. By this strategy, significant inroads were made into the regular parties' support. Henry George, on a social welfare platform, ran second in the mayoral race in New York. In all of the cities mentioned, state legislators and some city aldermen were voted into office on the United Labor ticket, and in Milwaukee even a United States Congressman was elected. Second, in 1887 Democrats and Republicans in Chicago were forced to fuse in order to defeat the third-party challenge. Because of policy differences, the effort collapsed in 1888. But this initiative showed that despite Haymarket, dissent was still possible.

Further, a moderating influence was exerted on the labor movement. That is not necessarily commendable but in the mid-1890s it seemed so if labor organizations were to survive and grow. The Knights had declined drastically in 1887, well after Haymarket and for reasons unassociated with it. Their form of organization was too vulnerable to attack from the employers. They also had to rely too much on dramatic successes to gain support and could never consolidate their gains. The Knights' successors were the trade unions. The trade unions renamed their national organization in 1886, and, as the American Federation of Labor (A.F.L.), it dominated the scene for the next forty years. With skilled workers as its membership and using a strategy of moderation, the A.F.L. seemed to have learned the lessons of the Great Upheaval and Haymarket. Labor organizations found it necessary to reject violence and adventurism and to concentrate on organization and short-term goals. It was a prudent course in the circumstances, but it stamped United States unionism as conservative. Debs' industrial unionism, the I.W.W.'s efforts, and the formation of the Congress of Industrial Organizations (C.I.O.) in the 1930s—none could rid itself of the conservative label.

At first it seemed that Haymarket had left the labor movement weakened and open to attack, but Haymarket had become a rallying point and a warning of what misfortunes could occur unless precautions were taken in the future. Capital had gained the initiative, but the way labor responded in the aftermath of Haymarket demonstrated that labor would survive such setbacks even if, in the process, they took on different forms.

MICHAEL PERMAN

Municipal broadsheet banning public assemblies.

PROCLAMATIO
TO THE PEOPLE OF CHICAGO
MAYOR'S OFFICE, Chicago, May 5. 1:
WHEREAS, Great excitement e: among the people of this good city, growin of the LABOR TROUBLES, which excitement is in fied by the open defiance of the guardians of the by a body of lawless men, who, under the prete aiding the laboring men, are really endeavor destroy all law. And Whereas, last nigh men, by the use of weapons never resorted CIVILIZED LANDS, EXCEPT IN TIME WAR or for REVOLUTIONARY PURP CAUSED GREAT BLOODSHED AMONG ZENS AND AMONG OFFICERS of the MU PALITY who were simply in the performance o duties. And Whereas, the CITY AUTHORITIES PROPO PROTECT LIFE AND PROPERTY AT ALL HAZARDS, and in so will be compelled to break up all unlawful or dan gatherings; and
WHEREAS, Even when men pro to meet for lawful purposes, bad men will attempt gle with them, armed with cowardly missiles, purpose of bringing about bloodshed, thus endang innocent persons;
THEREFORE I, Carter H. Harr
MAYOR OF THE CITY OF CHICAGO, DO HEREBY PROCLAIM THAT C INGS OF PEOPLE IN CROWDS OR PROCESSIONS IN THE STRE PUBLIC PLACES OF THE CITY ARE DANGEROUS AND CANNOT I MITTED, AND ORDERS HAVE BEEN ISSUED TO THE POLICE TO I ALL SUCH GATHERINGS and TO BREAK UP AND DISPERSE ALL C TO PREVENT INJURY TO INNOCENT PERSONS.
I urge all law-abiding people to quietly attend to their own aff not to meet in crowds. If the police order any gatherings to disperse, be not obeyed, all persons so disobeying will be treated as law-breakers. surely incur the penalty of their disobedience.
I further assure the good people of Chicago that I believe the police took their lives and property and the good name of Chicago, and WILL
CARTER H. HARRISON.

120

The Riches of the Rand — 1886

In an attempt to preserve the isolated tranquility of their adopted homeland, the Boer farmers of the South African Republic shared a phenomenal secret for more than thirty years. From the 1850s until 1886, they alone knew that incalculably rich reefs of gold ore had been discovered on a plateau south of the capital city of Pretoria. Such momentous news could not be suppressed indefinitely, of course, and in the summer of 1886 gold was "rediscovered" in the Transvaal. On September 8, the gold fields of the Rand—as the main reef was called—were opened to public prospecting, and within a decade those fields were producing 2 million troy ounces of gold per year, or one quarter of the world's output. In that same decade the Transvaal experienced a wildly accelerated industrial revolution and a staggering population explosion that turned the once pastoral veld into a microcosm of modern capitalism.

Johannesburg owes its existence to an accident of geology, not to any conditions of geography, commerce, strategy or politics. The South African metropolis was, quite literally, founded on gold. In the 1880s, deposits of gold-bearing rock were discovered at various places in the pastoral republic of the Transvaal, an isolated territory that lacked both sea and rail connections with its neighbors. A well-established tradition holds that gold was first discovered in the Transvaal in the 1850s, but that the news was deliberately suppressed by the government in an effort to preserve the region's isolated tranquility. In 1877 the Transvaal Republic was annexed by the British, who returned it to the Boers (Afrikaner farmers) after the British defeat at Majuba in 1881.

Ironically, gold was "rediscovered" in the Transvaal less than two years after the Boers and the British negotiated the 1884 Convention of London, which granted the Afrikaners de facto independence in internal affairs. At that time, the white population of the Transvaal numbered perhaps 50,000, most of whom lived in Pretoria, the capital, or in one of two small towns, Potchefstroom and Rustenburg. There were, in addition, a dozen or so respectably sized villages, and a mining camp had recently sprung up in the east. The boundaries of this primitive republic were defined by the Vaal River in the south and the Limpopo in the north. Between these lines, and in the vaguely defined regions to the west and east, lived roughly three-quarters of a million African tribesmen. The revenue of the state, in the year preceding the founding of Johannesburg, amounted to £177,000.

By 1886, a number of prospectors claimed they had found gold deposits in payable quantities on the plateau south of Pretoria. In February of that year, an adventurer named George Walker came upon what was later identified as the Main Reef Leader, an outcrop of gold-bearing rock that stretched down thousands of feet below the surface.

If a date can be ascribed to the founding of Johannesburg, it is September 8, 1886, the day that the gold fields of the Main Reef were proclaimed public diggings. The isolation of the Transvaal had ended.

The center of the new deposits seemed to be under a ridge called the Witwatersrand ("the ridge of white waters") not because it was abundant in streams but because mica deposits in the rocks gave the illusion, from a distance, of cascades. The surroundings were bleak and arid, and the essential characteristic of the Rand, as the ridge came to be called, was that the gold was hard to reach. This was no Klondike or Yukon in which the lone prospector might make his fortune. Its development depended upon the application of the skills of the engineer, the geologist and the chemist, backed by a large labor force and sustained by immense capital investment. In the words of Professor S. E. Frankel:

> The geological character of the gold field is unique. It is marked by the exceptional continuity in length and breadth of its general low grade ore deposits. The history of the Rand is the history of the adaptation of modern industrial and financial methods to the exploitation of a mining field, continually dumbfounding the prophets both as to the area and the scale of operations economically most suited to it.

The discovery of the gold fields had far-reaching implications; the vibrations could be felt throughout the Western world. In 1888, the Rand produced 230,000 troy ounces of gold; in 1889 it produced 369,000 ounces; in 1892, 1,210,000; and in 1894, over 2 million—more than a quarter of the world's output. Within a few years, the Rand had become linked to the money markets of the world, and investors throughout Europe and the Americas felt that they had a stake in the Transvaal Republic. The nature of the industry led naturally to a high level of combinations, and great mining firms began to emerge. Many of the "Randlords," as the mining magnates came to be called, had already made

Cecil Rhodes, Prime Minister of Cape Colony. He aimed at uniting the races of South Africa under the British crown.

Opposite Boers returning from hunting. The Boers were descended from Dutch farmers who settled in Cape Colony and the Transvaal.

Diggers at work in the Transvaal gold fields.

their fortunes in the exploitation of the diamond fields of Kimberley in the 1870s. Their backgrounds were diverse. The great capitalists included such men as Julius Wernher and Alfred Beit, Cecil Rhodes and Barney Barnato, Adolf Goertz and George Albu, Sammy Marks and Abe Bailey. In the wake of the giants came the lesser men. The Johannesburg Stock Exchange became a lively, and sometimes a frenetic, center of speculation. John X. Merriman, a politician of Whiggish outlook, described Johannesburg as "Monte Carlo superimposed upon Sodom and Gomorrah"; J. A. Hobson referred to it as "the new Jerusalem."

The name of the town was intended as a compliment to two officials of the Transvaal Republic—Johannes Rissik, the surveyor, and Christian Johannes Joubert, the head of the Department of Mines.

The settlement's European population is said to have reached three thousand within a year, but the first census in the Transvaal was not taken until 1896. According to that survey, Johannesburg contained some 50,000 whites and roughly 50,000 Africans, Indians and "Coloureds" (persons of mixed race). Less than seven thousand of the whites were Transvaalers; the remainder came from Britain, the British colonies, Russia, France, the United States, Germany and Holland. Johannesburg was a polyglot metropolis, overshadowing the Transvaal and threatening to transform the nature of the entire region. For that reason the hospitality that the Transvaal government had originally showed toward the developers of Johannesburg swiftly turned to mistrust. At the same time, the new wealth that the gold fields brought to the Transvaal treasury

gave the government command of resources that it had never previously possessed. Revenue increased from £177,000 in 1885 to £1,557,000 in 1889. By 1896 that figure had reached £3,912,000. President Kruger's republic had become spectacularly solvent, but as Kruger viewed the situation, the new wealth flooding the Transvaal brought with it a serious threat to the highly priced independence of his nation.

The history of the Boers was one of continuous struggle to escape from the jurisdiction of Britain. The Boers were descendants of the *Voortrekkers* who had emigrated from the Cape Colony in the 1830s, had moved north into the wilderness and had come at last to the Transvaal, their Promised Land. Britain had engulfed them in 1877, but they had won back their independence in 1881. Now it was threatened again, this time by "the money power." To assert his republic's independence, President Kruger successfully revived the construction of a railway line to the port of Lourenço Marques, giving the Transvaal an outlet to the sea that was beyond British control. He regarded the inhabitants of Johannesburg as foreign fortune hunters—*Uitlanders*, or "men from outside"—who were not to be regarded as equal to the older inhabitants, the burghers of the republic.

In the 1880s, the law governing the acquisition of Transvaal citizenship was reasonably hospitable to the newcomer—five years' residence and the payment of a fee of £25. Nonwhites were excluded from political rights and were not regarded as citizens. Male citizens elected the *Volksraad*, or legislative assembly, the President of the Republic and the Commandant General. In 1890, the voting law was changed to require a minimum of fourteen years' residence and the attainment of the age of forty. That move effectively disfranchised the majority of the Uitlanders. (Independence, Kruger knew, could be lost as easily through the ballot box as at the mouth of a gun.) Those who chose might acquire the right—after two years' residence—to vote in elections to fill the newly created "second Volksraad."

One of the characteristics of South Africa was that the region, from the beginning, was less a multiracial society than a geographical expression. As the suffrage dispute indicated, South Africa was a territory in which people of different origins, language, color and religion coexisted without forming a community. Uitlanders and Boers regarded each other with hostile incomprehension. James Bryce wrote:

Hearing nothing but English spoken, seeing nothing all round them that was not far more English than Dutch … it was natural that the bulk of the Uitlanders should deem themselves to be in a country which had become virtually English and should see something unreasonable and even grotesque in the control of a small body of persons whom they deemed in every way their inferiors.

Flora Shaw, a redoubtable woman journalist, wrote in 1892 that:

Johannesburg at present has no politics. It is much too busy with material problems. It is hideous and detestable, luxury without order; sensual enjoyment without art; riches without refinement; display without dignity.

The Johannesburgers might have had no politics, but they had, or thought they had, grievances about the way in which they were governed. Among other things, they considered themselves overtaxed, and the Randlords objected to the official policy of granting monopolies for the manufacture of dynamite, which was indispensable for mining operations. In retrospect, the grievances appear small, even illusory. It was W. E. H. Lecky who argued that if the Uitlanders suffered the disadvantages of aliens, it was because they had deliberately placed themselves under a "detestable government" for the sake of making money. The fact of the matter was that the Transvaal was experiencing, in accelerated form, the wrenching dislocations of

Old Park Station, Johannesburg. The city developed rapidly after the Main Reef rocks were declared public diggings.

Bottom Simmonds Street, Johannesburg. At first dealings on the stock exchange took place in Simmonds Street between chains that closed the street to traffic.

Above President Kruger of the Transvaal. He tried hard to establish the Transvaal's independence of British jurisdiction.

Below left Joseph Chamberlain, British Colonial Secretary; he was strongly criticized for his handling of the Jameson Raid.

Below right Dr L. S. Jameson, leader of the abortive raid. The effect of the raid was to increase hatred between the British and Afrikaners, making the Boer War virtually inevitable.

sudden industrialization, coupled with an influx of immigrants that produced the effects of a population explosion. Furthermore, the capitalists were there to stay. It had seemed at one time that the gold fields might be exhausted so far as profitable extraction went.

Johannesburg and Pretoria were thirty miles apart. To travel that distance was to move from one world to another. Two nationalisms were in conflict—a cocky jingoism in Johannesburg, a farouche hatred of foreigners in Pretoria. The conflict became violent in 1895, when a plot was hatched in Johannesburg to support a rising led by a detachment of volunteers from Cecil Rhodes' chartered territory to the north. Certain aspects of that rising, known as the Jameson Raid, resemble a musical comedy staged in a casino, and English poet and traveler Wilfred Blunt called it a "gangrene of Colonial rowdyism." The consequences were tragic, however. Dr. Jameson's force was rounded up by a Boer commando unit fifteen miles from Johannesburg, and Jameson himself was handed over to the British government for trial.

Four members of the Johannesburg plotters were sentenced to death for their part in the abortive coup, but all four were allowed to ransom themselves. Cecil Rhodes, then Prime Minister of the Cape, was deeply implicated, and the finger of suspicion was also pointed at Joseph Chamberlain, the Colonial Secretary. There is no proof of Chamberlain's complicity, but the manner of the inquiry in London—"the lying-in-state at Westminster," as one skeptic described it—gave the strong impression that a great deal was being suppressed. The Kaiser, with characteristic impetuosity, sent a telegram of support to Kruger that momentarily lifted the episode to the level of an international incident. In South Africa, the raid sharpened the racial animosities between English and Afrikaner. It was, in fact, the preliminary skirmish that made the Boer War a virtual inevitability.

That war, when it came in 1899, was at bottom a conflict of nationalisms, fought to secure British paramountcy in South Africa. The conflict has frequently been portrayed as a consequence of capitalism—and in that sense, Johannesburg provided the impetus for a new development of Marxist theory. The progenitor of that theory was J. A. Hobson, who generalized what he understood to be the experience of South Africa into a theory of imperialism. (Lenin, building on Hobson's foundations, portrayed imperialism as the .last stage of capitalism.) But to the men who made the decisions at the time, the issue was one of politics rather than economics. To Sir Alfred Milner, the High Commissioner at the Cape, the importance of the gold strike lay in the fact that power was being transferred from the Cape Colony to the Transvaal Republic. In that shift he saw a danger to British power. As far as the British High Commissioner was concerned, the war was fought to preserve the imperial position and to destroy Afrikaner nationalism by force. Britain ultimately achieved a military victory in South

Africa, but in so doing it endowed the Afrikaners with a permanent resentment of British rule.

The history of Johannesburg might be regarded as a textbook demonstration of the errors in the cruder forms of the Marxist thesis. The city's wealth has grown continuously throughout the twentieth century; at the same time, its political importance has declined. It is the metropolis of South Africa, and yet it has never been a dominating center of politics. In this weakness may be seen the failure of the South African English to develop skills in the theory or practice of government.

For a brief period after the Boer War, Milner conducted the government of the Transvaal from Johannesburg. If he had been allowed to do so, he would have made Johannesburg the capital city.

The more I see of Pretoria, the more I am impressed by its unfitness to be the capital of anything. . . . It will certainly never be the capital of British South Africa, if that country is going to remain part of the Empire.

The British government refused to agree. In the opinion of Joseph Chamberlain, Johannesburg was disqualified because of the preeminence of the mining industry:

I do not wish to be understood as holding that the moral tone of Johannesburg society is lower than that of similar society elsewhere; my objection is that it necessarily lacks that diversity which in other great cities renders public opinion healthy and impartial.

And so the curious duality has continued: wealth lies in Johannesburg, but political decisions are made in Pretoria.

G. H. LE MAY

Above A Boer farmhouse in the Transvaal showing the influence of Dutch domestic architecture; and (*below*) a Boer family at rest. The discovery of gold in the Transvaal brought to an end the peaceful and isolated existence of the Boers.

As world frontiers shrink, a new spirit

Scramble for Africa

The competition, which had begun in the 1870s, between the Europeans for territory in Africa reached its height in the 1880s. The sentiment of imperialism was most marked in Britain, where books such as *Greater Britain* (1868) by Sir Charles Dilke (1843–1911) and *The Expansion of England* (1883) by Sir John Seeley (1834–95) gave the colonial idea a powerful stimulus, and it soon spread to Germany, France and Italy. Even William Gladstone, condemned by his Tory opponents as "a little Englander," could write of empire as "part of our patrimony," and the great colonial figure of the era, Cecil Rhodes (1853–1902), was a national hero without equal.

But the fascination that Africa held at the time was best exemplified by the activities of Leopold II, King of the Belgians. He poured all his personal fortune into acquiring millions of square miles of land in the Congo Basin. He was, however, unable to finance its development effectively, and his treatment of the natives was so barbaric that in 1908 the area was acquired from the King by his country and became the Belgian Congo. The French acquired far more territory but the sands of the Sahara covered most of it.

Leopold II of the Belgians.

The other nations of Europe, too—including Germany and Italy—seized what they could and laid hopeful claims to what they could not. Yet in a real sense the colonial scramble was a reflection of Europe's weakness. The older colonies were demanding an ever-increasing measure of self-government, and Africa and Asia were the only regions left where the European powers could demonstrate their power to their rivals and the rest of the world. What was really at issue was the role that the European states were to play in the coming century, and what was at stake had as much importance for Europe as it had for Africa and Asia. It was almost by accident that the local battles that took place between colonial officials of different nations during the rush for Africa did not lead to a European war.

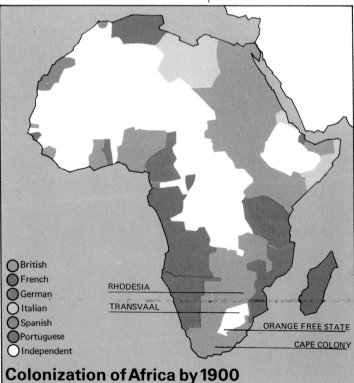

Colonization of Africa by 1900

- British
- French
- German
- Italian
- Spanish
- Portuguese
- Independent

RHODESIA

TRANSVAAL

ORANGE FREE STATE

CAPE COLONY

Africa and Asia

Two of the main areas of imperial dispute, southern Africa and the Nile Valley, were in Africa, the third, northern China, was in Asia. The sympathy of Germany—which had occupied Southwest Africa in 1884 and Tanganyika the following year—for the Boer (Afrikaner) Republic of the Transvaal, led, in 1896, to the first serious rift in Anglo-German relations—a coolness that continued until the end of the war waged by the British against the Boers from 1899 to 1902. The outcome of the Boer War was that the British came to control most of southern Africa, but the war had been fought at tremendous cost, both in men and in money, and was in a real sense a Pyrrhic victory, as the later history of South Africa was to show. It was also, despite its lack of success, the first war of decolonization. The war was unpopular in Britain almost from the beginning, and even the Prime Minister, Lord Salisbury, admitted that it was fought "for territory which will bring no profit and no power for England." As the death toll mounted and the war dragged on, public feeling turned increasingly against the continuation of the useless struggle. As a result the government was forced to negotiate a treaty that provided the Boers with a large measure of self-government.

British coolness toward Germany did not last, however, for Britain regarded the understanding between France and Russia to be a more serious threat to its imperial ambitions than it did the German participation in the Triple Alliance with Austria and Italy. Consequently, friendly relations with Germany were soon resumed.

After 1882, British troops occupied Egypt, and British proconsuls administered the country in much the same way that their counterparts did India. In 1885, however, the revolt led by the Moslem religious fanatic Mohammed Ahmed (*c.* 1843–85), known as the Mahdi, forced the British to withdraw garrisons from the Sudan, an area closely linked with Egypt by the waters of the Nile River. The rebuff that the British had suffered at the hands of the Mahdi was intensified by his massacre of the garrison, including General Charles "Chinese" Gordon, another great

hero of Victorian England, when he took Khartoum at the beginning of 1885.

In 1896, the knowledge that the French were sending an expedition eastward across Africa to the Sudan led Lord Salisbury to authorize a campaign to avenge the death of Gordon and overthrow the tyrannical rule of the Mahdi's successor, Abdullah et Taaisha, called the

General Charles Gordon; after a distinguished career in China he was killed at the siege of Khartoum.

Khalifa. General Kitchener defeated the Khalifa's dervishes at Omdurman in the first weeks of September, 1898, and proceeded up the Nile to the small town of Fashoda (already occupied by the French). For a few weeks it seemed that Britain and France would go to war over the future status of the Sudan, but the French ultimately gave way and agreed to withdraw. Kitchener was left as master of the Nile, but the humiliation imposed by the British at Fashoda rankled France for years to come.

At the same time the British were close to war with France's ally, Russia. The Tsar's armies were the only troops in the world who could be transported across the globe without running the gauntlet of British sea power, for after 1891 the thin steel line of the Trans-Siberian Railroad began to link European Russia with the farthest regions of Asia. Influential groups in St. Petersburg and Moscow wanted to carry the Russian frontier southward into Manchuria and Korea, and Lord Salisbury believed that Anglo-Russian friction in the Far East could only be resolved by a preliminary agreement defining the respective spheres of influence. The growing power of Japan, however, added a new and dangerous dimension to Far Eastern politics, as was to be shown at the beginning of the twentieth century by the Russo-Japanese War.

Bloody Sunday

The Haymarket riots were not an isolated example of violence in an industrial society. The general mood, both in Europe and in the United States, was more aggressive in the last years of the nineteenth century than it had been for several decades. Tension between classes mounted in the various countries and there were ugly instances of racial rioting. Peasant risings in Sicily led to the arrest of socialist leaders, and riots in Milan in 1898 caused the imposition of martial law in northern Italy. The 1894 Pullman strike in Illinois was in some ways a forecast of the troubles of 1896. In November, 1887, members of the royal family's household guard were called to London to clear Trafalgar Square of radical demonstrators; there were a hundred casualties—including two men so seriously injured that they later died. The bitterness caused by this incident (known as Bloody Sunday) led to greater militancy in the socialist movement in the remaining years before World War I. Anarchism and syndicalism and consequently the accomplishment of workers' control of industry through strike action hampered industrial developments in France and Spain as well.

Unrelated but no less violent outbreaks of violence occurred in France in 1898. These were prompted by the anti-Semitism of the French general staff, which had imprisoned a Jewish captain, Alfred Dreyfus (1859–1935), in 1894 and continued to deny him justice even when it became clear that he was the innocent victim of the army's dislike for Jews.

A new spirit of reaction was abroad among French intellectuals, which did much to contribute to the popularity of racist ideas. Count Joseph de Gobineau (1816–82), for example, had argued as early as 1854 that the races were unequal and different. Although few other French writers of the period were openly racist in their attitudes, the predominant tone in

Bloody Sunday; guardsmen arrive in Trafalgar Square to quell an early socialist riot.

French literary circles, so liberal early in the century, was now reactionary.

Racial envy also led to serious riots in a number of cities in the Hapsburg Empire, notably Prague, and throughout Eastern Europe the Jews were rapidly becoming the whipping boys of nationalist demagogues. In Russia, a forgery known as *The Protocols of the Elders of Zion* (1903) persuaded many that there was a Jewish conspiracy to take over the state—if not the whole world. *The Protocols* became the basis of most later anti-

The trial of Dreyfus; anti-Semitic attitudes were deeply rooted in the French army.

Semitic literature and were used as an excuse for pogroms by the Russian government. Even in Britain there were race riots in the early years of the twentieth century.

It was not only in France that liberal ideas were being abandoned by intellectuals. The ideas of the German philosopher Friedrich Nietzsche (1844–1900), first put forward in the 1880s, gained rapid popularity. Like Rousseau in France, Nietzsche was misunderstood and misrepresented. His followers read into his texts what they themselves wanted to read— a call for greater authority in the state, unrestrained by morality. It was a sorry prospect for the twentieth century.

The new internationalism

A number of writers and public figures were alive to the dangers of that warlike atmosphere, however, and were anxious to counter the hostile fragmentation of the European community. There had been a growing movement for international arbitration since 1872, when Gladstone submitted an Anglo-American quarrel to a five-nation tribunal. (The dispute involved compensation claimed by the United States for damage inflicted by the *Alabama* and the other commerce raiders built in Britain for the Confederate navy during the Civil War.) The foundation of an Interparliamentary Union in 1889—and the establishment of the Second Socialist International the same year— pointed the way toward closer

collaboration between different nations and peoples. So too did the decision to revive the Olympic Games after a lapse of more than fifteen hundred years (although only nine countries sent participants to the first modern Olympiad, held in Athens in 1896).

Alfred Nobel, the Swedish inventor of dynamite, who died in 1896, left his money in a trust fund that was to award annual prizes not only for literature and the sciences, but also for the encouragement of peace between nations. And in August of 1898, Tsar Nicholas II of Russia proposed an international conference to limit armaments and check the drift to war. The Tsar's motives were mixed— Russia was feeling the financial burden of maintaining a large fleet and a modern army—but a conference attended by representatives of twenty-six nations did gather at The Hague in May, 1899. Little was achieved on disarmament, but an International Court of Arbitration was established "to resolve disputes involving neither honor nor vital questions." Slowly and hesitantly the conscience of mankind was beginning to react against the shadow of war. It was ironical that this should be at the very time when Europe was preparing to fight a war on a scale larger than any previously imagined. The colonial squabblings in Africa, which were to leave Britain the master of half the continent, were a reflection of the jockeying for position among the powers that accorded ill with the internationalist aspirations they were proclaiming to the world.

The Olympic Games and The Hague peace conference attracted wide attention in the press, but another momentous gathering passed almost unnoticed. The Jewish people of Europe had taken a greater part in the political life of the Continent during the nineteenth century than ever before, but practicing Jews had attained cabinet rank only in Holland, France and Italy. Their share of political responsibilities, even in countries where they were not actively oppressed, was out of all proportion to the contribution they made to economic and intellectual life. By the 1890s a number of them sought to solve their dilemma by establishing a Jewish national state. And in the summer of 1897 the First Zionist Conference opened in Basel.

"Next year, in Jerusalem"

For nearly two thousand years, Jews in all corners of the globe have concluded the celebration of the Passover feast with the ritual line "Next year, in Jerusalem." That phrase expresses an ancient dream, one that centuries of persecution failed to extinguish. The Zionist dream—of one day returning to the ancestral homeland in Israel—became a tangible possibility on August 29, 1897, when the First Zionist Congress met in Basel, Switzerland. But for the singleminded dedication of Theodore Herzl, a Paris-based correspondent for a Viennese newspaper, the congress might never have been convened. Shocked out of his political complacency some five years earlier by the Dreyfus Affair, Herzl had begun to study, to discuss—and ultimately to promote—the idea of a separate Jewish state. The modern Zionist movement that Herzl founded was to survive his own untimely death, two world wars, and half a century of waiting before that dream was finally realized.

Dr. Theodore Herzl, who first suggested the idea of a separate Jewish state and called the Zionist Congress to work for this aim.

Opposite The Rabbi by Marc Chagall, who was a Russian Jew.

On August 29, 1897, Dr. Isidore Schalit, a man with a wide forehead and a small goatee, hoisted a strange-looking blue and white flag with the Star of David emblazoned on it above the Petit Casino in Basel. He then entered the large concert hall, mounted the dais, struck the podium with his gavel and solemnly informed his tense, expectant audience: "The Zionist Congress is open."

Dr. Schalit's pronouncement opened the First Zionist Congress in Basel, and it marked the first international conference of delegates of the Jewish people, who had been living a life of exile for two thousand years. The congress had been convened to determine the situation of Jews all over the world and to find a solution to what was popularly known as the "Jewish question." There were 202 delegates, hundreds of curious onlookers and dozens of journalists crowded together in the large hall when the congress came to an end on August 31. By that time the delegates had formulated one of the most momentous resolutions in the history of the Jewish people: "Zionism seeks to secure for the Jewish people a legally guaranteed home in Palestine."

That official resolution was to be the cornerstone of Zionist policy in the years to come and was to lead ultimately to the creation of the State of Israel. The resolution itself was largely the result of the untiring efforts of a Viennese journalist, Dr. Theodore Herzl, who had been advocating such a declaration since 1895. But the idea was not a new one. Indeed, ever since the dispersal of the Jewish people following Emperor Titus' destruction of the Second Temple in Jerusalem in A.D. 70, the hope of a return to Zion had dominated the prayers and dreams of the Jewish people. From time to time, various groups and individuals had tried to return to the Promised Land, but those attempts were isolated and doomed to failure. It was not until the nineteenth century that the Jews' centuries-old longing was transformed into a political and social philosophy, one that gave birth to a movement of renaissance and national liberation.

To a certain extent that movement was the result of the disappointment experienced by Jews who had tried to become assimilated into non-Jewish society. Their failure to do so prompted Jewish intellectuals such as Moses Hess and Peretz Smolenskin to preach a nebulous form of nationalism that advocated a return to Palestine. The movement was given impetus by a wave of anti-Semitism in Eastern Europe. In 1881 a series of bloody pogroms spread through tsarist Russia, beginning with a pogrom at Elisabethgard in April. A month later disturbances occurred in Kiev and Odessa, and by Christmastime more than 150 Jewish communities in Russia had been devastated by pogroms.

As a result of those pogroms, a Jewish doctor from Odessa named Leo Pinsker published a pamphlet entitled *Auto-Emancipation* in which he suggested that the Jews were deluding themselves about their future. According to Pinsker there was only one solution for them: the creation of a Jewish home in Palestine. Responding to the doctor's exhortations, a small group of students set out for Palestine, where they hoped to establish a settlement. With the generous help of Baron Edmund Rothschild, they created the first agricultural colonies in the land of Israel. Interest in Pinsker's proposal continued to grow, and in 1884 the inaugural congress of a new Jewish society was held at Katowice. That society was called *Hoveve Zion* (Lovers of Zion), and its primary aim was the return of the Jews to the Middle East and the acquisition of Palestine as a Jewish home.

The first man who dared to pronounce the words "Jewish state" was Dr. Theodore Herzl. Curiously, Herzl was the last Jew one would have expected to be nationalistic. He was thoroughly cosmopolitan and totally integrated into non-Jewish society, and

The entrance to the ancient Jewish ghetto in Prague. For two thousand years the Jewish people had been living in exile.

he had even gone so far as to propose that all children, Christian and Jewish alike, should have a common baptism to erase all differences of race. Herzl, who was employed as Paris correspondent of the great Viennese newspaper *Neue Freie Presse*, was a brilliant journalist who mixed with French writers and artists and lived and worked in a world where Jewish problems were rarely discussed. His majestic figure, deep magnetic eyes and long black beard were familiar in the corridors of the Palais Bourbon and the Parisian literary salons.

In 1894, a scandal known as the Dreyfus Affair shook Paris. Dreyfus' trial, which began on December 19, radically altered Herzl's life. The agitated doctor later wrote:

I became a Zionist as a result of the Dreyfus trial. I can still see the accused entering the court, dressed in his artillery uniform, decorated with gold stripes; the shouts of the frenzied crowd jamming the street in front of the Ecole Militaire still resound in my ears: "Death to the Jews!" Death to all the Jews because one of them was a traitor? And was he really a traitor? The Dreyfus case represents more than an error in the law. It expresses the desire of the vast majority of people in France: to condemn a Jew and, through him, all Jews. Since that time "down with the Jews" has become a war-cry.

Herzl found the trial profoundly disturbing. For two months he shut himself away in his home, and during that time he produced a pamphlet entitled *The Jewish State*. In it Herzl argued that Jews provoke anti-Semitism wherever they live and that their weakness makes them the scapegoats of every misfortune that occurs. Moreover, Herzl observed, the inner strength of Jews and their money make them the object of jealousy and hatred. Herzl's solution to the dilemma was a political one: the creation of a separate Jewish state, legally guaranteed by the civilized nations.

When Herzl showed his manuscript to a friend, the journalist Friedrich Schiff, the latter burst into tears. Herzl naturally assumed that his friend's tears were tears of emotion, but in reality Schiff was

crying because he believed that the doctor had gone mad. Schiff advised Herzl to see a psychiatrist, and in following his friend's advice Herzl met Dr. Max Nordau, a man of great spiritual and moral authority in the Jewish world. After reading *The Jewish State*, Nordau said to its author: "If you are mad, then that makes two of us. I am absolutely with you."

The idea of a separate Jewish state had been launched. Herzl, neglecting his other work, arranged to have his pamphlet printed and threw himself into the struggle. By then that struggle had become a political one, aimed at convincing heads of state that they should give the Jewish people a home in Palestine, then a part of the Ottoman Empire. At the same time Herzl sought to convince the Jews themselves that his solution was the right one. He was beset with difficulties and disappointments in his attempts to do so. Herzl did succeed in obtaining audiences with kings and princes, statesmen, ministers, royal councilors. He met Kaiser William, the Turkish Sultan, the King of Italy and the Pope as his fiery enthusiasm, his cultivation and his radiant belief opened all doors to him. Herzl's idea was that the Jewish people, if they made a tremendous financial effort, could succeed in finding the necessary money to restore the catastrophic finances of the Ottoman Empire. In return, the doctor asked for Turkish permission to create a Jewish national home in Palestine.

The kings of Europe received Herzl courteously, even warmly, and the Sultan himself appeared to be interested in the plan. It was only after several years of exhausting journeys and long negotiations that Herzl realized that all his efforts had been in vain. No one was going to let him have Palestine.

The Jewish reaction to his plan was an even greater disappointment for him. The Lovers of Zion had no faith in his solution; they were not interested in political action, and they were suspicious of this man who played the diplomat in royal courts. They continued to advocate their own solution: the colonization of Palestine, acre by acre, village after village. Moreover, the Lovers of Zion feared that Herzl's efforts would harm the Zionist movement by raising the issue in public. They were astounded and baffled by this proud, distinguished Jew who did not suffer from an inferiority complex and who dared to talk as an equal to kings. In their opinion, silence and discretion were the necessary conditions of success.

The Jews who favored integration also attacked Herzl, and he soon discovered that there were very few Jews in the world who were ready to demand their own state. The harried doctor did find one supporter, however: in an obscure synagogue in Plonsk, Poland, a ten-year-old boy declared that the true Messiah had just appeared on earth and that he would lead the children of Israel back to their country. The boy, who was to make the Zionist cause his personal religion, was named David Grin. He later changed his name to David Ben-Gurion.

In 1897, in spite of the persistent opposition to his

plans, Herzl decided to convene a Zionist Congress, one that would guarantee widespread Jewish support of Zionism. Difficulties arose almost immediately: the congress, which had originally been scheduled to convene in Munich, had to be postponed because of the violent opposition of the Bavarian rabbis, who embarked on a furious propaganda campaign against Zionism. Basel was hurriedly selected as an alternate location, and Herzl then turned his attention to the problem of rounding up delegates.

Herzl's fund-raising campaign was a dismal failure: only several tens of thousands of the world's 10 to 12 million Jews voted—and a mere 202 delegates actually attended the congress. Their ranks did include a number of distinguished personalities of the contemporary Jewish world, however—among them the writer Ahad Ha-am; the Jewish leaders Ussischkin, Sokolov, Motzkin and Sirkin; and the future historian, Joseph Klausner. The congress also included businessmen who happened to be on holiday in Switzerland, and some European university students who had been mandated by their countries to attend the congress.

As the date set for the opening of the congress approached, it appeared that the meeting hall would be half empty during the discussions. Such a brutal rebuff to the Zionists spelled disaster for the movement. And then a master stroke was devised by Herzl, an astute psychologist. He informed the delegates that they were to attend the inaugural meeting of the congress wearing evening dress and white tie—thus creating a most solemn and dignified atmosphere at the opening session. It was an inspiring sight: the huge hall, sober and elegant in appearance, the flags of Israel bedecking the walls, the feeling of the audience that they were taking part in a historic event. Herzl himself dazzled the delegates, and one witness of the occasion wrote:

It was quite extraordinary; what had happened? This man was not the Dr. Herzl that I had seen before, and with whom I was in discussion as recently as the night before. Before us stood a marvelous superior being, kingly in bearing and stature, with profound eyes in which could

be seen a quiet majesty and an indescribable sadness. This was not the elegant Dr. Herzl of Vienna; this man was a royal scion of the House of David, risen from the dead, clothed in legend, fantasy and beauty. Everyone remained seated, holding their breath, as if in the presence of a miracle. . . . Then, a burst of applause filled the hall; for fifteen minutes, the delegates clapped, shouted and waved their handkerchiefs. The dream of two thousand years was just about to come true; it was as if Messiah, son of David, had appeared amongst us; and in the middle of this joyous tumult, I was filled with an overpowering desire to cry out at the top of my voice so that everyone would hear: "*Yehi hamelech* Long live the King!"

Herzl, calm and solemn, walked up to the podium. As newly elected President of the Congress, he proceeded to make his inaugural address, elaborating on his main idea: the creation of a Jewish state in Palestine. Max Nordau, Herzl's faithful friend and colleague, spoke next. He described the situation of the Jews throughout the world, and that topic served as the theme of most of the speeches.

The last day of the meeting, August 31, was devoted to questions of finance. Before adjourning,

Early settlers in Ekron, Palestine. Small groups of Jews had gone to Palestine to set up agricultural colonies before the idea of a Jewish state was seriously considered.

The Second Zionist Congress in Basel in 1898. The Zionist Congress became an institution in Jewish life and took place annually.

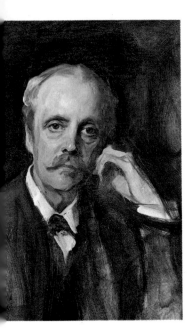

Arthur Balfour. The Balfour Declaration of 1917 promised British support for the creation of a Jewish national home in Palestine.

the delegates decided on the creation of a Jewish Colonial Bank and a Jewish National Fund—the *Keren Kayemet Leisrael*—which was empowered to purchase plots of land in Palestine and hand them out to Jewish immigrants.

The congress had tremendous repercussions throughout the Jewish world. Zionism had replaced the nostalgia and ineffectual hopes of a return to Zion with a clearly defined program that crystallized all previous efforts and showed world Jewry the road to follow. The struggle was far from over, however. During the years that followed, Herzl traveled across Europe and the Middle East, attempting without success to arouse interest in the Zionist cause among Europe's political powers. Herzl—who had given up journalism to devote himself full-time to the political struggle and to the publication of the Zionist journal *Die Welt,* which he had launched—was frequently in financial difficulty during this period. The Zionist Congress had become an institution in Jewish life, however, and it took place regularly year after year.

The first great crisis of Zionism occurred in 1903. On the evening of Easter Sunday, an atrocious pogrom broke out in Kishinev, Russia. Before it ran its course, 45 men, women and children were massacred, 1,000 were wounded and more than 1,500 houses were destroyed. Horrified by the catastrophe, the leaders of the Zionist movement began to cast about for a speedy solution to the Jewish problem. Herzl allowed himself to be talked into accepting a proposition made by the British government for Jewish immigration to Kenya (a plan that the Zionists mistakenly called "The Uganda Plan").

Dr. Chaim Weizmann, who took over the leadership of the Zionist movement after World War I.

Herzl considered that plan little more than one that would deal only with the most urgent problems. He put this proposition before the Zionist Congress that was in session in Basel, and chaos erupted at the meeting. The principal leaders of the revolt were the Russian delegates, for whom it was a case of "Palestine or nothing." Herzl, red with anger, got up in the midst of the violent discussion and quoted a famous line from the Bible: "If I forget thee, O Jerusalem, may my right hand wither." He managed to convince the Russian delegation not to walk out of the congress, but the Uganda Plan was doomed. A commission sent to Kenya by the congress reached a negative conclusion, and the plan was finally dropped by the Zionist organization.

In 1904, Herzl, who had become sick and worn out by his strenuous efforts to promote a Jewish state, died at the age of forty-four. His death came as a tragic shock to the Zionist movement. At Plonsk, David Ben-Gurion wrote to his friend Fuchs: "The loss is as great and as cruel as the eternal suffering of a race as unfortunate as ours.... The sun has gone down, but its light shines as brightly as ever." A new crisis threatened the very existence of the Zionist movement. Groups and associations began to break away from the main body of the movement, which Herzl's untimely death had left leaderless. The English Zionist leader, Israel Zangwill, left the Zionist movement in order to found the Jewish Territorial Organization. Zangwill's organization, whose mission was to find land in Palestine or elsewhere suitable for the founding of a Jewish colony, did not return to the main Zionist movement until 1917.

That year—1917—was to be the great turning point in the history of Zionism. In 1917 a new man, one who had not previously played a leading role in the movement, appeared on the scene. That man was Chaim Weizmann, a Russian-born chemist who had settled in Manchester, England. Weizmann worked for the British government during World War I. At its height, he solved England's acute shortage of explosives by discovering synthetic acetone, a chemical that made the continuing manufacture of munitions possible. The president of the committee for war munitions, David Lloyd George, was said to be grateful to Weizmann and to want to reward him for his valuable work. Weizmann asked him "to do something for his people." It happened that Britain was seeking the support of the Jewish community at this time and Lloyd George, then Prime Minister, was only too happy to oblige. His government therefore proposed the formation of a Jewish national home in Palestine, although this was contradictory to assurances that had already been given to various Arab leaders about the future of the Arab regions of the Ottoman Empire. (The creation of a national home in Palestine –under British protection—would also enable His Majesty's government to control that country.) England's offer was made in the middle of the war, at a time when it was easy to promise land

and countries that had not even been conquered. Thus, on November 2, 1917, Arthur James Balfour, British Secretary of State for Foreign Affairs, wrote a letter to Lord Rothschild that read:

His Majesty's government views with favour the establishment in Palestine of a national home for the Jewish people, and will use their best endeavours to facilitate the achievement of this object, it being clearly understood that nothing shall be done which may prejudice the civil and religious rights of existing non-Jewish communities in Palestine, or the rights and political status enjoyed by Jews in any other country.

I should be grateful if you would bring this declaration to the knowledge of the Zionist Federation.

The Balfour Declaration was received with both joy and surprise by the Jewish world. Surprise—since it far exceeded the wildest dreams of the Zionist leaders. For the first time, Zionist leaders really began to believe in their movement; they could suddenly entertain the hope that Herzl's dream would actually come true. The Zionist leaders' rejoicing over the Balfour Declaration was premature, however. Many believed that the Jewish state would be handed to them as soon as the war was over, and few saw clearly what lay ahead. Among those who did remain cool and calm was Ben-Gurion, who wrote:

England has not given us back Palestine. Even if the whole country were conquered by England, it would not be ours just because Great Britain agreed to it and because the other countries gave their assent.... Only the Hebrew people themselves can transform their right to the country into a tangible fact, and they must, with their bodies and with their souls, with their strength and with their capital, build a National Home for themselves, and achieve their national redemption.

At the end of World War I, Great Britain obtained a mandate over Palestine. The Jewish National Home became a reality. During the thirty years that followed, Weizmann and Ben-Gurion became the two great leaders of the Zionist world; yet their points of view on the best methods of creating a Jewish state were very different. Dr. Weizmann appeared as the natural successor to Herzl; he believed that the Jewish people would achieve their aims through diplomatic action vis-à-vis the great powers—in this instance, Great Britain. Ben-Gurion, on the other hand, was a realist. He advocated mass immigration to Palestine, reclamation of the land, the founding of new towns and colonies, and the creation of a Jewish economic, social and military force in Palestine itself. He realized that Great Britain's interests in the Arab world would eventually lead to a reevaluation of England's pro-Zionist policy—and might even cause the British government to change that policy radically. For this reason the Jews had to establish themselves firmly in the country and be prepared to fight not only the Arabs but also the British.

Tension between Jews and Arabs increased over the years, and bloody clashes broke out between the two communities in 1920–21, 1929–30 and 1936. In 1936 the British change of policy in favor of the Arabs that Ben-Gurion had long feared took place.

At the end of World War II the Jewish community in Palestine had increased to 600,000 people. It now found itself in conflict with both Great Britain and the Arabs, and this conflict increased in intensity. In addition to clashes between Jews and Arabs, anti-British terrorism began to develop. Finally, faced with a situation that had gotten entirely out of hand, Great Britain decided to evacuate Palestine and leave it to the people living there.

"At Basel I created the Jewish state," wrote Herzl in 1897. "If I stated that in public today, it would be received with laughter all over the world. Perhaps in five years time, however, and certainly within fifty, the whole world will understand."

On November 29, 1947—fifty years after the First Zionist Congress—the General Assembly of the United Nations voted in favor of the creation of a Jewish state in Palestine.

MICHAEL BAR-ZOHAR

A view of Jerusalem painted by Edward Lear in the latter half of the nineteenth century.

Urban developments

Although industry changed the character of all of Western Europe and the eastern United States by the start of the 1880s, it was only in Britain that town dwellers outnumbered the rural population. Two-thirds of the French people and seventy-two percent of the inhabitants of the United States still lived in communities of less than two thousand in 1880. Even by the end of the century the proportion in both countries was no more than sixty percent in rural settlements to forty percent in the towns. Conditions were only slightly different in the German Empire where the percentage of the urban population rose from 41.4 in 1880 to 54.4 in 1900. Elsewhere, despite heavy industrialization, most families continued to live in the country until the turn of the century.

By 1880 factories and mass production had imposed a common pattern of life, predominantly urban in form, upon most of these countries. That pattern was reflected in the architecture of the period, as the designs of public buildings and private houses sank to a nadir of unenterprising pretentiousness. The town halls of Victorian England were an acknowledged aesthetic joke, but such drab uniformity of ugliness was not the monopoly of any one country or continent. Buildings such as the Hôtel de Ville in Paris, the Metropolitan Museum of Art in New York, the vast Law Courts in London and the civic buildings along the Ringstrasse in Vienna

The Metropolitan Museum of Art, New York, which rapidly became the world's most extensive art collection.

were all in their different ways pastiches of earlier styles, alien to their environments. Some of them were, however, magnificent visually, and they expressed a real civic and national pride.

Private dwellings in most of the industrialized nations lost much of their character, largely as a result of the low cost of public transport, which enabled heavy materials to be carried over long distances, thereby destroying the local variations in construction that harmonized with the landscape. Brick walls and gray slate roofs invaded both the suburbs of the larger cities and the villages beyond as speculative builders followed the railroad lines deeper and deeper into the countryside. The threat of urban blight made legislation necessary to protect Epping Forest, near London, the Forest of Fontainebleau, outside Paris and the Vienna Woods.

There were a number of writers and artists in different countries who reacted against the encroachments of industry. In England, for example, William Morris (1834–96) sought to improve the standard

of furniture manufacture and in 1887 founded a Society for the Protection of Ancient Buildings. There were few manufacturers who shared Morris' naive aesthetic socialism, however, and the domestic arts suffered as much as architecture from urban uniformity. Yet it is not possible to condemn the public taste of the period

William Morris, poet and painter, whose designs for furniture and books helped improve public taste.

completely; its very uniformity shows that certain basic principles had come to be universally accepted and the buildings of the period provided better living conditions than most of their inhabitants had been used to.

In general, furniture manufacturers sacrificed good design for cheaper production costs and substituted decoration for craftsmanship. The clothing traditionally worn by various workers was giving way to cheap suits imitative

of those worn by clerical workers. All over Western Europe national costumes rapidly became archaic curiosities. Like folk music, they were preserved only by enthusiasts who had a sense of their people's heritage. Technological advance confounded and confused all the arts as machines turned out more and more commodities to standard patterns. In the 1830s Ralph Waldo Emerson had complained: "Things are in the saddle and ride mankind." The pace of change in the next five decades served only to underline the frightening wisdom of his words.

At the time, however, men believed that they were more civilized than ever before, and perhaps they were right. Slavery, except in the darkest recesses of the hidden continents, had been abolished by the 1880s. There was no killing in the name of religious conformity, and, west of the Asian border, there were virtually no political prisoners. Almost every government had accepted an obligation to mitigate the rigors of poverty, and advocates of penal reform had secured the abolition of the more barbaric punishments, although it is sometimes forgotten that the last public hanging in Britain—one of the most "advanced" countries—took place in the summer of 1868.

Evolution and education

The most encouraging improvement both in Europe and in the United States at the end of the century was in education. In 1850, over one-third of the adult population of Britain and the German states and half of the adult population of France and Belgium were illiterate. Standards were far lower in southern and eastern Europe, and even in the United States well over a million adult whites could neither read nor write. However, great advances were made in the latter years of the century: the state assumed responsibility for primary education in Austria in 1868, Britain in 1870, Germany in 1872, Switzerland in 1874, Italy in 1877, France and Holland in 1878 and Belgium in 1879. Almost everywhere the role of the Churches in education—for so long dominant—was gradually lessening and even ceasing. The conspicuous failure of private charity and the voluntary system to provide for the needs of an advanced society

The Hôtel de Ville in Paris; large-scale architecture in the late nineteenth century consisted chiefly of revivals of earlier styles.

Andrew Carnegie, who made a great fortune in steel and used much of it to endow libraries and universities in the United States and Britain.

led to a rapid growth in the power of the state. The number of high schools in the United States grew rapidly after the Civil War, and the establishment of the United States Office of Education in 1867 tacitly recognized federal responsibilities for teaching facilities, even if administration was left primarily to the individual state authorities.

By 1900, illiteracy had fallen to less than five percent in Britain, France, Germany and Scandinavia, and to ten percent for the total population (black and white) of the United States. But in Russia, the eastern provinces of Austria-Hungary and the Balkan, Italian and Iberian peninsulas, the proportion of illiterates remained high. At the turn of the century half the population of Europe was still unable to read or write. The figure was far higher in Latin America and Asia, while in Africa literacy was a rarity.

The spread of literacy in Europe and the United States had profound social consequences. A "popular" press was created in Britain, France, Germany and Italy, while in the United States, William Randolph Hearst (1863–1951) was merely the most successful of a number of newspaper proprietors. Popular journalism was introduced into America by Joseph Pulitzer (1847–1911) in the early 1880s (and was soon carried to extremes by Hearst). More newspapers were sold than was ever believed possible, and twice as many books were printed in 1900 as in 1880. Free public libraries seemed a natural corollary to free public education,

and many were established by local authorities.

In the last decade of the century industrial magnates came forward as patrons of the new mass culture. The Scottish-born American steel king, Andrew Carnegie (1835–1919), endowed libraries on a large scale. Over 2,800 Carnegie libraries were set up in America alone between 1889 and 1919; the British people also benefited from his philanthropy. Carnegie's example was quickly followed by other millionaires on both sides of the Atlantic, although many preferred to limit their endowments to higher education—presumably in the belief that their nations needed trained engineers, administrators and technicians in order to maintain a high level of prosperity in an increasingly competitive world.

The new luxury: leisure

Leisure habits were also changing by the second half of the nineteenth century. With the spread of organized work, sports became less casually haphazard, for both participants and spectators had begun to expect regulation and control in their recreation as well as in their daily life. The establishment of the Football Association in London in 1863 was of historic importance for Britain and the world; within half a century, the Association's code was to become England's first universally accepted cultural export since William Shakespeare.

The game ceased to be a preserve of the English upper classes in the 1870s when local churches began to organize Association Football (soccer) clubs as healthy alternatives to less morally acceptable pastimes. Professional players were authorized by the Association in 1885, and three years later twelve clubs formed the first league. At the same time the version of football originally played at Rugby school was growing in popularity (although the relative sophistication of its rules denied it the mass appeal of soccer). The English Rugby Union was established in 1871, and the first international match (between England and Scotland) was played that same year—a full season before the first soccer international. Significantly, American football became an organized game in the same period. The first intercollegiate

William Gilbert Grace, whose skill made cricket a popular sport in most parts of the British Empire and almost a symbol of British sovereignty.

match was played between Rutgers and Princeton in 1869, and a code of rules was drawn up in 1873.

Summer sports were more highly organized in the United States than in Europe. The rules of baseball had been drawn up in 1858, and even before the Civil War fifty clubs were playing a regular series of matches, watched by admission-paying spectators. Professional teams appeared after 1869, and in 1876 the National League was founded. Lawn tennis was recognized as a sport in 1877 (the year in which the first Wimbledon championship was held) and the United States Lawn Tennis Association was formed in 1881. Golf, which had become very popular in Britain in the 1880s, was introduced into Pennsylvania in 1887.

Cricket had long been the national sport of England, but it took the skill of Dr. W. G. Grace (1848–1915)—in the years between

1870 and 1886—to bring spectators into the cricket grounds in large numbers. The first team to leave England visited the United States and Canada in 1859, but the sport never took root in America and it was left to the Australians to raise it to international level. The first test matches between England and Australia were played at Melbourne in 1876–77, but a far greater stimulus to the game sprang from the Australian team's successful visit to London in 1878. There had been cricket clubs in Paris, Berlin, Frankfurt and other European cities from the early 1860s, and a successful "cricket week" was held at Hamburg in 1865. But from 1878 onward cricket became almost a symbol of British sovereignty. Cricket fields, like the roads of classical Rome, were to survive the collapse of the Empire, a legacy for later generations.

American imperialism

Although America appeared less imperialist than the great powers of Europe, this was mainly because rapid settlement of the enormous expanses of the Midwest and the Pacific coast had absorbed its energies. By the end of the century the United States was looking abroad for the opportunity to expand its influence. The younger Republican Party politicians, backed by the Hearst press, wanted to expand in the Pacific. At the same time the Republicans were protesting the brutally repressive colonial administration of Spanish Cuba, where an insurrection broke out in 1895. The mysterious loss of the American battleship *Maine* in Havana in February, 1898, provided the opportunity that many Americans had been waiting for.

The United States in the Caribbean

FLORIDA 1819

○ United States territory

○ United States military occupation

By the 1898 Treaty of Paris the United States also gained the Philippines and Guam

CUBA 1898-1902

BAHAMAS

CAICOS ISLANDS

HAITI 1914-1934

CAYMAN ISLANDS

Guantanamo 1898

PUERTO RICO 1898

JAMAICA

SWAN ISLAND 1863

DOMINICAN REPUBLIC 1916-1924

"Remember the *Maine!*"

After the Civil War, America turned inward and became self-absorbed with such matters as settling the Great Plains and developing industry. A few voices, however, spoke out for imperialism and expansion, notably the taking over of the Spanish colonies of Cuba, Puerto Rico, and the Philippines. When the Cubans rebelled against Spain, the U.S.S. Maine was sent to Havana to safeguard American lives. Mysteriously it exploded, and with the brief war that followed the United States took the first steps toward becoming a world power.

Admiral George Dewey, who led the U.S. Pacific fleet.

Opposite The charge of the Rough Riders at San Juan hill, led by Theodore Roosevelt.

On February 15, 1898, the United States battleship *Maine* blew up in Havana harbor, with a loss of more than 260 officers and men. The men on the *Maine* displayed exemplary calm. Captain Sigsbee cabled: "Public opinion should be suspended until further report." The official board of inquiry that reported at the end of March attributed the explosion to a submarine mine, but declined to make any accusations. By then, however, it was too late. Public opinion could not be "suspended," and war fever, encouraged by the yellow press, outran sober considerations of international responsibility. By the end of April the United States was at war with Spain; the sinking of the *Maine* had provided the excuse for war and an opportunity for overseas expansion. A new era in American national development had begun.

Cuba in 1898 was the scene of a bitter and bloody conflict between the Spanish colonial regime and Cuban rebels championing independence. Whereas Spain had lost the bulk of her American colonies in the early nineteenth century, her Caribbean possessions—Cuba and Puerto Rico—remained loyal, their commitment to plantation slavery carrying with it a commitment to continued colonial rule. But in the course of the century resentments against Spanish rule multiplied, culminating in the Ten Years War (1868–78), in which the independence movement was temporarily crushed. In 1895 revolt flared up again. The Spanish government, facing rampant guerrilla warfare, resorted to harsh repressive measures. General Valeriano Weyler, who was known as "the Butcher," herded the civilian population into concentration camps to isolate rebel units in the countryside.

Meanwhile, the United States watched these developments taking place ninety miles off the Florida coast. American interest in Cuba stemmed from a variety of considerations—historic, economic, strategic and moral.

American territorial designs on Cuba were as old as the Republic itself. In 1825, John Quincy Adams had asserted that the annexation of Cuba "will be indispensable to the continuance and integrity of the Union." As the expanding Republic absorbed Louisiana, Florida and Texas, plans for adding Cuba were shelved but not forgotten. In the 1850s the Pierce administration considered purchasing the island, now a major sugar producer, from the Spanish government, but northern opinion, because of the slavery question, opposed the idea. Again in the late 1860s, the slavery question settled, American expansionists included the Caribbean in their ambitions, but their cause lacked popular support and their only achievement was instead the acquisition of Alaska.

The American people had enough challenges at home. Overseas commitments did not interest them. The South experienced the ordeal of reconstruction; the Great Plains were being settled. Questions of governmental corruption and currency reform dominated politics. In foreign affairs, the post-Civil War years were characterized by an isolationism that even excluded American participation in the International Red Cross.

During these years American population and industry grew at a tremendous rate. Immigration from Western Europe provided an annual influx of manpower that reached a peak of 640,000 in 1882. A continental railway system was completed. By 1890 the Census Bureau was able to announce that the frontier—for generations the symbol of the expanding Republic—had finally "disappeared." The early 1890s also saw the end of the United States' unfavorable trade balance; by 1898 exports of manufactured goods exceeded imports by six million and, as the foreign debt was redeemed, the gap between debtor and creditor status was closing quickly. American steel production had surpassed that of the British and Pittsburgh steel was

underselling Sheffield steel in world markets. In 1897 the State Department Bureau of Foreign Commerce announced that "what may be termed an American invasion of the markets of the world" had begun. That same year, American foreign investments stood at $700 million, and were concentrated in Canada, Mexico and in Cuba, where investments in sugar plantations were over $30 million and rising rapidly.

The United States had, with its vast resources, become an industrial power that could rival the powers of the Old World. By the 1880s, a significant group of American politicians and writers were agitating for new policies to meet this new situation. They demanded the development of a merchant marine and a battle fleet capable of maintaining an American presence on the high seas; the establishment of overseas naval bases and the building of a canal across Central America; and the aggressive pursuit and protection of overseas markets for American commerce. Even President Cleveland, who adhered to the tradition of isolation, recognized the "irresistible tide of commercial expansion," and it was during his administration that appropriations were made for five new cruisers and two battleships —one of them the ill-fated u.s.s. *Maine*.

With the 1890s, in both Europe and America, came imperialist ideas and policies. These included a desire for commercial and territorial expansion, a concern for naval power and a belief in the racial superiority of whites. In the United States, academics argued that the white race enjoyed a unique political genius and had an obligation to introduce political civilization to the barbaric races. Advocates of a strong colonial policy also quoted Admiral Alfred Thayer Mahan, the influential historian, who stressed the importance of sea-power in history and urged a big navy, a merchant marine, and an Isthmian canal.

Some politicians—chiefly Republicans—responded to these ideas and tried to implement them. James G. Blaine, Republican presidential candidate in 1884 and Secretary of State (1889–92), worked for a canal across the Central American Isthmus under United States control, strove to increase American trade with Latin America and anticipated that the United States would eventually have to annex Cuba and Puerto Rico. Senator Henry Cabot Lodge in 1895 castigated the administration's policy of "retreat and surrender" in foreign affairs, urging United States' control of Samoa and Hawaii, absorption of Canada and a naval presence in the Caribbean. The young Theodore Roosevelt denounced the "animal sloth and ease" which he believed marred American society. Roosevelt, along with Cabot Lodge, John Hay and Henry Adams, formed the nucleus of a small but vociferous group dedicated to imperialism and expansion.

Domestic and international events encouraged this trend in the years immediately before matters came to a head in Havana. At home, economic depression produced Populism, the radical demands of which alarmed conservative groups. To some observers this underscored the need for new overseas markets and revitalized trade. In addition, expansion was seen as a means of diverting attention from internal troubles and fostering national unity. After the bitterly fought presidential election of 1896, the *Richmond Times* argued that war over Cuba "would undoubtedly have a wholesome effect in knitting the bonds of the Union closer together and in allaying sectional and class strife."

On the international front, the major European powers were setting an example of imperialist expansion in Africa and Asia, and clashes with European and non-European powers projected the United States onto the world stage and encouraged growing confidence and belligerency. Disputes with

Roosevelt and his Rough Riders relaxing after the capture of San Juan hill.

Germany over Samoa, with Great Britain over fishing rights, with Chile over the deaths of two American sailors in Valparaiso—all produced jingoistic outbursts in the United States. In 1891 only a full apology from the Chilean government averted a war which many Americans—notably Roosevelt, who earned himself the nickname of "the Chilean volunteer"—were eager to undertake. In 1895 the United States government intervened in the boundary dispute between Venezuela and British Guiana, warning Britain that, under the Monroe Doctrine, the United States would not permit European interference in the western hemisphere, where "the United States is practically sovereign and its fiat is law . . . ."

Thus, when the Cuban War of Independence erupted in February, 1895, the United States had several reasons for taking notice. Cuba's strategic location in the Caribbean was emphasized by the plans for an Isthmian canal. Some Americans therefore wanted Cuba under the American flag; at the very least, European rivals had to be kept out. On the material side, American investments in sugar, railroads and mining demanded protection, and continued civil war on the island seriously affected American trading interests. On the moral side, there was widespread sympathy for the Cuban rebels, fighting for national independence against an oppressive colonial regime. Protestant opinion was hostile to Roman Catholic Spain (though not to Roman Catholic Cuba) and looked to the overthrow of "the intolerable yoke of Spanish oppression"

as the curtain-raiser to Protestant missionary endeavor in the island. Opinion generally was agitated by sensational press disclosures of Spanish atrocities, as Joseph Pulitzer's *New York World* and William Randolph Hearst's *New York Journal* battled to gain readers. In this climate, some politicians saw "free Cuba" as a likely vote winner; others, like the Democrat Henry Watterson, looked further and saw additional bonuses: "We escape the menace and peril of socialism and agrarianism . . . by a policy of colonization and conquest."

These varied motives produced a series of resolutions and speeches in Congress calling for the recognition of the Cuban rebels' belligerency, or for the annexation of this "natural part of our geographical domain." The Republican platform in the 1896 presidential campaign promised a vigorous assertion of the Monroe Doctrine and the pursuit of peace and independence in Cuba. The victory of the Republican William McKinley over the Democrat William Jennings Bryan represented a victory for domestic conservatism and overseas expansion; although McKinley promised "there will be no jingo nonsense under my administration," he consented to Hawaiian annexation, gave the go-ahead for the Nicaraguan Canal and promoted committed expansionists like Theodore Roosevelt within the administration.

In fact, war was nearly averted. Late in 1897 a new Spanish administration withdrew General Weyler, used the concentration camps less and agreed to give Cuba a measure of autonomy. "No

American generals Miles, Shafter and Wheeler conferring during the siege of Santiago de Cuba, July, 1898. Old Civil War rivalries were apparent among the generals.

139

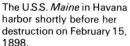
The U.S.S. *Maine* in Havana harbor shortly before her destruction on February 15, 1898.

war with Spain—all indications point to peace" declared the *Washington Post* on November 6. But early in the new year, pacifist hopes—and jingoist fears—were confounded. A leak from the Spanish Embassy in Washington implied criticism of McKinley as a weak glutton for popularity; a report by Senator Proctor highlighted the abuses of Spanish rule in Cuba; and, most important of all, the U.S.S. *Maine*, sent to protect American lives and property in Cuba, was blown out of the water in Havana harbor. War fever swept the country. Congress appropriated $50 million for national defense, and troops were mobilized. The popular cry was:

> Remember the *Maine*!
> To Hell with Spain!

European and papal diplomatic appeals and the readiness of the Spanish government to grant an immediate armistice in Cuba could not counteract the force of indignant public opinion in the United States. McKinley, who later admitted he could have secured Spanish withdrawal from Cuba without a war, bowed to pressure; tired and overworked, he requested congressional authority to order United States forces into action.

One important group in American society did not succumb to hysteria: big business. As the "new imperialism" of the 1890s developed, American

business leaders were more concerned with the domestic issues of economic depression and Populism. Overseas markets were desirable, but there was no guarantee that armed conquest would provide them. Throughout the Cuban crisis, business leaders feared that war would upset the current economic revival and undermine the currency. The peaceful attitude of the commercial and banking journals contrasted sharply with the belligerency of the yellow press. Wall Street stocks declined when war seemed likely and climbed when hopes of a peaceful settlement were raised.

Even American interests in Cuba itself were divided over the war issue. Some, facing bankruptcy, favored intervention as the only solution; others, such as planters who had managed to police their estates with company guards, or the iron and manganese miners whose operations had been relatively unaffected, regarded war and intervention as an evil to be avoided.

Opinions soon changed, however, as the war got under way. The Spanish navy was no match for its more up-to-date American counterpart. Admiral George Dewey at Hong Kong had received orders that, in the event of war, he was to attack the Spanish fleet and possessions in the Philippines. The orders had been cabled, on his own responsibility, by the Assistant Secretary of the Navy,

The first hoisting of the Stars and Stripes on Cuban soil, June 11, 1898. Despite poor provisioning, illness and disagreements among the general staff, the conquest of Cuba was surprisingly rapid.

Fighting in the Philippines; the Philippines provided a useful base for American interests in the Far East.

New York newspaper report of the sinking of the *Maine*.

temperature, the poor provisioning and the ravages of malaria and dysentery took a greater toll than Spanish bullets. By the time the enemy surrendered on July 26, seven thousand men had died, nine out of ten from disease. Nearly half of Roosevelt's six hundred Rough Riders were dead, wounded or sick.

Despite the failings of the army, the Spaniards had been easily defeated. But the victory brought new problems and unforeseen consequences. Cuba, Puerto Rico and the Philippines were in American hands. The Cuban intervention had been covered by the Teller Amendment, which disclaimed United States annexation of the island, but opinion was sharply divided over the future of these territories. Business, which had been hostile toward the war, found that the economy had not suffered any ill effects. In fact, the United States had acquired a position in the Far East that might help to protect American commercial interests in that region and open up the prospective Chinese market. Many Christian groups saw the hand of Providence in the American victories and welcomed the chance to evangelize the Philippines. Since the Philippines could not be handed back to Spain, nor allowed to fall into French or German hands, and because "they were unfit for self-government—and would soon have anarchy and misrule over there worse than Spain's was," McKinley therefore decided that they would have to be retained and civilized. Under the treaty, Spain therefore ceded the Philippines, which became the United States' first full-fledged colony. Hawaii, meanwhile, had been annexed and granted self-government within the Union. Guam was held as a naval base. Cuba remained under military rule until 1902, when self-government was given under the terms of the Platt Amendment. This amendment was incorporated into the new Cuban constitution that empowered the United States to intervene in the island whenever it pleased for "the protection of life, property, and individual liberty."

This settlement did not go uncontested in the United States. Cleveland and Bryan were prominent among those in the Senate who opposed ratification of the peace treaty. They criticized acquiring subject populations without civil rights, deplored involvement in great-power rivalry, and attacked administration policy. After a bitter debate in the Senate the treaty was approved by fifty-seven to twenty-seven—the necessary two-thirds majority.

Already the problems of colonial rule were becoming evident. The Filipino nationalists had fought against the Spaniards and did not want to exchange one imperial master for another, and therefore continued to resist the Americans for the next three years. The American forces found themselves fighting the same war the Spaniards had. In Cuba, the three-year military protectorate realized some notable public services and medical improvements—in particular the conquest of malaria—but could not create a viable and satisfactory political settlement. In the face of continued instability, the

Theodore Roosevelt, and the Secretary of the Navy allowed them to stand. Dewey proceeded to Manila and engaged the Spanish fleet at 5 A.M. on May 1, initiating the battle with the order, "You may fire when you are ready, Gridley." The Spanish fleet was destroyed with 381 Spanish seamen killed. There were no American casualties.

In the Caribbean, Cuba was blockaded, and the Spanish fleet bottled up in Santiago harbor. An expeditionary force of 18,000 men mobilized at Tampa, Florida, amid confusion, sickness and administrative corruption, included the First Volunteer Cavalry Regiment, or "Rough Riders," recruited by Theodore Roosevelt, now the acting second-in-command. In June, Cuba was invaded, and a disorganized campaign began. Roosevelt gratified his taste for heroics by leading a victorious charge up San Juan hill—and Admiral Cervera's wooden-decked ships were blown out of the water when they tried to make for the open sea. One American was killed and four hundred Spaniards were killed or wounded. In other respects the war went less well. The American commander suffered from heat prostration, and his generals indulged in old Civil War rivalries. In the ranks, the extremes of

Americans intervened again in 1906, under the terms of the Platt Amendment. Another three years of military rule failed to implant democracy or endear American tutelage to the Cubans.

By then, imperial ardor had cooled. Roosevelt, becoming President on the assassination of McKinley in 1901, rejected demands for the outright annexation of Cuba in 1906. Annexation had gone out of style. But the United States' new naval and imperial commitments were self-perpetuating. An Isthmian canal was all the more essential, and when Colombia proved uncooperative over the Panama route through Colombian territory, Roosevelt aided a provincial revolt that created the independent state of Panama. The completion of the Panama Canal in 1914 focused attention on the Caribbean, where the American intervention in Cuba was paralleled by later interventions in the Dominican Republic, Haiti, Nicaragua and Panama itself. Roosevelt justified interventions on the grounds of forestalling European involvement in areas of instability whereas Woodrow Wilson preferred to stress the inculcation of democratic processes. Either way, the American government had come to regard the Caribbean as its own. Armed interventions were dropped during Franklin Roosevelt's "Good Neighbor Policy" in the 1930s and 1940s, but they were revived by Eisenhower, Kennedy and Johnson to dislodge Communists, or supposed Communists, in the area. Meanwhile, in the Far East, the new American presence brought increasing involvement in great-power rivalry before and after World War 1, and increasing friction with the rising industrial and imperial power of Japan.

With the entry of America into the ranks of the imperial powers in 1898 came her new role—that of a world power.

ALAN KNIGHT

Above The Spanish fleet off Santiago ; the Spanish fleet proved no match for the American navy.

Left The bedecked wreck of the *Maine* in Havana habor on February 15, 1900, two years after it was blown up.

As a new century dawns, European

International friction

Throughout the last decade of the nineteenth century, international relations were in a continual state of flux, with new issues modifying traditional enmities. After Bismarck's departure from the German Chancery in 1890, military power on the Continent of Europe was evenly balanced between the Triple Alliance (Germany, Austria-Hungary and Italy) and the Franco-Russian Alliance. Bismarck had always feared a combination between France and Russia as the most dangerous to Germany, and it took only four years for one to come into being after his fall from power. Each bloc viewed the other with suspicion and hostility. The French still hankered for the return of Alsace-Lorraine, lost to Germany in 1871 after the Franco-Prussian War; the Russians distrusted Austrian projects for railroad construction in the Balkans; and the Italians resented the extent of French influence around the shores of the Mediterranean. Old problems persisted: Turkey, "the sick man of Europe" for half a century, was by now an incurable invalid; and so long as Strasbourg, the capital of Alsace, remained a German city, there was no possibility of reconciliation between the French Third Republic and Kaiser William II's Empire. But the existence of the two armed camps meant that, at least in Europe, there was deadlock over many questions. National prestige, as well as economic pressures, forced all of the great powers except Austria-Hungary, whose internal state was little healthier than that of Turkey, to seek expansion in other parts of the globe. From the founding of Johannesburg until the defeat of the Tsar's armies in the Russo-Japanese War of 1904–1905, imperial enterprise and rivalries in Africa and the Far East dominated world politics.

"The sun never sets . . ."

During these years Great Britain was in a unique position. Her widespread colonial possessions gave her an advantage over late starters in the scramble for empire, and they enabled her to avoid attachment to either of the opposing camps. Successive British gov-

Lord Salisbury, British Prime Minister at the turn of the century.

ernments accepted freedom from long-term commitments as a principle of conduct as sacrosanct as America's Monroe Doctrine. Lord Salisbury, who was both Prime Minister and Foreign Secretary from 1886 to 1892 and again from 1895 to 1902, declared that "British policy is to drift lazily downstream, occasionally putting out a boat-hook to avoid a collision."

Salisbury did not believe, as is sometimes maintained, that "splendid isolation" was a virtue in itself, for he was quite prepared to cooperate with other nations to preserve peace in the Mediterranean and the Far East. But he distrusted the apparent rigidity of the Bismarckian system of alliances. British independence relied instead upon the might of the Royal Navy.

Arms race

As the colonial struggle grew fiercer and disagreements between the European powers brought the threat of war nearer, the British government was forced to spend more and more on the upkeep of its fleet. A new standard, first declared publicly in 1889, was that the British fleet should be "at least equal to the naval strengths of any two other countries."

From 1890 the supremacy of British battleships and cruisers was maintained by ensuring that their numbers were at least ten percent higher than those of any two other combined fleets. Only a full-scale continental league (Germany, Russia and France, for example) could have limited the exercise of British naval power during this period. Although such a project was debated from time to time, especially by the Russians, old resentments within Europe rendered it impracticable.

But nonetheless foreign navies were growing faster than Britain's, and by 1904 Britain's supremacy at sea was challenged when the French and Germans had a total of sixty-nine battleships in service while Britain had no more than sixty-seven, encouraging the builders of a new class of super-battleships, the Dreadnoughts. Although the Royal Navy continued to have a numerical advantage among smaller warships, it was obvious from the rapid speed of German shipbuilding that Britain's standard would have to be abandoned,

and by 1908 the German and French fleets combined were larger than the British navy.

The Boxer Rebellion

The shock that China suffered in the second half of the nineteenth century from its defeat in the Opium Wars and the imposition of the "unequal treaties" was so great that the imperial government, whose authority had virtually disappeared, failed entirely in its efforts to modernize the administration of China. Heavy defeat by the traditionally weaker Japanese in the War of 1894 brought further

Execution of Chinese pirates in 1891.

humiliations. Anti-Western societies sprang up in many parts of China. One of these, the recently formed Society of the Harmonious Fist, popularly known as the Boxers, achieved an enormous popularity. Eventually the Chinese government took a few half-hearted measures to suppress the Boxers, but these only led to open rebellion against the government. Faced with rebellion, the government took no action at all; some ministers and courtiers supported the Boxers, and did not want to see them suppressed. As a result the Western powers became increasingly disturbed, and eventually, to force the suppression of the Boxers, declared war on the Chinese. Although the Western powers were able to end the rising in 1900, less than two years after its beginning, the effect on China was enormous.

The Third Republic

A major problem for Britain and France was the need to retain their independence of action in the

H.M.S. *Temeraire*, an early ironclad built for the Royal Navy.

battlelines begin to take shape

colonies and in independent countries such as China while satisfying public opinion at home. But foreign policy considerations in practice were often subordinated to other issues. The waves of anti-clericalism in France during the 1890s were evidence of the Republic's leaders' growing self-confidence. In 1871 it had seemed that the Third Republic would last no longer than either of its predecessors. The bloody suppression of the Paris Commune in May of that year had dealt a blow to French politics from which it had only just recovered. Socialism was in eclipse after 1871, and the French provinces imposed a socially conservative government on the chastened capital. From 1871 to 1876, the monarchists were actually in a majority in both chambers of the National Assembly. They were, however, divided among the supporters of the houses of Bourbon, Orleans and Bonaparte, and as Adolphe Thiers (1797–1877), who served as the first President of the Third Republic, declared: "There is only one throne and three people cannot sit on it." The French electorate gradually resigned itself to a moderately conservative republicanism (whose representatives gained control of the lower house, or Chamber of Deputies, in 1876 and of the upper house, or Senate, in 1879).

Administrations under the Third Republic were notoriously short-lived. Between 1871 and 1914 there were fifty-eight governments under thirty-four different prime ministers (compared with twelve governments and seven premiers in Britain). A complicated and variable system of proportional representation led to a multiplicity of political parties. Each government was a coalition formed for one political purpose, and once the purpose was achieved the coalition tended to disintegrate. Moreover, if deputies voted against a ministry and forced it to resign, their actions did not involve them in the risks and expense of a general election (as it would have done in Britain), and hence there was more willingness to overthrow governments in France than there was in countries with a more rigorous constitutional structure. The system also had the effect of keeping strong personalities who were unwilling to compromise with other political factions out of the highest office. Thus Léon Gambetta (1838–83), the archetypal republican of the 1870s, was Prime Minister for no more than nine weeks, and Georges Clemenceau (1841–1929), "the Tiger," whose biting tongue destroyed innumerable governments, did not become Prime Minister until 1906—after thirty years experience in the Chamber and Senate.

General Boulanger, leader of a proposed coup d'état in Paris, whose nerve failed at the last moment.

Critics of the Republic exploited instances of corruption to demand constitutional reform from time to time. Their favorite panacea was a strong executive, modeled on the American presidency, and in 1889 it seemed as if they might have their way. There was danger of a military coup d'état in Paris, for the political right had found a handsome and popular champion in General Georges Boulanger (1827–91). But the general's nerve failed at the last moment and the republican constitution remained fundamentally unchanged until the disasters of 1940. The Third Republic was a narrowly bourgeois regime, but it had qualities of durability unknown in France since the Revolution, and it ensured the French people a prosperity and world prestige that had seemed unattainable after the defeat of 1870.

Music

Although painting stagnated for part of the nineteenth century, musical life flourished throughout the century. While Romanticism in painting died a fairly speedy death, it continued to have a major impact on music. Despite the difficulties involved in providing full-scale orchestras for large works, composers poured forth a flood of compositions; although few of these were works of genius, formal musical culture in the nineteenth century reached a wider audience than ever before—or, perhaps, since.

The musicians of talent were, however, almost to a man natives of France, Russia, Italy, Germany or Austria-Hungary. Some countries —the Netherlands, Spain and Britain, for example—that in the past had produced composers of note, did so no longer. The spread of Romantic ideas, already apparent in Beethoven's work, was the most notable feature of nineteenth-century music, and it was often combined with nationalist sympathies.

Large-scale orchestral works were popular in most of Europe, but French composers, who had never looked with great favor on the classical symphony, continued to produce works on a more human scale. César Franck (1822–90), Camille Saint-Saëns (1835–1921), Jules Massenet (1842–1912) and Claude Debussy (1862–1918) managed to bring a sensual quality, which became a particular characteristic of French music, to their compositions. Those, like Hector Berlioz (1803–69) and Georges Bizet (1838–75), who tried to extend their work into opera and large-scale orchestral works, were not wholly successful, although the latter's *Carmen* has won a wide popularity. Yet, Paris remained a cultural center of international importance, and the brilliant Polish pianist and composer Frederic Chopin (1810–49) was only one among many who made their home there.

The nineteenth century was the great age of Italian opera. Gioacchino Rossini (1792–1868) and Gaetano Donizetti (1797–1848) formed a stylistic link with the eighteenth-century operatic composers. But the Italian Romantic opera reached its apogee in the works of Giuseppe Verdi (1813–1901), many of whose nineteen operas form the basis of the modern repertory.

Russia, for so long a musical wasteland, flowered suddenly in the nineteenth century, producing a strongly nationalistic style of operatic and symphonic composition. From the time of Mikhael Ivanovich Glinka (1803–57) until well into the twentieth century, Russian music—highly romantic, vibrant, forceful, yet capable of great depth of feeling—had a style all its own. Peter Ilich Tchaikovsky (1840–93) was the dominant musical figure for most of the second half of the century, but others such as Aleksandr Borodin (1834–87) and Nikolai Rimsky-Korsakov (1844–1908) were important in their own right.

The death of Beethoven in 1827 and of Franz Schubert the following year did not leave Germany devoid of musical talent. Felix Mendelssohn (1809–47), Robert Schumann (1810–56) and Franz Liszt (1811–86) were the main figures in the middle years of the century. Richard Wagner (1813–83) had an influence of a different

Liszt playing the piano.

kind; his operas became the anthems of German nationalism (although his own devotion had been to the mad King Louis of Bavaria).

It was, however, in Austria-Hungary that music flourished most toward the end of the century. The symphonies of Anton Bruckner (1824–96), Johannes Brahms (1833–97) and Gustav Mahler (1860–1911), the Czech nationalist composers Bedřich Smetana (1824–84) and Anton Dvořák (1841–1904), the waltzes of Johann Strauss (1825–99) and the operas of Richard Strauss (1864–1949) show the wealth of musical tradition that could be found in the Dual Monarchy. It was a tradition that was centered on Vienna, which, despite the political decline of Austria-Hungary, remained a great cultural center in which literature and philosophy as well as music flourished. The new and somewhat arcane study of the human mind also found supporters in Vienna; among them Sigmund Freud, whose *Traumdeutung* (*The Interpretation of Dreams*) established psychology as a respectable subject.

Publication of "The Interpretation of Dreams"

Dreams were long interpreted as omens of things to come or as merely responses to outside stimuli—like the ringing of the alarm clock. When Sigmund Freud suggested that instead they were a reflection of a self the conscious mind was unaware of, a part of the mind holding all the strong and forbidden thoughts and emotions the conscious mind had repressed, he was greeted with outrage. However, with The Interpretation of Dreams *and the unfolding of his psychoanalytical theory, Freud changed the way man looked at himself and his world, and ultimately changed the world as well.*

It would be misleading indeed to imagine that the year 1900—when Freud published *The Interpretation of Dreams*—was the year the nineteenth century ended, and the twentieth century began. In Freud's Vienna the nineteenth century remained virtually intact, sealed off from the next era by tradition, prejudice, custom and complacency. It was a world that had moved from the eighteenth century's Age of Reason into that of the Machine Age, where the mainly unspoken philosophy of the middle and upper classes was that the steam engine, in conjunction with stifling religious attitudes, would produce a sum of human happiness never before known to man. It was a philosophy that operated to keep the social order intact, and each man in his place. Freud's work, and in particular this book, played a considerable part in making way for the great social clashes and the growing liberalism of the twentieth century.

Vienna at the end of the nineteenth century epitomized a world of elaborate manners, of formalities between friends that might lead to a first-name basis only after years of close acquaintanceship. It was a society that believed that individuals were responsible for their actions in every way. It was a society in which the middle classes behaved as if sexuality were a sinful activity to be secretly enjoyed by men and heroically suffered by women; a society too in which the working class was a half-slave class that consoled itself with unfettered sexuality, and in which women supplemented their meager income by prostituting themselves.

Freud was well aware of the hypocrisy and inequality of the society in which he lived, yet one of the most fascinating paradoxes about this man is that he lived a life as decorous as the demanding Vienna of his day could have wished for. He was, nevertheless, attacked by critics not only for his views about sexuality, but also for the allegation that his treatment consisted in part of arousing patients to sexual frenzies. Indeed, he was regarded by many as a sexual monster, when in truth he was not only thoroughly conformist in his behavior, but also had only the smallest personal interest in sex, and might even be described in his own terminology as sexually repressed.

It was perhaps just as paradoxical that this respectable doctor and scientist, this solid family man and good Austrian should propose that dreams can be investigated as a source of valuable and sound scientific evidence about the way men's minds work. Freud also said these insights into the underlying emotional problems that beset people could reveal what makes them neurotic. This was heresy indeed, since dreams were widely regarded as prophecies of the future by the superstitious, or as mere twitchings of the mind during sleep—a kind of random image-making that occurred as a result of some kind of irritation or interference such as a stomach ache, or the sound of a banging door. That a doctor should look not at physical symptoms, that he should not administer medicines and physical treatments but instead should talk with his patients about their dreams and hope thereby to achieve a cure seemed mad to the doctors and scientists of his day. Also, it was generally felt that this was either a new and particularly cynical way to make money, or that it was a venture into realms no doctor should consider.

The insight that dreams were direct evidence of the functioning of the unconscious mind came only slowly to Freud. The significant event which led to Freud's dream theory was his visit to the famous Dr. Charcot some years earlier. Charcot was practicing hypnotism on hysterics, and his demonstration that ideas put in a subject's mind during a trance could be unknown to the subject, yet could cause certain acts when he awoke, struck Freud like a thunderbolt; it clearly proved that unconscious ideas—ideas of which the individual had no aware-

DIE

TRAUMDEUTUNG

VON

DR. SIGM. FREUD.

FLECTERE SI NEQUEO SUPEROS, ACHERONTA MOVEBO.

LEIPZIG UND WIEN.
FRANZ DEUTICKE.
1900.

Title-page of the first edition of *The Interpretation of Dreams*. Freud's work established the close link between dreams and the unconscious.

Opposite Detail from the *Garden of Earthly Delights* by Hieronymus Bosch. In *The Interpretation of Dreams* Freud made frequent use of artistic and literary theories to support his ideas

Jean Martin Charcot, whose work at the Salpêtrière hospital in Paris influenced Freud in his psychological theories.

ness—could sway human behavior. He saw in this a connection with slips of the tongue, where a person often accidentally betrays a hidden motive by mispronouncing or mischoosing a word as, for example, the mayor who was so eager to be off on his annual vacation that in opening a fair he was "happy to declare this fair closed." It was typical of Freud that he should see a connection between the unusual state of hypnosis and one of the commonest of human experiences, and that he should perceive running through them a thread that indicated the pervasive and dynamic nature of man's unconscious mind.

For a while Freud practiced hypnosis, but he found it unsatisfactory. Patients could be brought to recall the events that led to their current difficulties, but they could rarely, while under hypnosis, manage the emotional catharsis, or release, that was essential to a cure. He turned therefore to what he called free association. This technique required the patient to say exactly what came into his mind. The principle was that any connection that occurred between ideas was significant, and that if he tracked back through these connections he would ultimately approach the source of the idea pattern. In the case of neurotics this would be some unsolved emotional problem. Freud discovered that if he free associated to a dream, more emerged than by just free associating itself. This was the key to dream interpretation—an entirely new and fruitful technique.

Freud's first step was the realization that the dream has meaning. The dream had always been seen as meaningful but throughout the ages the meaning of dreams had been regarded as clairvoyant in nature and dreams were regarded as omens. Freud was now arguing something quite different, that we dream because stimuli of various kinds are disturbing the mind, and that the dream is the means by which we deal with these stimuli and actually prevent ourselves from waking up. He went on to argue that although a dream might be sparked by an external or a bodily stimulus—the sound of a bell, the pains of indigestion—the content of the dream was variable, and the variation depended on the stimulus plus other factors.

Freud drew an analogy with daydreams, and pointed out that what we imagine in daydreams are events that satisfy our "egoistic needs and cravings." We dream that we can conquer love-objects we admire only from afar and that we can strike down with ease enemies who in real life frighten us. As in daydreams, so in night dreams. Our unexpressed needs and cravings—our unfulfilled wishes—provide the content of the night dream, and these are states of the unconscious mind that we are loath to admit.

In that case, how do we know of these unfulfilled wishes? How can we find out about them? The answer, Freud argues, is to ask the dreamer himself. But how can we ask the dreamer when he doesn't know? But he does know; he just doesn't know he knows. Freud knew very well that an answer of that kind would not satisfy the intelligent skeptic. Also, if the dreamer were asked to free associate to the content of the dream, convincing explanations of the dream events would begin to present themselves to him. To the question of why the dreamer can free associate back to the right answer, but cannot say directly what the dream means, Freud responds that the dreamer cannot say what it means; it is as if there are two of him, the person who knows the answer, and the person—the conscious self—who is not supposed to find out. And because free association allows a kind of oblique approach to the source of the dreams, the conscious

Vienna in 1900; the vigorous cultural life of Vienna was an important part of the background to Freud's ideas.

Laboratory of the Institute of Physiology, where Freud worked from 1876 to 1882.

person can sometimes get around the defenses of the unconscious self that has the answer. In this way, what Freud termed "resistance" and later "repression" could be overcome.

If all this is accepted, there is another important question to be answered: why does our unconscious self keep its needs and cravings hidden or at least disguised? In Freud's conception of psychology, the answer lies in our childhood, a period of our lives when our many antisocial or purely selfish needs were initially tolerated or satisfied by our parents; as we grew older these needs came to be seen as wrong or inappropriate and were punished when they appeared. It was as if these punished wishes retreated into the unconscious, only to appear as a fairly regular event on the semiconscious stage of the dream. But the greedy, domineering, aggressive, even murderous child lives on eternally within each of us.

Freud argued, therefore, that what we experience in the dreaming state is a substitute for the thought processes that exist in the unconscious. We cannot experience them directly simply because having been punished until they retreated into the unconscious they are now too painful for us to face directly. He calls the dream we actually experience the manifest content, and the threatening needs and wishes that cause them the latent thoughts, and

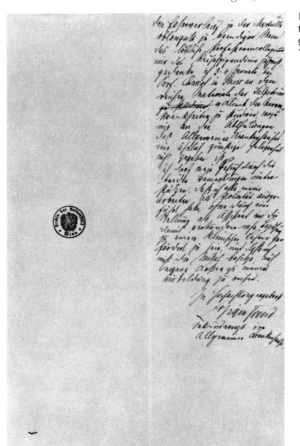

Letter from Freud applying to the Faculty of Medicine for a grant to see Charcot in Paris, 1885–86.

maintains that the strangeness of the dream is due to the action of the dream censorship and the dream work.

The object of dream censorship is to prevent us from directly confronting the real meaning of the dream and it operates in a number of ways. First, it creates odd gaps. The dream will quite often break off or change as the dreamer approaches a sensitive or critical area. In fact, the dreamer may even awake, perhaps in a fright. Second, it operates by expressing the latent thoughts in the forms of allusions, hints or parallels which tend to throw the dreamer off the trail. Third, it works through what Freud called a displacement of accent—the dream emphasizes and builds up minor elements and plays down sensitive ones in order to mislead the conscious mind, and it is this displacement which is one of the major causes of the strangeness of dreams.

But the dream is doubly confusing because of the operation of the dream work. By this Freud meant the process by which the latent thoughts are transformed into the manifest dream—the dream as we experience it. The dream work causes the transformation of latent thoughts into visual images—the dream is in effect a series of visual hallucinations—and thus difficult to understand. Many of our thoughts are highly abstract, and the process of turning them into visual images is an involved one. Since it is also impossible for concrete images to represent such thoughts as "yes" and "no" and "because" and "thereby," the dream becomes even more impenetrable to ordinary analysis. The dream work also operates through condensation. Condensation causes the latent thoughts to become concentrated through the action of the dream work into a smaller number of idea pictures. The dream work achieves this by omitting pieces of the latent

Above The Café Giensteidl in Vienna. Viennese café society provided a stimulating intellectual background for philosophers, artists and writers.

Right The Staircase, by Paul Delvaux. Many surrealist painters found dream imagery a rich source of material.

Opposite Salome, by Gustave Klimt. The rich sensuality of painters of the Vienna Secession, such as Klimt provided Freud with the backdrop for his ideas on the roots of the sexual impulse.

150

thoughts, by allowing only fragments of them to pass into the dream, and by blending elements of different latent thoughts into a single whole, or composite figure. Finally, there is displacement, which as we have already noted is operated by the dream censorship.

All these processes operate together to make the dream difficult for both dreamer and observer to understand. But Freud also claimed that another legitimate approach to the interpretation of dreams was the understanding of dream symbols. Freud maintains that dream symbols are a primitive and universal language known to all of us in some obscure way. This argument has failed to convince any but the most orthodox psychoanalysts, and fixed dream symbolism has played only a minor part in the profession. However, it is true that in the popular mind it is precisely this element of Freud's dream interpretation that has become widespread and influential.

Since it was Freud's belief that sexuality plays a dominant part in human behavior, it follows that he interpreted dreams as mainly sexual in nature; he particularly noted the very large number of fixed symbols that represented sexual activity, and it was

this perhaps that confirmed him in his view that repressed sexuality is the main reason for emotional disturbance in adults.

He was not surprised that his theory of dreams met with resistance, dismay, skepticism and anger, for it was central to his theory that dreams are what they are *because* we are unable to face real truths about our deepest selves. It follows that when we are presented with the facts about dreams we are likely to reject them too, for in opening the forbidden doors to the unconscious, we are threatened. But despite the attacks and the skepticism, psychoanalysis probably would never have survived, let alone flourished, as a therapeutic discipline had it not been for *The Interpretation of Dreams*. For dreams are, as Freud said, the royal road to the unconscious; they give psychoanalysts their most direct insight into the functioning of the personality, and they offer a means by which the analyst can, with the patient, pursue the patient's emotional life and help him come to terms with himself. The symptoms of the neurotic's illness often have some of the characteristics of dreams. They symbolize or represent an underlying conflict in the same way, as, for example, the possibility of writer's cramp being an hysterical condition that can point to the writer's unknown anxiety about his own talent. The cramp, conveniently enough, prevents him from putting his talent to the test. The exploration of the neurotic's dreams will show him the corollaries among the dream content, the latent thoughts and his everyday difficulties. Seeing these connections is essential in coming to terms with his difficulties.

Fixed symbolism has not been as popular with analysts as the free association technique, but in conjunction with the general theory of dream interpretation it has been very influential outside the realm of medicine and psychotherapy. This is particularly true of the arts, especially pictorial art, for artists have found in the fantastic world of the unconscious a source of new material. Novelists and poets have seen in the dream and in dream processes a new range of approaches and techniques.

The theory of dreams has been influential in the arts and also has played its part in molding social attitudes in the twentieth century. In showing us that we all have undesirable or even horrendous unconscious wishes, it has tended to make us more tolerant of those who act out their wishes. This century has seen an increasingly more understanding approach to criminal behavior, a non-punitive reaction to mental disease and emotional disturbances and a growing tolerance of those that the majority still regard as sexual deviants. Changes in child rearing, greater sexual permissiveness, and perhaps even the Women's Movement, owe something to the quest for self-knowledge that Freud's theories encouraged.

The interpretation of dreams and Freud's psychoanalytic theory have proved to be one of the richest and most persuasive influences in twentieth century Western society. MALCOLM LEVENE

Thomas Jefferson 1743–1826
U.S. President

John Quincy Adams 1767–1848
U.S. President

J. M. W. Turner
British painter

Francisco Goya 1746–1828
Spanish painter

Francis I 1768–1835
Emperor of Austria

Alexande
Tsar of R

Jeremy Bentham 1748–1832
British philosopher

Napoleon Bonaparte 1769–1821
Emperor of the French

Nathai
Londo

Charles James Fox 1749–1806
British statesman

Lord Castlereagh 1769–1822
British statesman

Henry
U.S.

Francisco de Miranda 1750–1816
Venezueluan patriot

Mohammed Ali 1769–1849
Pasha of Egypt

Ber
Chi

Charles Maurice de Talleyrand 1754–1838
French statesman

Arthur Wellesley, Duke of Wellington
1769–1852 *British statesman and soldier*

Jo:
So

Louis XVIII 1755–1824
King of France

Alexander von Humboldt 1769–1859
German explorer and scientist

William Blake 1757–1827
British poet and artist

Ludwig van Beethoven 1770–1827
German composer

Horatio, Lord Nelson 1758–1805
British admiral

George Canning 1770–1827
British statesman

James Monroe 1758–1831
U.S. President

Georg Hegel 1770–1831
German philosopher

William Pitt the Younger 1759–1806
British statesman

Frederick William III 1770–1840
King of Prussia

William Wilberforce 1759–1833
British statesman

William Wordsworth 1770–1850
British poet

Claude Henri de Saint-Simon 1760–1825
French philosopher and social scientist

Walter Scott 1771–1832
Scottish writer

George IV 1762–1830
King of Great Britain and Ireland

Robert Owen 1771–1858
British socialist

William Cobbett 1763–1835
British political writer

Samuel Taylor Coleridge 1772–
British poet

Charles, Earl Grey 1764–1845
British statesman

Charles Fourier 1772–1837
French social scientist and refor

Robert Fulton 1765–1815
U.S. engineer and inventor

Chaka 1773–1828
Zulu chief

Michel Ney 1767–1815
Marshal of France

Louis Philippe 1773–185(
King of France

Joachim Murat 1767–1815
King of Naples, Marshal of France

Klemens von Metternich
1773–1859 *Austrian state*

Andrew Jackson 1767–1845
U.S. President

Jane Austen 1775–
British novelist

51

?–1825

schild 1777–1836
:er

?–1852
:sman

ggins 1778–1842
:sman and soldier

Martin 1778–1850
:rican revolutionary

Melbourne 1779–1848
:h statesman

von Clausewitz 1780–1831
:ssian military theorist

Ingres 1780–1867
:ch painter

George Stephenson 1781–1848
English inventor and engineer

John C. Calhoun 1782–1850
U.S. statesman

Martin Van Buren 1782–1862
U.S. President

Simón Bolívar 1783–1830
South American revolutionary

Stendhal (Henri Beyle) 1783–1842
French writer

Lord Palmerston 1784–1865
British statesman

Alessandro Manzoni 1785–1873
Italian writer

François Guizot 1787–1874
French statesman and historian

Lord Byron 1788–1824
British poet

Robert Peel 1788–1850
British statesman

Percy Bysshe Shelley 1792–1822
British poet

Pius IX 1792–1878
Pope

Sam Houston 1793–1863
U.S. soldier and political leader

Matthew C. Perry 1794–1868
U.S. naval officer

John Keats 1795–1821
British poet

James Polk 1795–1849
U.S. President

Antonio López de Santa Anna *c.* 1795–1876
Mexican revolutionary

Thomas Carlyle 1795–1881
British essayist and historian

Frederick William IV 1795–1881
King of Prussia

Leopold von Ranke 1795–1886
German historian

Nicholas I 1796–1855
Tsar of Russia

Franz Schubert 1797–1828
Austrian composer

Adolphe Thiers 1797–1877
French statesman

William I 1797–1888
King of Prussia, Emperor of Germany

Auguste Comte 1798–1857
French philosopher

Eugène Delacroix 1798–1863
French painter

Alexander Pushkin 1799–1837
Russian poet

Honoré de Balzac 1799–1850
French novelist

Felix Schwarzenberg 1800–52
Austrian statesman

Cetewayo ?–1884
Zulu chief

Helmuth von Moltke 1800–91
Prussian field-marshal

Victor Hugo 1802–85
French writer

Lajos Kossuth 1802–94
Hungarian statesman

Ralph Waldo Emerson 1803–82
U.S. man of letters

Richard Cobden 1804–65
British statesman

Benjamin Disraeli 1804–81
British statesman

Giuseppe Mazzini 1805–72
Italian statesman

Ferdinand de Lesseps 1805–94
French engineer and diplomat

Isambard Kingdom Brunel 1806–59
British engineer

Benito Juarez 1806–72
Mexican statesman

John Stuart Mill 1806–73
British political philosopher

1804 ●
French *Code Civile* instituted

1804 ●
Coronation of Napoleon as
Emperor

● **1805**
Napoleon defeats
Russians and Austrians at
Austerlitz; British defeat
French at Trafalgar

●
1808–14
Peninsular War in Spain

●
1812 Spencer Perceval, British
Prime Minister, assassinated

●
1812–14 Anglo-American War

●
1815 Prussia initiates a German
Confederation, including
Austria-Hungary

1820 ●
Liberia founded

1820 ●
Missouri Compromise: no new
slave states in U.S.A. north of
36° 30′ latitude

The Unnecessary War   **1854**
Russia's expansion at Turkey's expense sparks off a wasteful struggle in the Crimea that fails to alter the European balance of power

The Emergence of Italy
Sardinia's astute Prime Minister capitalize[s] European rivalries to piece together the fir[st] modern Italian state

Mutiny in India   **1857**
Upper-caste Hindus serving in the British-led Bengal Army rebel against the reforms instituted by their English overlords

Realism and Revolution   **1855**
Courbet's art relies on the power of paint to "translate the customs, the ideas, the appearances" of the times, and inspires the future founders of Impressionism

Ape or Angel
British naturalist Charles Darwin's scan[dal] provoking "monkey-theory" of natural selection denies Genesis and advocates evolution

---

Robert E. Lee 1807–70
U.S. Confederate general

Otto von Bismarck 1815–98
German statesman

Ferdinand Lassalle 1825–64
German socialist

Paul Cézanne 1839–1906
French painter

Giuseppe Garibaldi 1807–82
Italian patriot

Charlotte Brontë 1816–55
British novelist

Paul Kruger 1825–1904
South African statesman

John D. Rockefeller 1839–1937
U.S. industralist and philanthropist

Louis Napoleon Bonaparte
(Napoleon I'') 1808–73 *King of France*

Henry Thoreau 1817–62
U.S. man of letters

Francisco López 1827–70
President of Paraguay

Peter Ilich Tchaikovsky 1840–93
Russian composer

Abraham Lincoln 1809–65
U.S. President

Alexander II 1818–81
Tsar of Russia

Joseph Lister 1827–1912
British surgeon

Emile Zola 1840–1902
French novelist

Pierre Joseph Proudhon 1809–65
French anarchist

Karl Marx 1818–83
German political philosopher

Hippolyte Adolphe Taine 1828–93
French philosopher and critic

Anton Dvořák 1841–1904
Czech composer

Charles Darwin 1809–82
British naturalist

Gustave Courbet 1819–77
French painter

Henrik Ibsen 1828–1906
Norwegian poet and dramatist

Pierre Renoir 1841–1919
French painter

Cyrus Hall McCormick 1809–84
U.S. inventor

George Eliot (Mary Ann Evans)
1819–80 *British novelist*

Leo Tolstoy 1828–1910
Russian writer

Georges Clemenceau 1841–1929
French statesman

Alfred, Lord Tennyson 1809–92
British poet

John Ruskin 1819–1900
British art critic and sociological writer

Porfirio Diaz 1830–1915
Mexican statesman

The Mahdi (Mohammed Ahmed) c. 1843–8[5]
Sudanese rebel leader

William Ewart Gladstone 1809–98
British statesman

Victoria 1819–1901
Queen of Great Britain and Ireland

Francis Joseph 1830–1916
Emperor of Austria

William McKinley 1843–1901
U.S. President

Frederic Chopin 1810–49
Polish composer

Victor Emmanuel II 1820–78
King of Sardinia, then Italy

Maximilian of Hapsburg 1832–67
Emperor of Mexico

Robert Koch 1843–1910
German bacteriologist

Camillo Cavour 1810–61
Italian statesman

Friedrich Engels 1820–95
German political philosopher

Edouard Manet 1832–83
French painter

Henry James 1843–1916
U.S. novelist

William Thackeray 1811–63
British novelist

Herbert Spencer 1820–1903
British philosopher

Charles Gordon 1833–85
British general

Friedrich Nietzsche 1844–1900
German philosopher

Louis Blanc 1811–82
French socialist

Florence Nightingale 1820–1910
British nursing reformer

Alfred Nobel 1833–96
Swedish inventor and philanthropist

Alexander III 1845–94
Tsar of Russia

Charles Dickens 1812–70
British novelist

Charles Baudelaire 1821–67
French poet

Johannes Brahms 1833–97
German composer

Charles Stewart Parnell 1846–[91]
Irish statesman

Alexander Herzen 1812–70
Russian revolutionary writer

Gustave Flaubert 1821–80
French novelist

Sitting Bull 1834–90
American Sioux Indian leader

Alexander Graham Bell 184[7]–
1922 *U.S. inventor*

Søren Kierkegaard 1813–55
Danish philosopher

Fyodor Dostoevsky 1821–81
Russian novelist

William Morris 1834–96
British poet and artist

Thomas Edison 1847–1931
U.S. inventor

David Livingstone 1813–73
British missionary and explorer

Ulysses Simpson Grant 1822–85
U.S. President

James Abbott McNeill Whistler 1834–1903
American painter

Paul Gauguin 1848–19[03]
French painter

Richard Wagner 1813–83
German composer

Heinrich Schliemann 1822–90
German archaelogist

Andrew Carnegie 1835–1919
U.S. industrialist and philanthropist

Crazy Horse c. 184[9]
Sioux Indian chief

Giuseppe Verdi 1813–1901
Italian operatic composer

Louis Pasteur 1822–95
French chemist

Léon Gambetta 1838–83
French statesman

Meiji
Emper[or]

Mikhail Bakunin 1814–76
Russian anarchist and writer

Nana Sahib (Dandhu Panth) c.1825–60
Leader of Sepoy mutiny

George Armstrong Custer 1839–76
U.S. soldier

Vi[ncent]
Du[tch]

Brazilian independence from **1822**
Portugal

Reform Act enfranchises **1832**
middle-class men in Britain

1840 ●
Representative of Sultan of Oman establishes his capital at Zanzibar

Thomas Cook organizes trip **18[41]**
to Paris

1823 ●
Monroe Doctrine: no European interference in the Americas tolerated by U.S.A.

1835–37 ●
Great Trek by Boers of Cape Colony

● **1840**
New Zealand becomes British colony

● **1848** California gold

1850–64
Taiping Rebellion in Chin[a] Ch'ing dynasty retains po[wer] with aid of British under Gordon

1825 ●
Decembrist Revolt in Russia

1839 ●
Mohammed Ali's revolt in Asia Minor checked by European powers

1845 ●
Republic of Texas annexed to U.S.A., leading to U.S.-Mexican War (1846–48)

18[...]
Napoleon III's Unive[rsal] Exhibition

1830 ●
July Revolution in France; uprisings in Germany, Italy, Belgium, Poland (till 1831)

1839–42 ●
Sino-British Opium War: Hong Kong and trade concessions to Britain

1846 Irish Famine

Victoria gold rush in **1851** ●
Australia

A Proclamation at Versailles   **1871**
Bismarck's dream of a united Germany is
fulfilled when his sovereign, William I of
Prussia, is proclaimed Emperor of Germany in
Versailles' Hall of Mirrors

The Haymarket Affair   **1886**
The trial and execution of eight strike leaders
creates America's first labor martyrs and diverts
the energies of labor into more political channels

"Remember the *Maine!*"   **1898**
Sent to Havana to protect American lives during
the Cuban revolt, the U.S.S. *Maine*
mysteriously explodes and the United States
embarks on an aggressive policy of overseas
expansion

Custer's Last Stand   **1876**
Among the U.S. forces sent to quell the
Sioux Indian uprising is a vainglorious cavalry
officer who leads his troops into America's
most celebrated massacre

The Birth of Big Business   **1870**
Industrialist John D. Rockefeller forms the
Standard Oil Company and begins a strategy
of growth through combination that creates
the world's largest manufacturing firm

The Riches of the Rand   **1886**
The discovery of vast reefs of gold ore
transform the peaceful farmlands of the
Transvaal into a booming industrial center

"Next year in Jerusalem"   **1897**
The dedication of a single man brings the
centuries-old dream of a sovereign Jewish
state a step closer to realization

A Nation Divided   **1863**
The defeat of Robert E.
Lee's valiant army of
"starving ragamuffins"
at Gettysburg deals the
Confederacy a mortal blow

Assassination of Alexander II   **1881**
Political terrorists assassinate
Russia's reforming Tsar, and their
terrible deed is noted with alarm
by every autocrat in Russia

Publication of   **1900**
The Interpretation of Dreams
Sigmund Freud's psychoanalytical theory
shocks middle-class Vienna by postulating a
hidden, subconscious self as the repository
of forbidden thoughts and emotions

The Zulu War   **1879**
The martial Zulu nation routs a British army at
Isandhlwana, only to be finally crushed by
superior British firepower

Cecil Rhodes 1853–1902
British statesman and colonialist

Alfred Dreyfus 1859–1935
French soldier

William II 1859–1941
Emperor of Germany

Theodor Herzl 1860–1904
Austro-Hungarian founder of Zionism

Anton Chekhov 1860–1904
Russian writer

Mutsuhito 1852–1912
Emperor of Japan

Vincent van Gogh 1853–90
Dutch painter

1857–65 First transatlantic cable laid	
1864 War over Schleswig-Holstein: Prussia and Austria against Denmark	**1870** Paris Commune; shortlived attempt by radicals to revive the spirit of 1792
1859 War of Austria against France and Sardinia concluded at Solferino	**1871** Compulsory primary education in Japan
	1867 Alaska purchased by U.S.A. from Russia
1859 John Brown's raid on Harper's Ferry	**1866** Prussians defeat Austrians at Sadowa
	1875–78 Eastern Crisis; Treaty of Berlin (1878) destroys Pan-Slav Greater Bulgaria
	1870 Vatican Council pronounces on papal infallibility
1860–70 Maori Wars	**1867** Dual monarchy of Austria-Hungary created
	1871 Trade Unionism legalized in Britain
1865 President Lincoln assassinated	**1867** Canadian Federation
	1869 Suez Canal opened
1861 Liberation of 20 million serfs open Alexander II's program of reform in Russia	**1870** Unification of Italy completed
	1865–70 Paraguayan War against Argentina, Brazil and Uruguay

1879–91 Tariff walls erected by U.S.A. and Europe except Britain	**1893** Women gain vote in New Zealand; first instance of female suffrage
	1898 Kitchener defeats Khalifa at Omdurman
1886 American Federation of Labor founded	**1894–1906** Dreyfus Affair discredits French monarchists and clericalists
1886 Gladstone's Irish Home Rule Bill splits the British Liberal Party	**1894** Sino-Japanese War
1882 British occupation of Egypt and Sudan	**1887** Secret Russo-German "Reinsurance Treaty"
	1899–1900 Boxer Rebellion in China
1885 The Mahdi's revolt in Sudan	**1899** Hague Conference on arms limitation: establishment of International Court of Arbitration
Indian National Congress founded	**1889** Second International founded in Paris
1882 Triple Alliance between Germany, Austria-Hungary and Italy	**1889** Interparliamentary Union founded
	1899–1902 Boer War
	1887 Bloody Sunday; troops break up demonstration in Trafalgar Square
	1896 First Olympiad held

Acknowledgments

The authors and publishers wish to thank the following museums and collections by whose kind permission the illustrations are reproduced. Page numbers appear in bold, photographic sources in Italics.

12 By kind permission of the Lieutenant General Commanding Coldstream Guards: *A. C. Cooper*
13 *Weidenfeld and Nicolson Archive*
15 National Army Museum, London
16 (1) Victoria and Albert Museum, London: *Miki Slingsby* (2) National Army Museum
17 (1, 2) National Army Museum
18 (1) British Museum, London: *A. C. Cooper* (2) National Army Museum
19 By kind permission of the Lieutenant Colonel Commanding Scots Guards: *A. C. Cooper*
20 (1) British Museum: *John R. Freeman* (2) *Mary Evans Picture Library*
21 (1) City of Birmingham Museum and Art Gallery (2) *Holtermann Collection* (3) *Mansell Collection*
22 Kimbell Art Museum, Fort Worth, Texas
23 *Weidenfeld and Nicolson Archive*
24 *Photo Bulloz*
25 Musée Fabre, Montpellier: *Photo Bulloz*
26 (1, 2) Louvre, Paris: *Photo Bulloz*
27 Musée Fabre: *Photo Bulloz*
28 Musée Carnavalet, Paris: *Photo Bulloz*
29 (1) Petit Palais, Paris: *Photo Bulloz* (2) Petit Palais: *Cooper-Bridgeman Library*
30 (1) *Anthony Cohen* (2) Science Museum, London (3) Musée Mermottan, Paris: *Photo Routhier* (4) National Museum Vincent van Gogh, Amsterdam
31 *Christie Manson and Woods*
32 National Portrait Gallery, London
33 British Museum: *John R. Freeman*
34 India Office, London
35 (1, 2) *Mansell Collection*
36 (1) National Portrait Gallery (2) Victoria and Albert Museum: *John R. Freeman* (3) India Office, London: *R. B. Fleming*
37 British Museum: *John R. Freeman*
38 (1) National Portrait Gallery (2) *Mansell Collection* (3) *Mary Evans Picture Library*
39 (1) Science Museum (2) *Mansell Collection*
40 National Portrait Gallery
42 (1) Royal College of Surgeons, London (2) National Portrait Gallery
43 *Weidenfeld and Nicolson Archive*

44 National Maritime Museum, Greenwich, London
45 (1) British Museum (2) National Portrait Gallery
46 (1, 2) National Portrait Gallery
47 (1) *Mansell Collection* (2, 3) National Portrait Gallery
48 (1) National Portrait Gallery (2, 3) *Mansell Collection*
49 (1) Tate Gallery, London (2) *Weidenfeld and Nicolson Archive*
50 Museo del Risorgimento, Milan: *Scala*
51 *Mansell Collection*
52 Pinacoteca di Brera, Milan: *Anderson-Giraudon*
53 (1) Pinacoteca di Capodimonte, Naples (2, 3) *Mansell Collection*
54 (1) Museo del Risorgimento, Milan: *Scala* (2) Château de Versailles, Paris: *Giraudon* (3) Istituto del Risorgimento, Rome
55 (1) *Scala* (2) *Mansell Collection* (3) *Oliver Walston Collection*
56 (1) *Mansell Collection* (3) *Mary Evans Picture Library* (4) *Radio Times Hulton Picture Library*
57 *Radio Times Hulton Picture Library*
58 National Military Park, Gettysburg
60 Brady Collection, u.s. Signal Corps., Washington D.C. (2) *Mansell Collection*
61 Brady Collection, u.s. Signal Corps
62 (1) *Mansell Collection* (2) u.s. War Department, Washington D.C.
64 *Mansell Collection*
66 *Radio Times Hulton Picture Library*
67 (1) *Mansell Collection* (2) Guildhall Library, London (3) *Weidenfeld and Nicolson Archive* (4) Staatsbibliothek, Berlin
68 *Brown Brothers*
69 *Standard Oil of New Jersey*
70 (1, 2) Standard Oil of New Jersey Collection, University of Louisville, Kentucky
71 (1) Drake Well Museum, New York (2) *Sohio News Service*
72 (1) Standard Oil of New Jersey Collection, University of Louisville
73 (2) Standard Oil of New Jersey Collection, University of Louisville
74 (1, 2, 3, 4) *Mansell Collection*
75 (1) *Weidenfeld and Nicolson Archive* (2) *Photo Bulloz*
76 *Mansell Collection*
77 *Bildarchiv Photo Marburg*
78 (1) *Giraudon* (2) *Mansell Collection*
79 *Radio Times Hulton Picture Library*
80 (1) *Mansell Collection* (2) British Museum: *John R. Freeman*
81 *Radio Times Hulton Picture Library*

82 (1) Victoria and Albert Museum: *John R. Freeman* (2) *Radio Times Hulton Picture Library*
83 (1, 2) *Mansell Collection*
84 (1) *Paul Popper*
85 (1, 2, 3) *Radio Times Hulton Picture Library*
86 u.s. Signal Corps
87 *Western Americana Picture Library*
88 (1) Thomas Gilcrease Institute of American History and Art, Tulsa, Oklahoma (2) National Park Service, Department of the Interior, u.s.a.
89 Library of Congress, Washington: *Orbis Publishing Ltd*
90 (1) u.s. Signal Corps: *Orbis Publishing Ltd* (2) Naval Observatory, u.s.a.: *Orbis Publishing Ltd*
91 (1) u.s. Signal Corps (2) Denver Public Library, Colorado (3) *Western Americana Picture Library*
92 (1) National Park Service, Department of the Interior, u.s.a. (2) Naval Observatory, u.s.a.: *Orbis Publishing Ltd*
93 Southwest Museum, California
94 (1) *Radio Times Hulton Picture Library* (2) National Army Museum
95 (1) *Mansell Collection* (2) *Weidenfeld and Nicolson Archive*
96 National Army Museum
97 Durban Museum, Natal; reproduced by gracious permission of Her Majesty The Queen
98 National Army Museum
99 (1) National Army Museum (2) British Museum: *Phoebus Picture Library*
101 (1, 2) National Army Museum
102 National Army Museum
103 National Army Museum
104 (1, 2) *Weidenfeld and Nicolson Archive* (3) *Radio Times Hulton Picture Library*
105 *Radio Times Hulton Picture Library*
106 *Mansell Collection*
107 *Novosti Press Agency*
108 (1) *Radio Times Hulton Picture Library* (2, 3) *Mansell Collection*
109 (1) *Mansell Collection* (2) *Novosti Press Agency*
110 (1) *John R. Freeman* (2) *Novosti Press Agency*
111 *Novosti Press Agency*
112 (1) *Paul Popper* (2) National Portrait Gallery (3, 4) Guildhall Library: *Su Gooders* (5) *Weidenfeld and Nicolson Archive*
113 (1) National Portrait Gallery (2) Victoria and Albert Museum
115 *John Frost/Historical Newspaper Service*
117 (2) *Bob Natkin*
120 British Museum: *John R. Freeman*

121 National Portrait Gallery
122 (1, 2, 3, 4) Africana Museum, Johannesburg (5) *Mansell Collection*
123 (1, 2) South African Embassy, London
124 (1) South African Embassy, London (2) National Portrait Gallery (3) Africana Museum
125 (1, 2) British Museum: *John R. Freeman*
126 (1) *Radio Times Hulton Picture Library* (2) National Portrait Gallery
127 (1) *Mary Evans Picture Library* (2) *Radio Times Hulton Picture Library*
128 Jews' College Library, London: *R. B. Fleming*
129 Israel Museum, Jerusalem
130 (1) Central Zionist Archives, Jerusalem (2) *Paul Popper*
131 (1) *Jewish National Fund* (2) *Mansell Collection*
132 (1) National Portrait Gallery (2) Central Zionist Archives
133 Victoria and Albert Museum
134 (1) *Mary Evans Picture Library* (2) *Paul Popper* (3) National Portrait Gallery
135 (1) *Mansell Collection* (2) *Paul Popper*
136 u.s. Naval Academy Museum, Annapolis, Maryland
137 Library of Congress
138 Library of Congress
139 Library of Congress
140 u.s. Naval Academy Museum
141 (1, 2) The Free Library of Philadelphia: *Joseph Martin/Scala*
142 Library of Congress
143 (1) The Free Library of Philadelphia: *Joseph Martin/Scala* (2) Library of Congress
144 (1) National Portrait Gallery (2) Imperial War Museum, London (3) *Radio Times Hulton Picture Library*
145 (1, 2) *Mansell Collection*
146 Prado, Madrid: *Cooper-Bridgeman Library*
147 Österreichische National- bibliothek
148 (1) *Radio Times Hulton Picture Library* (2) Editions du Seuil
149 (1) Bildarchiv Instituts für Geschichte der Medezin (2) Österreichische Nationalbibliothek
150 (1) Österreichische National- bibliothek (2) Musée des Beaux Arts, Ghent: *Scala*
151 Ca' Pesaro, Venice: *Scala*
152 (1) *A. C. Cooper* (2) *Werner Forman*
153 (1) *Snark International* (2) *A. C. Cooper*

Managing Editor *Adrian Brink*
Assistant Editors *Geoffrey Chesler, Francesca Ronan*
Picture Editor *Julia Brown*
Consultant Designer *Tim Higgins*
Art Director *Anthony Cohen*

Index

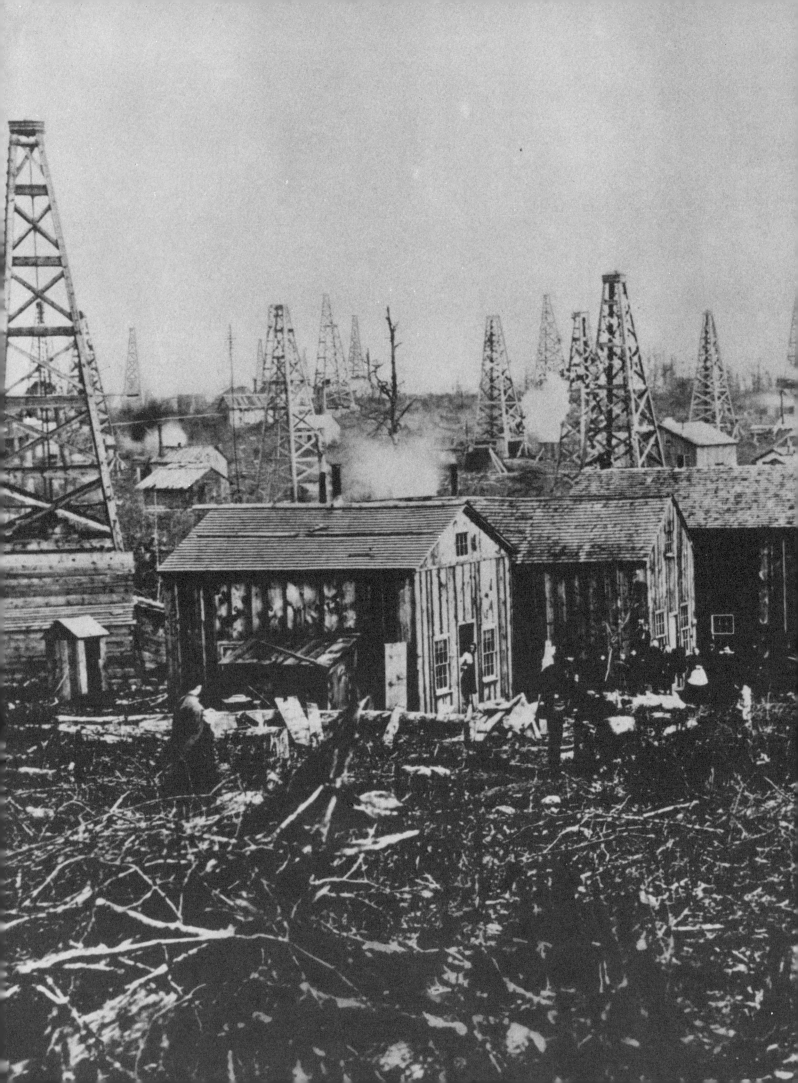